MAHATMA GANDHI
MAN OF THE MILLENNIUM

MAHATMA GANDHI

MAN OF THE MILLENNIUM

Ramjee Singh

Commonwealth

Mahatma Gandhi—Man of the Millennium

First Published : 2010

ISBN 978-81-311-0304-3

Published by :
COMMONWEALTH PUBLISHERS PVT. LTD.
4831/24, Prahlad Street,
Ansari Road, Darya Ganj,
New Delhi - 110002
Ph. : 23272541, 23257835
Fax : 91- 011- 23257835
e-mail : commonwealthbooks@gmail.com

Laser Typesetting by :
Dimple Computers
Delhi

Printed at :
Roshan Offset Printers
Delhi

Preface

Spirituality is neither the monopoly of the East or the West. It is the common heritage of the entire mankind. Honour, according to the cultural and social division of labour, we can satisfy say that both spirituality and practical outlook are the two most important factors of Indian culture. Philosophy is not only one in intellectual pastime, it is a way of life but as a boat without a rudder meets disaster, so even our practical outlook without an appropriate vision can not bring proper result.

The starting point of Indian thought and culture is rooted in spirituality. The Vedic RTA or inviolable order. We have a faith in the eternal moral order and that is spirituality. Today in the 21st century, when we are at the top of scientific knowledge feels and emptiness since without spirituality it explodes an atom bomb when children, sick persons, old people who were sleeping during dead of night. This is neither wisdom nor bravery.

In such a state of crises, Gandhi comes to our rescue with the truth and non-violence. He has neither dollars and pounds in his pocket, nor atomic arsenal in his store. Nor he is President or Prime-Minister of a country but people listen to him for he carries a moral weapon of Satyagraha, which hurts himself, not other. Gandhi is an important spiritual phenomenon to modern Indian Renaissance. Deeper the spirituality more effective it is. It is invisible power which can an resolve any small big crises of humanity.

Ramjee Singh

Contents

Preface (v)

Chapter *Pages*

1. Meditation : Pathway to Deepen Spirituality 1
2. Encounter with the Other : Illusion and Reality 6
3. Philosophy of a Karmyogi 13
4. Reason and Intuition in Indian Thought 18
5. The Holy Mother : True to the Kindred Points of Heaven and Earth 31
6. Unique Spirituality of Sri Ram Charita Manas 44
7. Universal Man and Universal Religion 50
8. Beyond All Frontiers : A Plea for World-Civilization 62
9. A Resolution of Indo-Pak Conflict : A Gandhian Approach 80
10. Freedom Through Non-violence 87
11. Puzzles and Paradoxes in the Contemporary Sarvodaya Movement 91
12. Good Government and Good Governance 102
13. J.P.—A Practical Idealist 108
14. Potentials of Gandhian Initiative in Bihar Retrospect and Prospect 114
15. The Message of Silent Revolution in Bihar 121
16. Reminiscences of Freedom Movement 127
17. Gandhian World Order and World Peace 130
18. In Lieu of a Foreword for 'Shanti-Sena' 138
19. In Defence of Value Education 144

Chapter	*Pages*
20. Inspiring Martyrdom of Mahatma Gandhi	154
21. Gandhi will Inspire Me even in My Next Birth	162
22. Vision of World Poverty : The Gandhian Perspective	166
23. Satyagraha : As a Moral Equivalent of Terrorism and Violence	177
24. Structural and Institutional Dimensions of Global Peace	182
25. Global Resistance Against the Globalisation : The Gandhian Way	188
26. Strategies and Stratagems in Gandhian Thought	194
27. The Relevance of Gandhian Economics for Modern Times	200
Index	214

1

Meditation : Pathway to Deepen Spirituality

Spirituality is deepening of our consciousness. When consciousness broadens or widens, it assumes the form of either physical or psychological but when it deepens, it becomes spiritual. It is entirely internal and subjective. It needs no prophets, no priests, no churches, no saviours, no popes, because spirituality is the flowering of our heart.

But spirituality is not over and above the human life. Human life is not divided into water tight compartment called social, political and religious. All act and react upon one another. The spiritual law works on a field of its own. On the contrary, it expresses itself only through the ordinary activities of life. It thus affects the economic, the social and the political fields.

But the question is how to deepen our spirituality or consciousness. I have only one pathway to peace *i.e.* meditation. The world faces two alternatives : global suicide or meditation. It is the science of deprogramming. But for this, we need no label of caste, class, religion, nation, or sex. He or she is now simply a human being. Deprogramming takes rubbish from us but it is difficult. But practice and intense practice will heep. The moment we are able to clean our dirt and filth and make ourselves empty, we shall begin to feel joy. This is meditation and nothing else. Hence there is no need for any complexity, institute, universities, class etc. There is a simple method of watching our breath is enough but everyday we have to repeat for one hour everyday. We have to sit silently and witness our mind-process, while keeping our attention on the breath. We have not to do anything except remain as a witness, a watcher, an observer, locking at the traffic of the mind—passing thoughts, desires, memories, dreams, fantasies. Simply, we must stand aloof, cool, with no condemnation, no evaluations.

There are a few things to be kept in mind with regard to meditation. The first thing is that we must be, must remain relaxed. Second thing is watchfulness of our inner process. Then we must not have evaluation over it. We may remain as a witness or watcher. There is changes in body, mental states, and emotions but only the witness remains the same. The clouds of thoughts and emotions slowly begin to disperse and the vast blue sky of our inner being would appear. Then we can have a taste of going beyond the body-mind-heart complex. This is the state of meditation where we get joy and fulfilment. This transforms us. Unless something transforms us, it is not meditation. Prayers are all good but they are either longing for some desires and confessions of one's mistakes and guilt. Prayers are not complete deprogramming or complete emptying our mind from the dirt and filth. There are desires lurking into it, while meditation makes us new being, a new man, a new consciousness, which knows no fear, no seriousness, no greed, no hate, no dark emotions and no ugly, sick, nauseating sentiments.

This is called the Science of Yoga in India, where we observe the internal states, power of attention, analyse the mind, and illumine facts for us. The power of the mind are like rays of light dissipated; when they are concentrated, they illumine. Unfortunately, from our childhood upwards we have been taught only to pay attention to things external, but never to things internal, hence most of us have nearly lost the faculty of mind, as it were, inside, stop it from going outside, and then to concentrate all its powers, and throw them upon the mind itself, in order that it may know to own nature, analyse itself is very hard work. This is self-knowledge, which is itself the highest reward. Then there is also utility in it. It will take all our misery, anxiety. When analysing one's own mind, man comes face to face, as it were, with something which is never destroyed something which is, by its own nature, eternally pure and perfect. All misery comes from fear, from unsatisfied desire. We can achieve it through meditation and concentration. The more we can concentrate our thoughts, the more clearly we can grasp, the more concentrated it is, the more power is brought to bear on one point. It is easier to concentrate the mind on the external things as it always goes outwards, but in the case of deeper spirituality, religion, depth psychology, the object and subject are the same. We work and think at the same time, while a portion of our mind stands by and sees what we are thinking. The powers of the mind should be concentrated and turned back upon itself, and as the darkest places reveal this secrets before the penetrating rays of the sun, so will this concentrated mind penetrate its own innermost secrets.

All our knowledge which is called rational is referred to consciousness. But there is a very great part of my existence of which we are not conscious like assimilation, manufacturing of our blood, strengthening the body by the food etc. The conscious plane works with the feeling of egoism, while the unconscious plane, it works with the instinct. But there is a higher plane upon which the mind can work *i.e.* beyond consciousness. Just as, at the instinct level, our action takes place at the unconscious level, so also at the highest level, it also works beyond the conscious level or without the feeling of egoism or the feeling of "I". This is called superconsciousness or *Samadhi.* Here the man comes out enlightened, like a sage, a prophet, a saint. His whole character is changed, his life changed and illumined. This superconsciousness spontaneous, supra-logical and beyond sensory perceptions.

In order to reach the superconscious state in a scientific manner, it is necessary to pass through the various steps of *Yoga.* We begin with ethical disciplines called *Yama* and *Niyam,* then we lessens in bodily postures (*Asanana*) and vital breaths (*Pranayama*). Then we have the exercise of checking the outgoing powers of the mind, freeing it from the thralldom of the senses. The controlling of the mind and not allowing it to join itself to the centres is called *Pratyahara,* which can be achieved only through patient continuous struggle for years. The organs are separate states of the mind stuff. When I see a book the form is not the book, it is the mind. Something is outside which calls that form up. The colour is in the *Chitta*. The organs identify themselves with and take the forms of, whatever comes to them. If we can refrain from taking these forms, the mind will remain calm. This is *Pratyahara.* The next step is meditation on the heart that has given up all attachment to sense-objects, or by the meditation on anything that appeals to one as good. The mind by this practice, easily contemplates the most minute, as well as the biggest thing. Meditation is one of the great means of controlling the rising of the mind-waves. By meditation, we can make the mind subdue these waves, and if you go on practicing meditation for days, months and years, until it has become a habit, until it will come in spite of yourself, anger and hatred will be controlled and checked. The mind tries to think of one object, to hold itself to one particular spot, as the top of the head, the heart etc. and if the mind succeeds in keeping itself in that state for some time, it is called meditation (*Dhyana*).

We have tried politics for being our saviour but politicians, both in the East and the West, the South or the North, have dragged the whole of humanity to the point where humanity has to decide; "Now, either we can live, or these politicians can remain in power, both are not possible." Similarly, religion has also failed as they have been fighting, killing each other in the name of religion—a crusade, a Jihad, a holy war. Every religionist proclaim that "Their religion is the best", which means, other are inferior. In fact, one humanity or one religiousness should be enough—meditation, truth, love, sincerity, compassion—which is neither Christian nor Hindu nor Muslim. We want a quality, not something organised or regimented. A true religiousness needs no prophets, no saviors, no churches, no Popes, no priests because religiousness is the flowering of your heart. It is an individual affair—not dogma of the herd or crowd. It carries the message of love from one to the other. When religion and politics seem to have failed, we can try science, which has made more progress than man has made in the whole history of hundreds of thousands of years. But scientists too have become servants of nationalism, communism, fascism, capitalism. They are no more independent but part of vested interest. They work or discover but have no control over their own discoveries.

This can be changed if science should not only be an objective search, it should also open the subjective doors of consciousness. Uptill now, science has been denying his own consciousness or self-consciousness. This brings science closer to superstitions. Science will become of tremendous importance if it adds subjectivity and method of meditation to its methodology. Secondly, the scientist must refuse the politicians the possession of weapons of mass-destruction. He must learn to discriminate between which helps life and what destroys life. He must not serve death and destruction whatever the cost. So a scientist has to be a spiritual seeker first, and then he has also to be a revolutionary. Once scientists change their attitude and stops being supportive of politicians for war or destruction, so much energy will be released. But in order to make science more comfortable, more beautiful and more civilizational. We have to include meditation as an absolute part of education all over the world. Without meditation we cannot have the clarity and a grounding within ourselves and vision which is simple and innocent.

2

Encounter with the Other : Illusion and Reality

The problem of the "Other" is a problem of dualistic metaphysics. But to brush aside the duality or multiplicity and merge everything into a unity might be an interesting intellectual enterprise, but it suffers from oversimplification. The Universe, in fact, is a multiverse. Hence, encounter with the "other" is a fact of life. Atleast abstract unity is a grandiose but empty conception and hence, instead there is conception of concrete unity or unity-in-diversity. But even here, diversity retains its identity under the broad umbrella of a unity. It is, therefore, a metaphysical conflict resolution to say that there is unity in diversity.

There are obvious imperatives for metaphysical monism for example a barren dualism need a principle of interrelatedness without which duality cannot make a universe. But then, if we posit a principle of external relation, it involves the principle of regressus and finitinuum. The case of pluralistic metaphysics is still worse as one can ask why there are only 'seven categories' and not eight and soon. There are many other inconsistencies in supporting metaphysical dualism or pluralism.

Similarly, in the field of theology, polytheism or ditheism seems to have been gradually replaced by the faith in monotheism. Pluralistic theology is regarded as the faith of the primitive people. But even monotheism suffers from many inconsistencies. For example, why a perfect God needs a world or creation? If it is creation, it is beset with the problem of endless evil and if it is recreation, it looks as if even the perfect God needs, recreation or sport like the imperfect human beings. Hence monotheism does involve some sort of duality or plurality. Theology also presuopposes World and Man with God, thus God has to encounter with the "other". We have to solve the riddle of creation and explain the "fall of man" through mythologies. To posit God along with World or Man smacks of their independent identities and hence we have to devise various kinds of relationships like diesm, pantheism or pan-en-theism, each having its own structural philosophical defects. Then there are different monotheistic theological systems and yet they are at variance with each other. Islamic monotheism is qualitatively different from Christian Variety and Hindu monotheism is indescribable and basically different from Islam and Christian views. It means that in the same theological system of monotheism, there is encounter with the "other", hence one is not the other. Hence there is a clamour for "Universal Religion" or "Religion of Man". The days of personal religion, it seems, are over. But can we conceive of one single world religion and yet satisfy the individual sentiments and aspirations of all religionists? Buddha, Confusicues and Gandhi no doubt put forward the concept of Ethical Religion but people say that it takes away the essential theological element from religion. Hence, we need a religion which satisfies our heart and soul and yet in its encounter with the other does not generate hatred and animosity. Unless we are able to obliterate the emotional distinction between 'I' and "Thous' or 'mine' and 'thine' it is not possible. The Hindu religious metaphysics of Ramanuja, in order to reach this stage of non-confrontation between the multiple souls, holds that the individual soul is only a part (ansa) of God and hence it is divine and pure. Islam also holds a that "Man is not God but neither he is not different from the rays of God." (Adam Khuda nahi, Lekin Khuda Ke noor se Adam Juda nahi.) However, it does not fully stop the scope of encounter of the one soul with the other. Hence, Advaita Vedanta of Sankar, propounds the theory of 'That Those Art' (Tat Tvam Asi) or Man is God himself. Thus there is no encounter with the other. There is absolute identity. There is an intricate logic to explain the import of the meaning of the sentence "That Thou Art". This is not a tautological judgement as it might appear. It is not the base raptun of the slave before the mighty, that has overawed him for ever. It is not a product. It is the realisation of the essential non-composite universal nature of man. It affirms the fundamental oneness of Reality. The self is universal and one. Hence the final salvation is not derivative, it is native to the soul of man. It is the birthright of man. It is for all and everyone—hence it stands for salvation for all--sarva-mukti. This is spiritual democracy, where we do not based the need of the conceptions of eternal domnalion or the pleasures of the paradise. Nor we have distinctions of the self and not-self. There is no hiatus between God and man, both are con-substantial. This spiritual realisation of the fundamental oneness of Reality that makes us feel effectively the truth of man.

Hence, to the Advaitin, this concept of brotherhood of man is not a social exhortation nor a mere doctrine, it is reality. Others who talk about it have no roots for their feelings. It becomes merely convention or a habit with them. Paul Deusses, at the end of his tour of India had said. "The gospels quite correctly establish as the highest law of morality," Love your neighbour as yourselves. But why should I do so sense by the order of nature I feel pain and pleasure only in myself not in my neighbour? The answer is not in the Bible,... but it is in the Vedas, in the great formula—'That art Thou.' You should love your neighbour as yourself because you are your neighbour. It is therefore spiritual humanism.

It is only in Brahman realisation that joy infinite can be had. The result of Brahman realisation is fearlessness or abhay. Fear or sorrow result from a second (dvitiyad vai bhayam bhavati, Brahadaranyaka Upanisad, I.4.2). The monistic-faith and to realisation abolishes the scope for fear or sorrow. No serious attempt is made to define the term "identity". Mr. Johnson says : "the conception of identity and of otherness are two independent indefinable, the understanding of which is required in order intelligently to accept the truth...of any... proposition which explicitly or implicitly involves the notions of identity or of otherness." (Logic, Part-I, pp. 195-196). Identity comes to mean only negation of difference (abheda). When we have only negated otherness, the original term is left as no new content is added in our thought. Gadadhara in his famous treatise on Vyutpattivada has explicitly taken non-difference in the sense of identity (tadatmya). The identity of a thing in this sense, is found ultimately to consist in the particular nature of the thing which is not shared by anything else. The identity of meaning, in this sense, will be, in the last resort, the meaning itself.

The saying, "That Thou Art" also means that there is an unqualified identity between the soul that underlies the apparently finite man and God. It is true that if we take the word "Thou" in the sense of the empirical individual limited and conditioned by its body, and the word, "Thest" the reality beyond the world, there cannot be an identity between "Thou" and "That". We have to understand therefore the word "Thou" to imply pure consciousness underlying main and "That" to imply also pure consciousness which ferms the essence of God. Between these two complete identity exists and is taught by the Vedanta. There cannot be any identity between the man qualified by one set of conditions with the man qualified by another set. In short, it means that man, viewed apart from the different conditions is the same. So is the identity taught between Self and God. The Self apart from the conditions that differentiates it from the attributes that differentiate them from pure consciousness. Such identity judgement, therefore, is not tautological and superfluous, because it serves the purpose of pointing out that what are illusory taken as different are really one. The identity between terms appear as different. Being identical with God, the soul is in reality what God also really is. It is the supreme Braham—the self-luminous, infinite, consciousness, The soul appears as the limited, finite self because of its association with the body which is the product of ignorance.

In fact, all life is spiritual. The world is not a delusion or unreal. Life is Brahman. Hence non-violence is the greatest of all spirituality. Equally it is spiritually to save a life and to help a life to continue and do progress. Thus the whole course of evolution is repeated in the daily life of a man. The whole existence is Brahman and there is nothing except Brahman (Chandogya Upanisad, 1.3). Verily the whole existence is the Brahman says the Chandogya Upanisad (III. 14.1). As the spider produces the thread and absorbs it again, as the herbs grow on earth, as the hairs come out from a living man, even so does the Universe spring forth from the Imperishable Brahman, (Mundaka Upanisad, 1.17). The Upanisad says 'Life is Brahman' (Taittiriya Upanisad, III. 3), "Mind is Brahma" (T.U, III.4), the "Self is Brahman" (Mundukya Upanisad, 2). Thus when the seeker realises that his own Self is the Brahman and he is that Self, he boldly assests "I am the Brahman, which is the final divine dictum of wisdom appearing in the Brahadaranyaka Upanisad (I.IV.10).

If one is able to achieve this mental frame of identity between "I" and "Thou" or "Mine" and "Thine", the very basis of envy or jealousy, hatred and anger, will be most minimized if not completely liquidated. In fact, envy or jealousy, hatred or ill-will arise from a sense of duality or encounter with the other. If we can treat the other as oneself, there will be no such problem. The question is how this is possible? The attitude of distinction "between mine and thine," should not be treated only as an ethical sermon but also as a sociological imperative. After all, the root of all religious, ethenic or social conflicts lie in the distinction of "mine" and "thine". Hence, Socrates says that he is neither an Athenian nor a Greek but a citizen of the world. Similarly, Swami Viveknand decried the emphasis upon 'personal religion' and advocated "Universal Religion". Tagore talked about 'Religion of Man' went to the extent of practising each religion, Vedanta, Islam, Christianity etc. for specified duration in his personal life. Gandhi advocated treating all religions alike. He said "I am a Hindu, I am a Muslim, I am a Christian". Peace must be based on understanding and tolerance concerning the acceptance of different values. No doubt, encounters between different cultures can contribute to the preservation of peculiarities and promote a constructive dialogue the peace cannot manifest itself on the long run as a monotone standardised culture, *e.g.* as a forced form of an intellectual and ideological 'absolute monism', which would suppress or obstruct free individual. The "protest against the unity in the name of a sûbdued diversity" manifests itself in the end of the modern era as a monistic understanding. A book of prayer (Sivamahimna stotra) says : "As the different streams having their sources in different places all mingle their water in the sea, so Lord, the different paths which men take through different tendencies, various though they appear, crooked or straight, all lead to Thee" The Upanisads are full of such ideas. "Reality is one, seers call if differently". The Vedantic Absolutism is rooted in such experiences of reality. Here the subjectivity and objectivity, the internal world and the external world are fused into one. So also science and religion are fused together. Thus, the idea of oneness of things and universality of all religions are rooted here. It establishes not only the unity of man with other men, and with other living beings but also with the supreme reality of the universe or Brahman. The sun, the moon, stars, tire, air and every particle of cosmos is surcharged with the same radiation of the supreme Reality. It reveals itself in each and every mode of knowledge. (Pratibodh Viditam), in short, oneness and non-duality of the Supreme Reality (Ekmeva dvitiyam). The Gita also corroborates this unitary stand and says : "He who seens the Supreme Lord dwelling alike in all things, the imperishable in things that perish, he sees indeed. For seeing the Lord as the same, everywhere present, he does not destroy the Self by the Self, and thus he goes to the highest soul (Gita VI.30). This reveals the experience of the profound unity of all things in One who is the personal God. The deeper the self, the wider is its comprehension. When we are one with the Divine in us, we become one with the whole stream of life.

This spiritual unity is essential for the elevation of the

entire humanity. Act the evils—jealousy, hatred, grude, fear etc. are due to the ignorance of this unity of existence or the essential divinity of human race. Usually, we try to understand difference as otherness or the other as different. In the Greek language, the "other" not only meant "foreigner", but also the unintelligible, the inhuman. However, the Vedantic attitude is the treat the "other" as "oneself", hence there is likely to be less problem.

3

Philosophy of a Karmyogi

True to the Indian Philosophical tradition, Professor D.M. Datta believed that to be philosopher is not merely to have subth thoughts; but to love wisdom as to live according to its dictates. To him, philosophy was not merely an intellectual gymnastic or a recreation, but in the art and law of life which teaches us what to do in all cases and like the good marksmen to hit the white at any distance. Infact, spirituality and practical outlook are the two important features of Indian philosophy and Dr. D.M. Datta has applied & inherited these two attributes in his own life. Like Wordsworth's Skylorck, Dr. Datta was true to the kindred thought of heaven and earth. His head was no doubt in the Advaitic philosophy of the Upanishad—That Thou Art, but his feet were firmly on earth practicing the Kantian. Gita doctrine of the Categorical Imperative or Niskama Karma-Yoga. Hence, when we were giving Dr. Datta a hearty send off for his great visit to America, our teacher and beloved disciple of Dr. Datta himself, Late Professor Harimohan Jha, in his usual intelligent and cryptic way said : "D.M. Datta stands for three letter", D.M.D. in which the first 'D' stands for Duty and the last 'D' stands for Duty. This means Duty first and Duty Last. But the intervening term "M" is still more significant which stands for "More" so D.M.D. means "Duty and More Duty". Though this was uttered in a lighter win but this truly depicts his life's idea. He taught philosophy all his life and taught so well that he was admired and adored by both his students and scholars in India and abroad. He was so much conscientious to his teaching profession that he put his heart and soul into it and to do anything else to develop his career. Even so as a writer, he did not write very much but what he wrote became masterpieces in that field. About his 'Introduction to the Indian Philosophy', even Dr. Radhakrishnan had to say that there was no better 'Introduction' than this. About his 'Chief Currents' of Contemporary Philosophy, the great philosopher J.B. Pratt had said : "I am constrained to believe that there are a few philosopher East and West so well equipped as Dr. Datta." Late Professor Charles A. Moore of East-West Philosopher Conference was perhaps his greatest admirer in the west, who had invited him to Hawai to participate in the East-West Philosopher Conference. Dr. Datta not only contributed his harned paper but helped a lot to establish the center of East and West. Although he had penetrating grasp in Indian Philosophy, he would like to evolve a 'World Philosophy'. For this purpose, he had turned towards deep study into the trends of modern Indian philosophy, after he had written his magnum opus Six Ways of Knowing. In its depth and comparative approach, perhaps no other work on Indian epistemology has come to light. In course of his study of contemporary thought for about 12 years he became influenced by some western thinkers and charmed by a wonderful openness of such great souls as William James and A.N. Whitehead. An unconscious change was wrought on the earlier partriotic impulse of defending Indian culture as such. A wider human perspective began to take its place, which was further strengthened by his participation in the East-West Philosopher Conference. One great lesson, in his natural humility, he learnt from that Conference is that, it is easier to silence another person by argument than to convince him. To quote his memorable words : "So long as the inner motive of scoring victory (vigisa) was not replaced by a selfless devotion to truth and a genuine respect (sradha) for humanity, no amount or scholarship, orotatory or dialectical skill could produce any real and lasting effect". I found the spiritual influence on the teachers of the Dept. of Philosophy at Hawai, when I had the opportunity of participating in the East-West Philosopher Conference in 1995. He had global mind so he confesses that he has seen much of goodness in other countries and he no longer feels that old enthusiasm for proving the superiority of Indian thought and culture to those of other. He had seen so much goodness in other countries that he believed that there are other good ways of thinking and living that what we have achieved here, and that there is a good deal we can learn from other, as they also can perhaps from us. "But ideas", he says "can spread and last only if they emanate from a good life."

But as a tried and trusted Freedom Fighter under Mahatma Gandhi's leadership and as an Indologist of great name and fame, Dr. Datta admitted real sorrow that long foreign domination has crushed our self-confidence, which is the mark of a living nation. Hence, we have blindly imitated the West-particularly Great Britain. An unassimilable load of foreign ideas and customs come to on a deep under current on indigenous ones. There arise all the merbid psychological phenomena of a split personality. On the other hand, a reacher equally blind has now set in among a richer of our people to have nothing from the West. It is a danger symptom of self-sufficiency that would not only impoverish our culture, but also, hamper international understanding and our own ideal of treating the whole world as one family (Vasudhaiva Kutumbkam). According to Dr. D.M. Datta, the history of India, during at least the five hundred years has shown a remarkable capacity for such judicious assimilation and synthesis, as well as for appreciation of the universal ideals of humanity. Narrow and disruptive forces of the present time have been overpowered by the synthetic genius of Indian culture. But we should also take into account that there can be no rootless internationalism. There is no virtue in open mindedness which leads no where. Hence our first attempt today is to study with the Indian systems of thought then supplement and widen our knowledge by studying both the western as well as the eastern thought.

No doubt there is but Philosophy like science. But this refer to only with regard to fundamental problems—matter, soul, God, truth but even the philosophical discussions of such universal topics arises out of certain concepts beliefs relating to particular times and place. In other words philosophy arises not out of vacuum and hence it is not separable from the social background. Dr. Datta is therefore critical of the tendency to confine the work 'philosophy' only to discussion of term abstract, theoretical, logical and metaphysical problems, which would have nothing to do with practical aspects of philosophy, society, religion and politics. To treat philosophy as mere 'linguistic analysis' is an example of decadent phase of Western Philosophy. Indian Philosophy has always regarded philosophy as a guide to life as we find in the teaching of Buddha, Mahavira or Sankara. Philosophy as a corner has become an artificial and dead affair out of touch with life. Therefore, we have made so little contribution to modern thought. Hence Dr. Datta, at the cost of cheap popularity in philosophical realm by peonpooring the traditional conondrums took up the cause of propagating the contemporary Indian Philosophical thought. There he found an earnest search for truth and unity in diverse peoples and cultures, an effort to assimilate the synthesis of the best wisdom of the East to the West, an international outlook, a regard for other religions and cultures, an integral view of life, special emphasis on the necessity of moral discipline, recognition of morality and spiritual realisation, belief in inner goodness of man, supreme concern for the individual and constructive synthetic view of the universe.

True modern Indian Philosophers like Vivekanand, Tagore, Gandhi, Sri Aurobindo might have dwelt upon the themes of the Vedas and Upanisads but their interpretations are original and much more vital. They are the live roots from which even out technical philosophy springs. Their contribution or Datta does not believe in such cheap and unthoughtful; criticisms against Philosophy that, philosophy is useless, irrelevant. Not to go far as Buddha, Jesus, Socrates, even in modern times, we find unmistakable practical role is playing and is destined to play in the present world. Markist philosophy did cast a great influence on the world so to check the spread of Communism, politicians and war veterans have tried to confront Communism with ideas of democracy.

Scientists are seeking some direction and Einstein plead strongly for a synthesis of seva and spirituality. Modern Philosophers like James, Jeans, Eddington, Herigedoing show severe idealistic landless in modern science. The great Indian thinkers from Raja Ram Mohan Roy upto Tilak and Gandhi have led cultural renaissance. Mahatma Gandhi has not only helped in freeing idea but he has given an alternative philosophy of war (Satyagraha) and a new philosophy of civilization for the 21st century. Gandhi had time only to finish a part of his experiment but it as been acclaimed by the greatest leader of modern times inside and outside India. Martin Lutter King adopting the Gandhian technique of non-violent resistance has successfully solve the problem of racial discrimination; Leh Walessa challenged the might of military rule in Poland with performed success, the Great Powers are trying hard to stop nuclear harakin but their vested interest are the greatest shimbling. In order to advocate singing C.T.B.T. they should pledge to destroy thousands of nuclear arsenals with them. In India, through the Gandhian method of non-violent, Gandhi's spiritual heir Acharya Vinoba launched land-gift and village gift (Bhoodan-Gramdan) movement which is a significant achievement to root out economic injustice. So also Jaya Prakash Narain aroused national consciousness against a total atrium attempt to suppress civil and political rights through non-violence.

To conclude, Dr. D. M. Datta not only taught philosophy but also living philosophy. His life was worthy of evolution by other. He never hankered after any power and position with the greatest humility, he had turned down many covetous offer like that of Padma Bhusan, Vice-Chancellorship and membership in UNESCO delegation. In fact, this was height of greatness. His whole mission of his life was to make philosophy a living and useful discipline that it used to be in the past in India. His philosophical pilgrimage began with the study of abstruse Indian texts, which nourished him throughout his life to go deep and deep to defend Indian thought and culture without slightest hatred to the western thought. Thus he has shown that true Indian Philosophy is cosmic in its scope, integral in its sweep and practical in life.

4

Reason and Intuition in Indian Thought

1. Background

Hindu thought, no doubt is predominant in India but its germs lie in the Indus Valley civilization and more so in Mohanjodaro civilization. Before the Aryans came, there were Nisads, Kirats etc. But Indian civilization through its alchemy has integrated them all without eliminating the divestiture. But for academic purposes, when I am supposed to discuss "Hindu Thought", I am constrained to leave aside "The Buddhist" and the Jaina" thought.

As a matter of fact, there are three important strands of ancient Indian culture : (1) Vedic (which is now mainly Hindu) (2) Sramanic (Evangelical or Missionary) having two sub-strands *(a)* Jainism *(b)* Buddhism and (3) the Lokayat or the school Materialism. All these three have got great antiquity and great heritage in philosophy, religion and culture. In broader sense, Hinduism is said to include Vedic religion (mainly Vaishnava, Shiva and Shakta) Buddhism, Jainism, Sikhism, Arya Samaj, Brahma Samaj, Prathana Samaj etc. So it is quite necessary to understand the unique nature of Hinduism as a religious thought. In a narrow and accepted sense of the term of 'religion' Hinduism may not be called a religion. There is no central book of reference as we find Holy Quran for the Muslims, or the Holy Bible for the Christians. Even those who believe in the inviolability of the Vedas, they are Hindus but those who do not accept in testimony like Buddhists, Jainas and the Lokayats and many others, they are also Hindus. What to speak of the Vedas, those who cannot read a single word of the Vedas, it does not matter. He might read true the Gita or the Ramayan or even Hanuman Chalisa, that is enough. Similarly, those who believe in the existence of God, they are Hindus but there are many who refute it, like the famous philosophical orthodox schools of Sankhya, Mimamsa, even Advait Vedanta (God is illusion) are accepted as Hindus. The Jainas, the Buddhists and Indian materialists are frankly atheists. Similarly, this is no one way for final self-realization. Those who follow the Path of Knowledge, they are Hindus, those who reject it and accept the path of devotion, they are also Hindus and so on. Hence in the accepted narrow sense of the term 'religion', Hinduism can not be called a religion. But who can deny that Hinduism is an established and powerful religion. This only shows that it covers rigidity and regimentation. Ofcourse, this does never mean that there is no fixed base of its own. Infact, Spiritualism is its supreme ideal.

2. Hindu View of Religion

Broadly, religions of the world can be distinguished into (1) those which emphasize the object (2) and those which insist on experience. For the former, religion is an attitude of faith and conduct directed to a power without; for the second, it is an experience of which the individual attaches supreme value. For the Hindus (including the Buddhist and the Jainas), religion is salvation. It is more a transforming experience than a notion of God. Hence, according to it, a real religion cannot exist without a definite conception of deity, but well without a distinction between the spiritual and the profane, the sacred and the secular. Even in primitive religions, we have religion, though not a belief in God. In Hinduism even in its theistic systems, the essential thing is not a belief in God or deity, but its power to transform man. Belief and conduct, rites and ceremonies, authorities and dogma are assigned a place subordinate to the art of conscious self-discovery and contact with the divine. Therefore Philostratus says "All wish to live in the nearness of God, but only the Hindus bring it to pass". Spiritual experience has been confirmed by the experience of men whose writings testify to their intellectual power and has commanded the respect of the masses. It cannot be explained away as hallucination or charlatanism. Brahma is the principle of search as well as the object sought, the animating ideal and its fulfillment. The very fact that we seek God clearly proves that life cannot be without Him. God is life and recognition of this fact is spiritual consciousness. When man apprehends the supreme being, returns to the concrete, and controls his life in the light of its truth, he is a complete man. He reaches an almost inconceivable Universality. All his power which have been hither to bound up with narrow pursuits are liberated for larger ends.

We fall away from our authentic being if we are lost in the world of empirical objects and earthly desires, turning our back on the reality, which gives them value. He is in whom the spark of spirit glows and grows into a new man. The divine penetrates his self, wells up and flows through him, absorbing him and enriching him within it. God is not another self, He is the real self closer than his own ego. "I live, yet not I, but it is Christ who liveth in me."

Hence, the fundamental truths of Hinduism are that our real self is the supreme being which is our business to discover and consciously become, and this being is one in all. This is 'Thou in me and I in thee'. Fellowship is life, lack of fellowship is death. The secret solidarity of the human race cannot be abolished by the passing insanities of the world. The collapse of a civilization built on the audacities of speculative doubt, moral impressionism, and the fierce and the confused enthusiasms of races and nations need not dishearten us. Intellectually the world is bound together in a web of common ideas and reciprocal knowledge. Even the obstacles of religious dogmas are not so formidable as in past. 'Religious fundamentalism coupled with terrorism, that we see today, is neither 'religious' nor even 'fair' politics'. They are bound to pass away.

The Hindu Ideal of Life and Knowledge

There is only our ideals for man, to make himself profoundly human, perfectly human. "Be ye perfect". The whole man, the complete man, is the ideal man, the divine man. "You are complete in the Godhead" said St. Paul. Hence the seeking for our highest and inmost self is the seeking of God. India has adored and idealized most not soldiers and statesman, not men of technology and heads of industry, not even pacts and philosophers but those rarer and more chastened spirits whose greatness lies in what they are and not in what they do; men who have stamped infinity on thought and life of the country, men who have added to the invisible forces of goodness in the world. While we start with the immediate and the actual our limited consciousness, we can constantly increase and enrich it to the seen and unseen of the world around us and above us. The instinctive and the intellectual both attain their fruition in the spiritual personality. The flesh is sanctified and harmonized with the spirit; the intellectual is illumined and increased with intuition and revelation of the spirit. Body and mind, instinct and intellect become the willing servants of the spirit and not its tyrannical master.

Today, this is a tendency to overlook the spiritual and exalt the intellectual. Everything is stripped of soul, of inner life. The world is all, and we must rest content with it. We live on the surface and are afraid of thinking because it is all so and discordant and divided self, leading to universal barbarism? Why cannot have the courage and selflessness, the vision and the generosity to regulate our affairs on principles, of equity and justice?

Here the Hindus, Buddhists and the Jainas make out that ignorance (avidya) is the root cause of all the anguish and afflictions. Hence knowledge (Vidya wisdom bodhi—enlightenment) is our salvation. So there are two kinds of knowledge : 1. Intellectual and 2. Spiritual. There is no conflict between them but their domains are different. The Upanishads compares the temporal knowledge with the self-knowledge

(Atma Jnana) and comes to the conclusion that unless we have self-knowledge, we cannot get peace and immortality. The famous learned sage Narada had therefore gone to the spiritual Seer Sanat Kumar even though he had acquired knowledge of the entire world. But the knowledge of the self is superior to the knowledge of the temporal world. So the Gita says that corresponding to higher and lower nature of God, there are two kinds of knowledge—higher (Para) and lower (apara). (Gita VII 5, 3.42; 18.50). Isa Upanishad, even transcends the division between knowledge (vidya) and ignorance (avidya) (Isa, 9) and finally comes to the conclusion that it is the self-knowledge which gives us immortality and bliss (Isa, 11). Infact, self-knowledge (adhyatma, vidya) is the knowledge par-excellence. (Gita, 10.33; 13.11). As becoming is a lapse from being, so is avidya or ignorance a fall from vidya or knowledge. To know the truth, to apprehend reality, we have to get rid of avidya and its intellectual moulds, which all crack the movement we try to force reality into them.

Inspite of elevating the self-knowledge to the supreme status, Hindu thought has distinctly shown the two tends—the rationalistic and the intuitionistic, from the very beginning. There is not an excuse for indolence of thought. Philosophy as logic on this view persuades us to give up the employment of the intellectual concepts which are relative to our practical needs and the world of becoming. So long we are bound by intellect and are lost in the world of many. We shall seek in vain to get back to the simplicity of one. We can think it out, defend it logically and help its propagation. With its distinctions of logic and intuition, reality and world of existence, we meet in the Upanishads, Nagarjuna, Sankara in ultra philosophical moods, and echoes of it are heard in Parmenides, Plato, Spinoza, Pobinus, Bradley and Bergson, not to speak of the mystics in the west. Whatever the being, pure and simple, may be called intuition, that is nothing more or less than an absolute abstraction, it is intellect Intuition is supposed to continue when every fact and form of existence is abolished. It is the residue left behind when abstractions is made from the whole world.

When an effort is made to abolish the whole universe, sublate all existence, nothing seems, to remain for thought. Thought, finite and relational finds to its utter despair that, there is just nothing remaining for thought. To the conceptual mind the central proposition of intuition" "Being only is", means that there is just nothing at all. Thought, as Hegel says, can only work with determinate realities, concrete things. To it all affirmation implies negation and *vice-versa*. So those who are not satisfied with the intuited being, and wish to have a synthesis capable of being attained by thought which has a natural instinct for the concrete, are attained to a system of objective idealism. These are those who hold that the rationality of the real with the reservation that reality is not mere reason. In 'that' exceeds 'what' in Bradley's, words. Thought gives us knowledge of reality, but it is only knowledge, and not reality. Thought works with the opposition of subject and object, and the absolute real is something in which these anti-thesis are annulled. The most concrete thought, combining many in one, is still abstract because it is self-contradictory, and if we want to grasp first the real, we have to give up thought. What thought reveals is not opposed to reality, but it is the revelatory part of it. Secondly reality is to be attained in its fullness by a form of feeling or intuition.

However, Hindu thought uses the term darshana, which is neither perceptual observation not conceptual knowledge or intuitional experience, but a synthesis of all. It indicates a thought system required by intuitive experience and sustained by logical argument. Conceptual constructions do not possess the certainty of experienced facts. Again, an opinion or logical view becomes truth only if it stands the test of life. Darshana is a spiritual perception, a holistic view revealed to the soul-sense, which is possible only when and where philosophy is lived, and not merely and intellectual gymnastic.

The Western mind lays great stress on science, logic and humanism, where as Hindu thought thinks that we possess a power more interior than intellect. For Hindus, a system of philosophy is an insight-vision of truth and not merely a matter of logical argument. Intuitive insight is identical with freedom. Brahma which symbolizes the absolute reality as well as the intuitive wisdom, which Sankara regards as integral experience, Buddha emphasizes the importance of bodhi or enlightenment. The Sophistication of the intellect are hindrances to higher life. In early Buddhism, Prajna or intuitive insight is the highest activity of the human mind—which amounts to realizing the spirit and in life the basic unity of existence. Even in Plato, Noesis is the highest kind of knowledge, immediate and supernatural, and believed that dialectic is the conversation of the soul with itself. Aristotle speaks of the absolute self-knowledge God. Platonists and Neo-Platonists were convinced that logical knowledge alone was inadequate. From Socratic insistence on the concept of Russell's mathematical logic, the history of western thought has been an illustration of the primacy of the logical.

True, these are different ways of knowing—sense experience, discursive reasoning and intuitive apprehension; the former two kinds are inadequate to apprehend the real. Plato therefore distinguishes between 'knowledge' and 'opinion' Bradley and Bergson took interest on the symbolic character of logical knowledge. Thought lives in the distinction between reality of that and the abstract character of what. However wide the 'what' may extend it can never embrace the whole of existing reality. Intellectual symbols are no substitutes for perceived realities. Besides the whole life of feeling and emotions, "the delights and pains of the flesh the agonies and raptures of the soul" remains outside of thought. Bradley too demand higher unity in which "thought, feeling and volition's are blended into a whole". It is the creative effort of the whole man. According to Bergson, conceptual analysis has its own qualities but it is separative utilitarian and partial. Reality is life, movement, duration, concrete continuity; and logic gives us concepts which are timeless, immobile, dead. He suggests intuition for intellect as the proper logical knowledge takes away from the individual and the actual into a world of abstractions, while intuitive knowledge gives us an insight into the individual. The deepest things of life are known only through intuitive apprehension. We recognize their truth but do not reason about them. According to Bergson, the life force evolves intellect as an instrument for the practical control of the environment. Intellect is useful for action; it is the tool making faculty by means of which life fashions inanimate matter into environments for extension of its own power but intuitive truths are simple acts of mental vision, free from doubt. So logical knowledge is non-knowledge (avidya) valid only till intuition arises. So Sankar says the "fruit of knowledge is manifest to intuition". (Anubharudham eva ca vidya phalam. Brahma Sutra, C.S.B), III.4-15; Katha UP., III.12. Both intellect and intuition are justified in their own rights and useful for their own specific purposes but the "direct vision" (Plato), "apprehension of the form of beauty" (Socrates) or intuition is the "perfect knowledge" (Samyak Jnana). Intuition is not a-logical but supra-logical. It is the wisdom gained by the whole spirit which is mere fragment thereof, be its feeling or intellect. The whole life of mind is more concrete than that of any specialized mode of it. Therefore, Hegel's criticism and misapprehension that the intuitive power is something cut off from the rest of mental life and the reality is unfounded. Intuition is not unrelated to intellect or other forms of knowledge but it is the fulfillment of all (Jnan Vijnanam Sahitam). Hence, Indian thought does not create a conflict between intellect and intuition. Sankar admires that intuitive certainly is reached after a long process of discursive analysis. Hegel, in his "intuitive understanding", exaggerating the importance of conceptual thinking is inclined to make reason organic to reality. Dialectic becomes not merely a method of philosophizing but also a description of reality. Thus Hegel reduces the rich life of concrete nature to a ballet of blooded categories. Hence T.H Green makes thought not merely revelatory but constitutive of reality. Thought is things and things are thought". (T.H. Green, works III, P:144). It is perhaps the heritage of Kant who does not believe in any unity prior to reflective thought.

In Indian thought, philosophy is not so much as a conceptual reconstruction as an exhibition of insights. If life is history, if reality is genuine becoming a perpetual renewal, and not mere repetition, then its apprehension cannot be merely dialectical. There is however, no break of continuity between intuition and intellect. In moving from intellect to intuition, we are not moving the direction of unreason but are getting into the deepest rationality of which human nature is capable. It is not non-rational ; it is only non-conceptual. Even intuition has an intellectual content, and by making it more intellectual we deepen the content. Intuition is neither abstract thought and analysis nor formless darkness and primitive sentience. It is the wisdom, the nous of which Aristotle speaks, the all-pervading intelligence of Dante. The order of nature is dependable unity. The ordered men of the universe is a conviction of life which is beyond mere logic. It will not do to be merely logical. It is reasonable to be reasonable. Intuition is as strong as life itself from whose soul it springs. Our whole life grows on the foundation of a deeper insight. It is this spiritual imperative born out of intuitive insight to seek not the safe and the expedient but the good, logic and ethics take for granted the meaningfulness of life, which they require but cannot establish. The heart of man craves for happiness. The rejection of pain is a sovereign instinct in our nature. Life is opposed to death. All growth in knowledge is an elaboration of this instinct our increasing assimilation of the mind of man to the spirit in him. All experiences issues forth from it and sets in it. It is beyond the reach of thought, sensors, etc. Major convictions of life are born of intuition. "The voice of inner demon" counted most for Socrates, so "Recollection" in Plato is the basis of logical process, Aristotle's "nous" represents "intuitive apprehension", even Descartes 'clara-et-distinctia' or clear perceptibility or intelligibility presuppose "intuitive knowledge". Spinosa, thinks that from intuitive vision arises the highest possible peace of mind". Leibniz's 'pure reason' cannot be tested by self-observation. According to Pascal, mind thinks in two ways—mathematics and the finer subtler. In latter case we see and feel the truth. Kant's chief contribution to the philosophy of religion is to show the 'logical indemonstrability of God'. The highest idea is not derived from sense, or proved by logic, but is founded in the secret places of the soul and its validity is self-established by reason or the soul's trust in itself. Leaving aside Hegel, Jacobi thinks that metaphysical truth can be reached not by immediate knowledge of ideas but by immediate insight or direct knowledge (faith).

Perhaps upholding the supremacy of intuition, Indian thought is misunderstood as being dogmatic and anti-rational. I will put before only five points in the background of what has been stated before regarding intuition :

(a) All systems of Indian philosophy starts discussion with epistemology-problem of knowledge, origin, kinds, validity, error etc. It is true that Veda or the shruti (scripture) is considered to be an authoritative source of knowledge but this is because that Vedic statements are sayings of the trustworthy (apta—vachana) but even there is always a saving clause that it satisfies your conscience and reason. What is dogma to the ordinary man is experience to the pure in heart.

(b) Infact, there are two trends in Indian thought *(a)* intuitionistic *(b)* Rationalistic from the very beginning of the Vedas. Intuitive trend emphasizes the value of intuitive knowledge, only through which we can grasp the ultimate reality. The Vedas says : "Andidvatam Swadhya Tad Ekam". In the beginning there is only one.

Neither our eyes can nor our mind, nor our consciousness ' can reach there—says the Upanishad. It means that the ultimate reality can be known only through intuitive insight. But the rationalistic trend is equally strong. We can see the great logical acumen of Indian scholars like Gargi, Maitreyi, Sankar, Ramanuja (Buddhist) Dignag, Asang, Vasubavodhu, Nagarjuna, Dhama Krist, Gautama, Prasastpada to Raghunath Siromani and Gangesh Upadhya etc. (Jaina), Samta Bhadra, Sidhsena, Hemchandon, Haribhadra, Yasovieya etc. The most important thing to note is that the logical trend has never died down. For example there has been commentaries upon commentaries on Gobana's Nyaye-Suba (Treatise of logic). Navya-Nyaya reminds us of symbolic logic and analytical philosophy of today. In short, we can fight the climax of logical acumen and sophistication in all systems of Indian philosophy whether it is Nyaya-vaisesika, Sankhya, Memasa and Vedanta.

3. Hinduism is its Own Best Critic

No religion admits of so much of varieties and so much of freedom of thought. We can be Hindu even by denying God, scripture or follow any particular path or ritual. This freedom of thought is the basis of rationality. In all system of Indian philosophy—there are two divisions.

4. The Spirit is Man

The roots of all great thinking and noble living lie deep in life itself and not in the dry light of mere reasoning. All creative work is science and philosophy, is art and life, is inspired by intuitive experience. Creative work is not blind imitation or mechanical repetition. It is a synthetic insight which advances by leaps. The successful practice of intuition requires previous study and assimilation of a multitude of facts and laws. Hence we can say that great intuitions arise out of a matrix of rationality. We invent by intuition though we prove by logic.

Intuition is not exclusive phenomenon in religion or spiritual experience, it is present in artistic achievements, poetry, artistic knowledge, and ethical life, religious consciousness and other values, creative work etc. Thus the spirit in man is neither the physical body or vital organism, the mind or the will, but something which underlies them all and sustains them. It is the basis and background of our being. But we should remember that though it cannot be gained by mere intellectual effort it is also true that it cannot be gained without it. Intellectual inaction seems to be the prelude to the intuitive flash.

5. Indian mind thinks not only of Righteousness but also of truth as constituting religion. It is not only a moralist but a rationalist in its outlook. Sankar says which is not rational or

logical has to be shunned. Even Gandhi says "I reject a very religious doctrine that does not appeal to reason and is in conflict with morality". He goes further "I do not believe in the exclusive divinity of the Vedas.... my belief in the Hindu scriptures does not require me to accept every verse as divinely inspired", I would reject all authority if it is in conflict with sober reason or the dictates of the heart. Authority sustains and ennobles the weak when it is the handiwork of reason, but it degrades them when it supplants reason sanctified by the still small voice within. Such a disregard of or limited regard for the Vedas is a thing not unknown to the students of Hinduism. The Gita says "Go beyond the three gunas which alone constitute the subject matter of the Vedas." (II.42-43) The Mundak Upanishad says "Those fools, who believe that only the performance of sacrificial ritual (istapurtam) is meritorious and nothing else is meritorious, come back to this mortal world" (Mundak I.2.10). So can we find such statement is Isa Upanishad (9.12) and Kathopnisad (II.5). Infact the Vedic Aryans were like glorious children in their eager acceptance of life. They represent the youth of humanity whose life was still fresh and sweet, undisturbed by disconcerting dreams.

Of course, it is not very fair to divide Hinduism into traditional and philosophical, for popular understanding and know that in the Indian tradition, the Vedas are spoken as Nigamas, constituting the authoritative religious scripture and Agamas, under whose fold the Vaishnawas, the Saivas, and the Saktas etc. come. But philosophical systems, orthodox and unorthodox, are examples of the best and the highest logical and philosophical traditions in the world. Each philosophical school has such a multitude literature of criticism and counter-criticism that it shudders to think that how traditional mind can be so much logical and philosophical.

Conclusion : Compared to such neatly formulated religious creeds as Christianity, Islam, Hinduism appears to be a matter of beliefs, doctrines and practices that defy the understanding and interpretative ingenuity of even sympathetic students and scholars. This complexity is due to racial and religious mixtures, its deep religious overtones in all walks of life (India is religion-cramb) "No people on earth took religion so seriously, none toiled on the way to salvation as they did"—Paul Deussen said. No doubt there was great regard for scriptural authority but the diluting factors are equally important. True there are mystical elements in Vedic religion in the concepts of Rigved (orderly function) Dhama (expression of universal order), Yajna (rituals). Tapas etc., but spirituality and intuition is the basis of everything—epistemology, logic, politics, art and literature. Intuition is an activity of the whole being. It is recognized factor in the discovery of scientific truth, in creative spirit, art and aesthetics, politics and economics. But, it has never disregarded logic and reason. If God is the whole of reality which intuitive knowledge affirms still as Aristotle told us in his Poetics no object is a whole which is not logically coherent.

Discovery becomes proof when that is revealed by intuition by the slower process of consecutive thinking. The general character of the universe as known is quite consistent with this intuited certainty of God. It is the only way by which religious truths can be recommended to the general people for whom religion is a matter of trust and inference. It is the safest way to defend from uncritical intuitions and dogmations which are prepared to find whatever they want.

5

The Holy Mother : True to the Kindred Points of Heaven and Earth

1. Holiness of the Mother

The Holy Mother's life was wonderfully earthly as well as perfectly divine. As a mundane being, her life appears to be just the lonely life of a Bengali Brahmin, almost unlettered and unsophisticated woman of a rural setting, who is sometimes a daughter, a sister, a wife and Guru-mata (Teacher's consort) but as a spiritual sould there is an unmistakable mark of superhuman love and consummation of purity and divinity. Swami Abhedananda said :

पवित्रं चरितं यस्याः पवित्रं जीवनं यथा।
पवित्रता स्वरूपिण्यै तस्यै कर्मो नमो नमः।।

"whose character is all pure and whose life is similarly pure, who is the embodiment of purity divine, that shinning goddess I salute again and again". Sri Ram Krishna himself said that there is no difference between him and Sri Sarda Devi. If the Master was a "renunciate of the world", the Holy Mother was a "renunciate in the world". The Master himself worshipped her as Supreme deity—Saraswati, Sodshi, Kali, Durga, Bhubneshwari etc. We all know that the Master knowing her divine power, established her one day on the divine throne of goddess Kali and performed Sodshi form of worship. Swami Vivekanand rationalised it by saying that without *Sakti*, there is no regeneration for the world. In her, one realised that wisdom and sweetness to which the simplest of the woman may attain. He was so much enamoured by the female-power that he believed that India has become the weakest and most backward in the world because Shakti is held in dishonour here. Mother has been born to revive that wonderful *Shakti* in India and make her the nucleus of world-power. Swami Vivekananda went further and said that "Father's grace is great but Mother's grace is paramount". To quote him again : "Mother's grace is a hundred thousand times more valuable than Father's". Another apostle Swami Purnananda ranks the Holy Mother higher place than even Sita, Savitri, Radha. She concelaed her spiritual powers. She appeared as the indigent woman, sweeping the floor, cleaning the utensils, husking the paddy and even removing the left over of the food of the devotees, with infinite patience, unbounded love, and negation of even the slightest trace of annoyance, and egotism. When a disciple opening her heart before Swami Sardanandji saying that he believes in the divinity of Swami Ramkrishna but he cannot comprehend that Mother (Sarda Devi) as divine. Swamiji asked : "Do you then mean to say that God (Ramkrishna) married the daughter of a cow-dung-cake-gathering woman?" The Holy Mother and Sri Ram Krishna used to mutually consider the other as Mother. When Ram Krishna entered Mahasamadhi, the Mother cried out "Mother, where are you gone?" "The Holy Mother is Saraswati herself, the bestower of knowledge, she again is Mahamaya, the giver of liberation."—say Swami Abhedananda. In her spiritual trance, he spoke about her as Radha Swami Vijnananand believes that the Master is indeed Rama and Krishna and the Holy Mother is none other than Sita and Yogamaya. This time the Master's advent on earth was in a disguised form (as woman). The spirit of Rama Krishna was unified with her. They were one in essence as the scriptures says : "Thou art man, thou art woman." (त्वं स्त्री त्वं प्रमान असि, त्वं कुमार उत वा कुमारी). So, "He is our all. He is our mother; He is our father; He is our brother, and friend."

2. Motherhood of God

If we move to the higher spirituality, there is only the great

Cosmic Energy which makes it possible for the divinity to assume human form. This is Infinite in the Finite form. If the Infinite is unrelated to the world of time, humanity cannot realize the Infinite. The Infinite, then must speak the language of the finite. So it is that whenever there is occasion and need, the Divine descends into humanity. The Infinite must take form and shape and live with the mortals. Hence there must be a combination of the Supreme Divinity (Paratva) and easy accessibility (Saulabhva). The great incarnations of the past revealed either of the two prominently. In the Avatara of this age, there was a confluence of Rama and Krishna. As if this was not enough, Sri Ram Krishna brought the Holy Mother with him to focus upon normalcy, naturality and easy accessibility. Ramkrishna was the high Himalayas, which average people could not reach but the Holy Mother was like the accessible Ganges, where anybody can take a bath and cool himself. The incarnation could show its divinity or miraculous powers. It is difficult to cover the super powers for an Avatara. But in the case of incarnation in the form of the Holy Mother, it was extremely difficult to comprehend her greatness because she lived like a very ordinary housewife doing all common duties like sweeping the floor, cooking and serving the food to all and sundry, even cleaning the plates in which the drunkard, the untouchables, the criminal etc. took food. One could not know the glory and grandeur of the Holy Mother as she chose to hide her divinity under a cover of commoners. There was hardly any external symbols of saintliness in her and it was far difficult to understand her divinity. Call it Maya-power of God or Holy Mother's spiritual modesty, she kept all these powers under veil. The Gita (IV.6) says :

> Though unborn and immortal, and also the Lord of all beings, I manifest Myself through My own Maya-Power, keeping my Prakrti under control.

In fact, there was no difference between Ram Krishna and Sri Sharda Devi, so Sri Rama Krishna himself said to his disciples—"There is no difference between me and Sharda". The Holy Mother also said that she and the Master were non-different. The same divinity, the same Supreme Spirit, manifested itself in two bodies. Because this age is a difficult age, it required two persons who were identical in order to spread the message of India's spirituality. It is said that Shiva's consort Parvati because of her intense love for Her Lord, occupied the half of his body (Ardha Narishwar). But even without her desire, even without a need for her wanting, the Holy Mother occupied the entire personality of Sri Ram Krishna. Hence, this maya is called the "Motherhood of God". They showed two paths "renunciation of the worldliness" and "renunciation in worldliness". Ram Krishna was a flaming example of spiritual renunciation so was the Holy Mother. Among the ten Avataras (incarnations) of God in the Hindu tradition, we do not find a place for women, so among the different Prophets in Islam, we do not have a woman prophet, among 24 Tirthankaras of the Jainas, only one is said to be a woman and that also doubtful, in Christianity perhaps there has not been a woman Pope. But Ram Krishna while following the Tantrik tradition, identifies the Holy Mother with Him "Who is she but my Shakti"—says Ram Krishna. Shakti is her manifestation. She is Saraswati or goddess of learning. She is Kali, Durga (Vivekananda), Supreme Prakriti (Abhedananda), Shodshi (Sankara) or Sri (Sri Yantra). Shiva is as good as Shava (dead body) with the power of Shakti. She is also triad of knowledge, feeling and desire. Shiva and Shakti, Ram Krishna and Sharda Mata are one in two or two in one. Hence the concept of Motherhood of God is not against the Indian spiritual tradition. Mother loves not on her own terms but on child's terms. She does not love her child because he or she is good but because he/she is her own child. When the Divine approaches man on his own terms, it is Motherhood of God. The Holy Mother loves the embodiment of the Motherhood of God. Ram Krishna had himself said that the spiritual heritage will be shared by her.

In our country, we characterise Shakti as a woman-power as being feminine. But in other lands especially in the West, power is pictured as being masculine, as a man. In India Shakti takes the form of a graceful woman as Mother. This is the message of India to the world. So long as power is brutal, and Shakti is of the animal virility, man cannot realise his goal. It is only when power is used in pursuit of the higher values of his life that man can come to know God at all. In India womanhood is being perfected in the Motherhood which is the symbol of service and sacrifice.

3. Transcendental Marriage

Hence marriage is not a business contract for sexual satisfaction but for a mutually elevating relationship between kindred souls. It is an ethical and spiritual relationship and from both sides the influence is more spiritual than secular. It is why that the Fatherhood and the Motherhood were both incarnated in the same Divinity. The Upanisad therefore declares : "You are woman, you are man". The male-principle and the female-principle are not distinct from each other. In each individual there are the manifestations of both these principles. No man is wholly a man; no woman is entirely a woman. There is always a combination of the two. By choosing to worship the Divine in the form of Kali or elevating the Holy Mother as the Supreme Power. Sri Ram Krishna taught that there in divinity in the Mother, or divinity in destruction. It is very difficult to combine motherliness and destructions, and here in the form of Kali, we have a combination of both and in Sri Ram Krishna there was the soul of Motherhood. So when the news of Mahasamadhi of the Master was conveyed to the Holy Mother, she burst into crying—"Oh Mother, where have you gone?" This is the Motherhood of God. Another very very significant episode comes when at Dakhineshwar one day while shapooning the feet of Sri Ram Krishna, the Holy Mother asked him "Who do you think I am ?" In which Shri Ram Krishna replied, "The Mother who is in the shrine, gave birth to this body and is now living in the Nahabat, a small room at some distance from the temple enclosure, intended for the temple music." It is found of many great men in different fields of life that much of their noble achievements were possible through the assistance of their wives. Even in the ease of Sri Ram Krishna without the noble and pure character of his wife, Sri Ram Krishna would not have reached the height of spiritual realization that he did. Though Sri Ram Krishna and the Holy Mother used to sleep in the same bed for months but she was completely free from all desires and body-consciousness. In mystical conversion it is not only that part of the libido specialised in the sex instinct but the whole of the libido employed in the activities and affections of this worldly life. Thus raise India's womenfolk from the social evils to the Divinised Humanity, the nearest approximation of the Virgin-Mother, Virgin-nun and Nun-Goddess of which Sri Sharda Devi was both the symbol and the substance. She was another representation of Khir Bhawani but Swami Bhuteshananda felt that "it should not be a matter of public talk". The disciples of the Holy Mother wanted to keep the Mother exclusively within their hearts and keep her away from public gaze thinking that the public would not understand her. Even when appearing before her devotees the Mother would like to conceal herself. The Master also did not like otherwise. Perhaps this was a part of training to the Mother. In fact, the Mother was the first disciple whom the Master began to teach not only things spiritual but even how to conduct herself in the world? How the household is to be managed? How to behave among the people? How to organise while on a journey? and so on. To my understanding, it means that Sri Ram Krishna wanted to hold before the world an example as to how married life is to be lived so that it can lead to God-realisation. When the disciples wanted to ask some spiritual questions, the Master would direct them to the Holy Mother, because he knew that she is the Goddess of Learning and she had come to give wisdom and knowledge to the world Sri Ram Krishna also regarded here as 'purity incarnate'. He said : "If she was not as pure as that, who knows whether I could have remained pure throughout". Once as a test case when Sri Ram Krishna asked to keep five rupees as he could not touch them. The Holy Mother said : "How can that be? If I keep that money, it will be spent for your service only. So it is as good as your accepting it." In the case of Avataras, there is not a single instance where the consorts of the Avataras became an actively associated with work of the spiritual uplift of the people. But the Holy Mother was almost as active associate of the Master as he himself was right up to the end.

4. Spirituality of Mother's Love

Spirituality was no deep in the Holy Mother that she was capable of hiding her spiritual and super-natural powers to the extreme so that nobody could have any glimpse of it. With difficulty, we could somehow understand the Master, but never the Holy Mother. Once Golap-Ma said : "Mother, you say you do not have Samadhi, but today I saw you in that state. "The Mother gently advised : "No, no, never mention that it is not Samadhi. Do not speak about it. Keep quiet. Do not make noise about it." She did not like her spiritual experiences to be talked about in public. This she did to restrain her children from evil path because whenever they thought of her as their affectionate 'mothers' they could never think of going astray. This is how she affected reforms, not by remonstration, not by chiding, not by any punishment but simply by abounding love that transformed people. "She binds our minds to you with the broad of affection, change our vices into virtues, for no reason."

The other uniqueness of the Holy Mother is that she appeared as the incarnation of God in the form of Mother. When the Divine approaches man on his own terms, it is Motherhood of God. The Holy Mother was the embodiment of God because she wanted to uplift the humanity at her awn cost. We have long heard about the Fatherhood of God but there are some differences between the Fatherhood and Motherhood of God. Father is bound with the world. He acts as the guide and hence he chides, and lifts while the Mother swings, feeds, nurses, nourishes whereas Father protects, Mother saves and loves the child even when the child is of unclean character. Mother's love is completely unselfish and one-sided. Whether the mother is in the kitchen or in some domestic work, she gives up those work when she hears the cry of her children as child is her first priority. Her love is unconditional and final Motherhood of Divinity is a new in Islam, Christianity and Judaism. In the semetic tradition of God is regarded as the Creator, the Ruler of the universe and the extra-cosmic being. But according to Hinduism, the Godhead is both efficient and the material cause, therefore the Shakti (power) which projects the universe is inseparable from Godhead. Nature is God's other aspect (Apara). Hence God is regarded in the Hindu tradition as both the Father and the Mother. A woman conceives her child, brings it forth in proper time, and afterwards nourishes it. The Divine Power performs the same functions with regard to creation. Thus woman is the earthly symbol of the Divine Power. Sri Ram Krishna therefore wanted to bring out the spiritual aspect of womanhood. Now if the woman sticks and emphasises physical aspect or physical pleasure (preya) she binds both herself as well as man to the phenomenal world, which is the result of ignorance (avidya). A man succumbing to a woman's physical charms, becomes entangled in worldliness. But if a woman is treated as a manifestation of Godhead, both man and woman can keep their lower nature under control and ultimately attains liberation. Adorned as 'Mother' a woman feels an exaltation of spirit and acts in a noble manner. So when Sri Ram Krishna criticised 'woman' and 'gold', he was only speaking of the physical aspect, otherwise he would not have treated the Holy Mother with such reverence. A man can escape the snare of lust not by hating woman and keeping her at distance, but by showing her respect as Mother-God. The Holy Mother is thus the triumph of womanhood. True there are a few examples of spiritually elevated souls with mystical experiences in the West like Angels of Foligno (13th century), Julian of Norwich (14th-15th centuries) and St. Teresa (1515-1582), however, the Holy Mother's spirituality is unique. She not only sublimated her sex libido but her whole body and mind. Madame Acarie (1566-1615) a married woman with six children and attending all domestic duties had become "Conscience of Paris". Lucie-Christine also performed duties to please the children who were not of her flesh and yet remained an elevated mystic. Marie Guyard or Madame Martime (1599-1672) known as Marie de Incarnation and Teresa of France Her intuition belongs to the highest order of mysticism. Jeanne de-Chautal (1572-1641) foundress of the visitation "never excused herself save for illness from being cook to her children. Mrs. Josephine Butler loved many girls who had been wronged before they had enough experience of the world. Elizabeth Fry (1780-1845), the quaker-saint and prison-reformer found in silence the Power which loves the unlovable into loveableness, which aroused loyalties even of convicts and all other who came to her willing influence. Similarly, there are other ladies who were endowed with high spiritual powers like Lucie-Christine, Madame Martin, Angela of Foligno etc. However, Christianity appears to be a Father-centred religion having little in common with the "Mother Worship" of India. When a child is a hurt as a dread, it runneth hastily to the mother for help, with all its might. The Holy Mother however, had two manners of beholding—one according to the common teaching of Hinduism and the other according to the 'she wing'. Not all the scruples, discretions and counsels of the orthodox could deter her from living and eating with European disciples like Sister Nivedita, as she believed in the whole world as our own and in the message "No one is stranger". Thus the Holy Mother was not only the last of an Old Order, she was also the beginning of a New Order. This was understood as the final word as in the ideal of Indian womanhood. She is full of motherly love. So she says "If my children smear themselves with dust it remains for me as their mother to remove that dust from the person and take them on my laps." However there is a remarkable difference between the concept of woman's perfection. In the west, there is news of worshipping of women. Every woman's face was that of Blissful Mother for the protection of human race. God was worshipped in the female aspect as Mother Goddess—Aditi, Prthvi, Sarasvati, Devi, Ambika, Uma, Durga, Brahmvadins, Viswavara, Apala, Ghosa, Godha, Lopamudra, Romasa, Vak in the Vedas are there. During the Upanisad period, the names of Gargi and Maitryi. In the west, there is news of worshipping of women but that is for her youth and beauty; in India, every woman's face is that of Blissful Mother. Sodshi is the first disciple of spiritual comradeship. Even in the present time, Vinoba Bhave, the spiritual disciple of Mahatma Gandhi has also highlighted the heritage of female-power in Indian culture. He even did not hesitate to propagate the legibility but also the desirability of study of the Vedas and other holy scriptures but also to observe life-long celibacy for the women.

5. Sri Sarda Devi—The Mother of All

The Holy Mother's religious faith places her far beyond the frontiers of all creeds, races and countries. She was unflagging in her Japas for all her disciples—Hindus and non-Hindus, Indians and European, Black or White. She did not distinguish between good and bad, rich and poor. There was no barrier of caste and temple to her overflowing love. Her love for others was no diffuse "altruism" which tires of its zeal. She had no blood children of her own but she was endearing Mother to all. Thus she lives the Vedanta, ideal which believes in the doctrine of "That Thou Art" (Tat tvam asi) and "I am Brahman" (Aham Brahma Asmi) or popular notion of "the whole world is my family" (Vasudheva Kutumbkam). The God realisation is to be found amongst all—Aryans and non-Aryans, Mlechas and barbarians. When we take stand on the basis of concrete spiritual experiences, it is not limited to any particular religion but is to be found among the followers of all religions. We are all members of the 'invisible church of God', though we may belong to the particular visible church of Christ, Muhamad or Buddha etc. In the field of Spirituality, there is eternal and all pervading democracy. There is only one distinction—between the lovers of God and those who are lacking in it, between good and the bad, righteousness and unrighteousness. All other distinctions are artificial, and anti-spiritual. Hence "The service of man is the service of God" (Manav seva is Madhava seva). Those who are indifferent to the work of the world, merely going about repeating the name of God are described as the enemies of God—says the Vishnu Purana. The essence of religion is love of humanity irrespective of any religion. "There is nothing higher than man." The Holy Mother's life always felt the visible man in the embodiment of the supreme. To serve him is the highest prayer we can offer to the Divine. The Knower of the Self sees action alike a learned Brahmin, a cow, an elephant, a dog and a pariah (Samdarsinah). The Holy Mother expresses her feelings : "If any children sneers themselves on dust, it remains for me as their mother to remove that dust from the person and take them on my laps."

Only a few examples will explain this more clearly. Once an immoral man wanting to visit the Holy Mother, Master Mahasaya instructed Sarat to stop but lo! the Mother came out herself and talked to the man and made him peaceful. Similarly an ill-reputed lady visited the Mother and the Holy Mother met her and showered affection like Lord Krishna. The Holy Mother says "Those who have taken refuge in me will come to her." When somebody objected to that lady's coming, the kind mother said : "If one does not come because another's coming what could I do? When a woman who had a sinful life, came and confused the Mother while the Holy Mother embraced her with great warmth and even accepted food from her hands." Every body known the famous story of accepting one Muslim with criminal antecedent and a drunkand with love. She not only fed him in her Ashram but cleaned his place with left over of food. In fact, the Holy Mother was purity incarnate. The Master himself proclaimed : "Had she (Mother) not been so pure who knows whether I might not have lost my self-control from her inducements?" To her, everything is Brahman (Sarvam Khalu idam Brahman) or God is everything (Isavasya idam Brahma). So if everyone is the divine manifestation, what is the sense in making distinction between high and low, religion and religion, Indian and non-Indian, even good and bad.

This is the core of highest spirituality. The Holy Mother also came in contact with some western devotees of Swami Vivekananda, who were all impressed tnough they could not understand their words. She accepted them as her children. Her western devotees and admirers are many like Elizabeth Davidson, Hartha Martens, Joan Rayne (Daysi), Cwendolyn Thomas, Marion Code (Mukti), Charlottee Bose (Sarla), Edle Alma Saxlund, Elinor Hill, Jane Brown, Ida Derby, Saral N. David, Anna Nylund, Rev. Andrew Blenko Nancy Pope

Mayarga, Mallika Clare Gupta, Roberts P. Utter, Jane Lewis etc.

Conclusion

When Sri Ram Krishna said to the Holy Mother "I have learnt to look upon every woman as Mother. That is the only idea that I can have about you. But if you wish to draw me into the world (of illusion), as I have married to you, I am at your service." The reply of the Holy Mother's answer was "No. Why should I drag you down to worldly ways. I have come to help you in your chosen path." To her, wife is not a plaything to the husband. Her contribution is two-fold. She is part of the Shakti or moral strength in man as well as companion. She treated all her husband's disciple and hers later and still others, who came in contact with her, as her own children. Thus she showed the highest example of universal love and motherhood. She demonstrated the quality of God's love in her life. She accepted all as her own and she poured her love unhesitatingly only, whether he is a thief like Amzad, an alcoholic like Padambinode, if they called her 'Mother'. She was as universal as the sky. She manifested motherhood and universality at the same time. Most human mothers are focussed and polarized in their love but in the Holy Mother, there was no focussing and no polarizing. She neither excluded nor hated. There is no question of great and small, saint or sinner.

"Mother of millions of world clusters. Yet Virgin by the Vedas called." Sister Nivedita addressed her in a letter : "You are full of love and it is not a flushed and violent love like ours and like the world's but a gentle peace that brings good to everything. Nobel Laureate Romain Rolland describes the episode of Sodshi Worship for the adoration of womanhood when Sri Sarda Devi was asked to sit in the seat of Kali. In the Indian tradition, the wife has a binding rights over her husband and hence she was so magnanimous enough to forgo those rights and encourage her husband to encourage in his high mission. She herself said that Sri Ram Krishna left her in this world in order to exemplify the Motherhood of God. Even after the death of Sri Ram Krishna, the Holy Mother lived in the world to fulfil his mission. The fundamental approach to all world problems concerns the individual man in a very practical sense. So the real constructive worker addresses himself to the individual who is ultimately the self. Therefore the self-culture or any form of personal Sadhana is vitally related with all true efforts for solving world problems. So the Holy Mother accepting the two ideals of renunciation and service, she asked to intensify her in those channels, and the rest will take care of itself. The knowers of the Self look with equal eye on the Brahman endowed with learning and humility, a cow, an elephant, a dog and a pariah. Such a can never be a cause of any suffering for anybody in the world. Contrariwise, he is a peace-generating institution by himself. Such was the Mother's life. Her life was her message. Hence five days before her passing away, when mother of Annapurna had come to see her, the Holy Mother consoling her in a low, almost inaudible voice said : "Why do you fear. You have seen the Master." After a pause, she added, "But I tell you one thing—if you want peace of mind, do not find fault with others. Rather see your own faults. Learn to make the whole world your own. No one is a stranger, my child : the whole world is your own". This is her last message to the world. Peace can come only peacefully. Agitation for peace is a contradiction in terms, objective peace is a misnomer. It is a subjective attainment. No real solution of any human problem can ever be based on a scheme of differentiation. This is arrogance to feel that an erstwhile sinner has to be made to pay. We commit a great sin in piously supposing that we have a share in that sin. While every suffering is justified no oppression is justifiable. We cannot be supercillious and yet be constructive. In short, we cannot understand world-problems in their proper perspective without self-discipline and self-love. An ungenerous man cannot help in solving the world problems. The Holy Mother had reduced herself to zero and made the entire humanity as her kith and kin. Hence the Mother was in the true path of world Peace as well as of individual peace. Om Shanti.

6

Unique Spirituality of Sri Ram Charita Manas

The Ramayana or the Rama-story is countless in tradition—*Ramayana Sat koti Apara.* Right from the inception of primeval poetic genius Valmiki, the greatest of the great sur and scholar Vyasa, the most shining star in Indian literary horizon. Kalidasa, and the most erudite and sophisticated poet Bhavabhuti etc. upto modern Rama-story poets like Maithili Saran Gupta, Nirala and others have sung the glory of Ram with extraordinary artistic poetic skill and ingenuity. But Sri Ram Charita Manas of Tulsidas is unique in its approach and passionate devotion. In fact, the personality of Ram is so magnetic that it has attracted a vast number of poets and writers to utilise their genius on the theme of Rama-story. However, Tulsi's depiction of Rama is neither a historical account, nor a mere flight of poetic imagination, but purely a Confession of faith' and a matter of 'personal encounter'. What he wrote about Ram was yearning of his soul as if Rama was face to face with him. For example, narrating about the very birth of Rama, Tulsi seems to be not only a personal witness on the blissful scene, he was himself in fact a participant in the collective song along with other ladies where Tulsi is also joining them. *Tanh Tulsi Mili gavai* (*Gitavali*). Tulsi's relation with Ram is so intimate that he would not like to live for a moment in a kingdom which is not the kingdom of Ram or kingdom of God on earth—

गुरु समाज भाइन्ह सहित राम राजु पुर होउ।
अछत राम राजा अवध, मारिए माँग सब कोउ।।

Hence, for him, the capital of India was neither Delhi nor Agra but Ayodhya or Chitrakoot. "Chitrakoot or our innermost self, where resides the Almighty is the real capital." (*Vinay Patrika*)

तुलसी तो को कृपाल जो कियो कोसल.......... ।
चित्रकूट को चरित्र चेतकार सो–

विनय पत्रिका

No doubt, Chitrakoot is geographical entity but symbolically it is the "innermost self" of man, which is the habitation of God, Sri Ram. Tulsi has absolute faith in the omnipotence of Ram who could protect him from all afflictions. This fearlessness is generated because of his faith in Ram. When a person has faith in God, he need not fear even death. We need not be afraid even during our dream from the dread of death provided we have God's grace. Even Valmiki and Bhavabhuti also might have some vision of God in the incarnation of Ram but Tulsi's perception of Ram as God was full and total. It was his intuitive and immediate perception of the divine. This is the direct intuitive perception which is the core of spirituality. Neither Valmiki nor Vyas nor even Kalidas had this sort of intuitive perception of Ram's entire *lila.* It was why he declared unhesitatingly and repeatedly about the Ram as God.

राम सच्चिदानन्द दिनेशा। राम सो परमात्मा भवानी,
सीय राम मय जब जग जानी........

Ram like sun is Truth-consciousness bliss. Ram is veritable supreme. Rama is God, yet a son, a father, a husband, a friend. This conception of the Absolute Brahman is more inspiring and much more intelligible to the common man. God's descent upon earth has a great purpose to banish the evil and establish the reign of righteousness.

असुर मार थापहि सुरहि रामचन्द्र के कारण।

The victory of the good over the evil is again an essential feature of spirituality. The truth triumphs, so there is victory of virtue over the vice. This is faith in the final victory of truth for which Tulsi's Rama had to suffer from birth to death imparting a lesson to us. In fact, we can try to understand symbolically the spiritual meaning of the fight between Ram and Ravana symbolised in the terms of good and evil. If we loose faith in the ultimate victory of truth over falsehood, good over evil, we shall also begin to loose faith in spiritual values. After all the Rg vedic concept of *Rta, Auprva* of Mimansa, *Adrsta* of Vaisesika, *Dhamma* of Buddha, and *Karma* of the Gita do emphasise regarding the conservation of eternal moral values which is spirituality in practice.

If spiritualism is faith in eternal moral order, the entire Ramcharit Manas is an epic of duty, love and other universal human values. For example, Ram symbolises the value of truth and justice, Ravana symbolises injustice, tyranny, violence and terror (*Balkanda,* 182.62) when Ravana walks in anger, on earth, creatures tremble like anything. (*Balkanda,* Lankakanda, 25.7.3). To Tulsi, Ram is the well wisher of humanity and embodiment of truth. Similarly, all human values of compassion, and well-being and love, friendship, respect for elder and love for younger, devotion to duty, love for nature, hate the sin, not the sinner, forgiveness etc. are demonstrated in the life and character of Rama. If God is both transcendent and immanent, we wish to see the concretisation of universal values in the life of Ram. To him therefore, there is hardly and difference between the transcendent and the immanent qualified divinity and unqualified Brahman.

Ramcharit Manas of Tulsidas also believes in the continuity of our life and existence. Unless we think that this physical-psychological life is not the end of life, there is no incentive to goodness or absence of fear from evil action. Hence, the law of Karma is inexonerable and it is the life-blood of spiritual faith. Hence Ramayan both proclaims the law of karma and also demonstrates that truth triumphs and falsity and fraud go down. The symbolic poem about the chariot of victory (*Vijaya Rath*) is the affirmation of the law of karma and the triumph and moral and spiritual powers.

Last but not the least, Tulsi's Ramcharita Manas believes

in the sanctity of all life, whether human beings, or animals and birds, even Rakshasas and Asuras. If we say that there is God in everybody, we cannot but treat equally human and subhuman beings on the same level of life.

Concluding Remarks

The centre of spirituality is self and its horizon is the Universe. It is neither abnegation of Self nor negation of the work. But "who am I"? It is not the body, vital breath or the senses. It is not even the mind. It is pure existence-consciousness-bliss. But how can we experience pure existence and pure consciousness unless we learn to reduce ourselves to zero, we cannot experience true spirituality. Hence to know is to become. If we know the essence of true self, we know about the Absolute Brahman. The life of Rama as the Supreme Self (Purushottama) is an object lesson in forbearance, suffering for others and a life of living crucification. Lord Rama's life is concretisation of ethical and spiritual values, which is the life blood of spirituality. For a devotee of Rama, there is no enemy, nor has any fight with anyone, has neither hope nor fear. All the corners of the world are full of delight to him. He does nothing for selfish reason, has no home, no pride, no anger and no ill-will against anyone. This is the ideal ethical-spiritual life-model. In short, Sri Ram Charita Manas presents the picture of spirituality in practical life. Spirituality is an illusion unless it has ethical basis. It is why almost every religion gives top priority to cultivate ethical life. The six-systems of Indian Philosophy, prescribe ethical discipline as path of self-realisation or salvation. Even the yoga system insist upon five ethical vows (*yama*) and five disciplines of self-control (*niyama*). So the Jainas ask to follow Right Conduct along with Right Faith and Right Knowledge. In the list of Right Conduct, the five vows (*Panch Mahavrata*) and Buddhist Five Moral Conducts (*Panchshila*) do emphasise ethical life as necessary step for attainment *of Moksa,* the Summum Bonum of life. Hence Sri Ram Charita Manas in the quest of spirituality emphasises upon ethical life from the very beginning. There is an ethical yardstick for the behaviour of all—son, father, teacher, husband, even enemy. It may be called as incarnation of spirituality (*sagun adhyatma*). Lord Ram himself is the embodiment of righteousness and highest moral standard. Only on one occasion *i.e.,* killing Bali, it seems that he transgressed the law of war but there are good many justification for that. Unlike Valmiki and Vyasa, Ram Charita Manas carefully avoids the slaughter of a Sudra named Shambook and banishment of Sita even when she had qualified the test of fire with regard to her purity and more so when she was in a family way. This means that spirituality is not something ethereal and does not rest on any ivory-tower, but rests with our day to day life. It covers our entire life—how I talk, walk, and behave. Life is not like a water-tight compartment between physical, psychological, moral and spiritual. They all act and react with each other. Hence Sri Ram Charita Manas presents an integral philosophy of spirituality combining the house-hold, neighbours, society and even the state. Even politics in Sri Ram Charita Manas gets a spiritual face. There is spiritualisation of politics and social life. It decries politics without principles and wealth without scruples, because they lead to total destruction of self. The very concept of Ram Rajya is the concept of Spiritual polity or "Kingdom of God on Earth". Similarly the ideal fraternity between Ram, Lakshman and Bharata is a concretisation of spirituality in family relationships. So Hanuman presents the picture of an ideal servant, while Ram as the ideal master, who loves him more than his own brother. Every character seems earthly and yet divine and spiritual. For Ram, whether it is coronation on throne of Ayodhya or banishment for 14 years in wilderness of forest, it makes no difference. This is an object lesson in the virtue of steadfast wisdom (*Sthit Pragna*), which is a true characteristics of spiritual life. For a spiritual man, the pairs of opposite like victory or defeat, praise or blame, pleasure and pain are treated at par. Last but not the least, there is the demonstration of supreme love called Bhakti in the Ram Charita Manas everywhere, whether it is of Ahalaya or Sabri, Lakshman or Bharata, Vibhisana or Hanuman etc. The whole book is a veritable compendium of supreme love of God incarnate—Rama. In fact, Manas is voice of divine oracle in the form of a dialogue between Shiva and Parvati, retold by Kakavusundi and Garuda, and Yagnavalkya and Bharadwaj. Hence it is a divine gospel propagating divine love through the story of Rama. The net result of listening is to get supreme peace and bliss.

7

Universal Man and Universal Religion

The test of every religious, political or educational system is the man that it forms. Alexander Pope rightly says : "The proper study of mankind is man". But what is man? "Half dust, half diety, alike unfit to sinks or soar" (Byron). Somebody sings his glory, somebody else treats him as beasts. Shakespeare exclaims—"What a piece of work is man! How noble in reason! How infinite is faculties! In form and moving how express and admirable! In action, heard like and angle! In apprehension, how like a God!" This is why, he is regarded as the crowning wonder of creation. But then there are other, who depict man as beasts—"a frowning dog, a roaring lion, a thieving fox, a robbing wolf, a dissembling crocodile, a trecherous decoy, and a rapacious vultures"—English poet Abhram Cowley. It seems that perhaps he is both. Hence it is dangerous to represent man as to how near he is to the level of beasts, without showing him at the same time his greatness. Similarly, it is dangerous to let him see his greatness without his meanness. "It is more dangerous yet to leave him ignorant of either; but every beneficial that he should be made sensible of both"—says Pascal.

None of the above views about man may be adequate because all of them try to understand human nature from a superficial standpoint, based on external behaviour. All of them emphasize upon the physical and material aspect of man. Indian Philosophy tries to harmonize the Psychologists and the metaphysicians because it is the search after unity. It also does not care for the particular; it is always after the general, may universal. But this universal cosmic entity splits into the soul of man. Though evil and good are both conditioned manifestations of the some, yet evil is the most external coating, and good is the nearer coating of the real man, the self. Unless a man cuts through the layer of evil, he cannot reach the layer of good, and unless he passes through both the layers of good and evil, he cannot reach the self. It is the universal cosmic mind that splits into many things and beyond mind we have found in soul in us. In the universal behind the Universal mind, this is the soul that exists all-comprehending existence, and that appears as manifold. This self, or soul, or substance, is all that exists in the universe, which appears as manifold by the utter position of name and form. It is like the sea and its waves. Not one wave is really different from the sea, but what makes the waves apparently different? Name and form, the form of the wave, and the name which we give to it, 'wave'. That is what makes it different from the sea. Not one wave is really different from the sea. When name and form go, it is the same sea. So this whole Universe is that One Unit Existence, name and form have created all these various differences. But it is in reality only one. There is no "I" nor "You", it is all One. It is neither all "I" or all "You". The idea of duality is entirely false. There is, therefore, oneself, eternally perfect, unchangeable, unchanged. Various changes in the universe are but appearances in that one Self. Each man consists of thou parts—the body, the internal organ of the mind, and behind that, what is called the Self (Atman). The body is the external coating, and the mind is the internal coating of the Atman who is the real perceiver the real enjoyer, the being in the body by means of the internal organ or the mind. The Self is the only existence in the human body which is immaterial, and since it is immaterial it is not a compound and because it is not compound, it does not obey the law of cause and effect, and so we can call it immortal, which has no beginning and hence no end. It must be also formless for there cannot be any form without matter. Our body will perish as it has a beginning but the Self having no form, cannot be bound by the law if beginning and end. It is in existence from infinite time; just as time is eternal, so is the self of man eternal. Secondly it must be all-pervading because that which is formless cannot be confined in space. So the Self is in me, in you, in everyone, and therefore omnipresent. It never comes as or goes, is never born nor dies. It miller move......... looms large on our mind when it says that man evolves out of animals. If we have a soul so they should have, and if they have none, neither have we. It is absurd to say that man alone has a soul, and the animals none. These are men worse than animals.

Modern man is in search of soul, says Jung. The scripture says—"I exist in all brings as the self." So "Know thyself" is the key-word of the Upanisads as well as of Socrates. One who sees the entire universe in his Self and Self in the entire Universe, there is no cause of any worry and anxiety for him.[1] Buy how can we understand this spiritual nature of man, if we treat him as the Economic Man (Adam Smith) or "Sexual Creature" (Freud) or as an animal engaged in the "Struggle for Existence" (Darwin)? Man is not all physical and psychological but essentially divine and spiritual. Hence logically he inherits the qualities of God, who is said to be the possessor of all excellences. Hence man's goodness follows from the goodness of God.

But, then how can we explain the presence of evil impulses in man? This is because man is not perfect being like God. He is not pure soul but a combination of body and soul. Hence be has emotions, passions and impulses also as they are necessary resultant of our physical frame. But they can be reformed. Hence there is the evolutionary progress of man. History is the sage of man's striving to discover his humanity, which is but a reflection of the Supreme. God is perfect hence man's goal is perfection. Man's nature is not essentially evil because he is definitely going higher everyday. Even follower and thoroughly debased man is capable of rising to the greatest height. Hence we find that in the midst of death, life persists, in the midst of hatred, love persists.

One can say that to regard human nature as basically good,

we indulge in false generalisation based on bad psychology. But supposing this is wrong and the critics are right and that man is by nature evil, then the result would be to draw a very dismal picture of life. All efforts at purification and reformation will go in vain. To consider man or woman as naturally evil is not only an insult to the whole human race, it is also a counsel of despair. True, we find anger, lust, envy in man but this is not his essential nature. They are due to his attachment to this body. Soul is pure, true and absolutely unattached with evil. He can true himself from evil through moral and spiritual discipline. This explains his potentials divinity.

Another criticism against such as view about Self is that it obliterates the distinction between the ideal and actual. From the position "man ought to be good" one derives the conclusion that "man is actually good". But this is not so. Nobody denies the presence of good and evil in man. Everyone of us is a combination of both good and evil. Spiritually he is pure and good but while he is in the body, he is tied down by the shackles of flesh. He is no doubt imperfect but he always endeavour to be perfect. In Short, he is a harmonious combination of gross animal body, intellect and heart of the soul. Outside universe is the reflection of the inside universe. The universe is universe compressed in the atoms. There is not one law for the atoms and another for the universe.

The concept of human nature and its progress is in conformity with the sociological findings. The human civilization has been a march from barbarity to civilization from egoistic struggle to altruistic existence. Mankind has steadily progressed towards love and it is bound to progress further. Perhaps we were cannibals in the beginning but many of us would not like to kill a beast or even hurt a fly. Vegetarianism as a food habit and pacifism as a social-political cult is growing popular.

But apart from his spirituality, man's sociality is also established. True, his physical body is personal and individual, his mind and heart is social and universal. Leave aside

Aristotle's thesis that "man is a social animal", the entire findings of modern science go to uphold this view. The perennial adventures in civilization are threefold :

1. To bringforth the integrated and complete kind of man—the Universal Man that has emerged in all epochs of human history.
2. To find out and achieve the intrinsic, ultimate and transcendent values that are more or less of perennial nature.
3. To establish a society or communion that passes towards the unlimited continuity which is the cosmos.

Civilization in spite of its manifoldness is fundamentally one. Each major culture spells out its own nation of the complete and Universal Person, its intrinsic and instrumental values of life and the wholeness and harmony with the cosmos, corresponding to its spirit and genius the accumulated force of myth, value and environment. It is false one-sided western philosophy of history, coming from Hegal and Marx that regards human cultures as more or less discrete and successive stages of phases in a unilinear, historical series. Infact cultures have parallel evolution, historically and logically contributing with its universally and rationally human elements towards and encircling the common heritage of mankind.

There is a tendency in civilizational dynamics of mankind to transcend time and changes in men and the flux of events into open pattern of persons values and cosmos. Hence, the key-notions of civilization are the unity and wholeness. The conception of Universal Man along with universal values and universal community is the transcending principal of knowledge of civilization grasped only as supra-historical reality. Universal Person is one's Neighbour. Every social relationship is the vehicle of Transcendence and every people, group or institution is an echo of cosmic community.

The three entities—'Universal Person, Tanscendent values and cosmic community are facts of the same dynamic of civilization. The twentieth century is perhaps the sickest, most wicked, and bloodiest in human annals, possesses the highest potentials for a complete transformation and fulfilment of man and civilization. With the possibilities of the emergence of Universal Man. Today, instruments and techniques of human degradation, mutilation and savegery thrive side by side with the great possibilities of the whole and Universal Man and Cosmic Community. Knowledge, art, religion and morality combine in envisioning a metaphysical, metacultural cosmic pattern of harmony, beauty and wholeness based on an ontological order encompassing man which alone can build up the unity and integrity of One world. One Civilization, One Noetic System, which can achieve the harmonious concord between man and society and civilization as a whole, and between man and the cosmos—total.[2]

The Universal Man is grounded in transhumanism as neither Ethical Humanism from Comte Russell confined mainly to the intellectual dimension nor Naturalistic Humanism from Marx to Freud which has become and anthropocentric, myopic and sterile crud, but when man reaches his highest when he thinks, feels and lives beyond humanity when infinitute and eternity exist in his spiritual dialectic. The Universal Man is finite and yet bound by the infinite.[3]

If we think of a Universal Man, we cannot think of a sectarian religion. Religion is the highest plane of thought and life but unfortunately on the one hand we find the intense love that humanity has ever known, on the other hand the most diabolical hatred that humanity has witnessed. No other human motive has deluged the world with blood so much as religion. It is said that about 86% of wars and bloodshed have been caused in the name of religion. The crux of the problem even at the end of this millennium is how to bring harmony among the religions.

Firstly, we have taken up religion as a mere play upon words and not a thing to be carried into practice. (The Universal Religion, a.v.p.8 Middle Sex. 1993). It becomes more or less like personal property as "my father's religion" or "nation's religion." In short, it becomes like a political phenomenon, a phase of narrow and sectarian patriotism. Hence as one ruler fight with the other, one religion does the same. Like Julious Caeser or Alexander, the religious leader want to have world empire. Christianity, Islam and Buddhism started with world-conquests, either through preaching, service, fraud or force. Jainism, Zorastrianism, Judaism and Hinduism perhaps did not believe in prostylisation. The root cause of this religious imperialism is that "ones own religion is the most ancient, most universal and most useful for the mankind." Hence there who think themselves as superior think as their divine right to not only to propagate but to convert other into their fold through wilful or manipulated and forced conversion. We forget that religions are different roads converging to the same point. What does it matter if we take different roads. Hence to think that one's own religion is the only way is undivine act. God has created different faiths just as He has the votaries thereof. Hence Gandhi asks : "How can I even secretly harbour the thought that my neighbour's faith is inferior to mine and wish that he should"[4] give up his faith and embrace mine? As a true and loyal friend, I can only wish and pray that he may live and grow perfect in his own faith. In God's house there are many mansions and they are equally holy.[5] Therefore, Gandhiji with all good intentions advised the Christian Missionaries : "your work will be all the richer if you accept as settled fact the faiths of the people you come to serve—faiths however crude, are valuable to there. I want you to complement the faith of the people instead I undermining it."[6] Hence a non-absolutistic attitude is necessary. To think that my religion is the best and the rest are in the clutches of devils and hence our sacred duty is to "civilize" them is a sacrilegious act. Hence, the institutions of conversion look like regiments of an army marching for aggression and carving out and empire. This has caused innumerable strifes, crusades, inquisitions and bloodshed in the world. Religion is a very sacred and personal affair. It is highly moral and spiritual phenomenon. No action which is not voluntary can be called a moral or spiritual and as soon as we loose the moral basis, we cease to be religious. All faiths constitute a revelation of Truth, but all are imperfect and liable to error. Besides, we cannot have the full vision of Truth, hence to think that our own faith is the best and the rest are inferior is again an indication imperialism in thought. Hence the best way is to develop sincere reverence for all other faiths. There may be faults in them but we should be keenly alive to the defects of our own faith also and try to overcome them we should alone try to blend into our faith every acceptable feature of other faiths. "True knowledge of religion breaks down the barriers between faith and faith."[7] Study and appreciation of other religions need not cause a weakening of that religion rather it should mean extension of the regard to other religions. Hence, it is better to allow our lives to speak for us than words than indulge in organized, preaching. Speaking to Christian friends, Gandhi Said "your work will be all richer if you accept as settled fact the faiths of the people you come to serve. He said "your work will be all the richer if you accept as settled fact the faiths of the people you come to serve faiths however crude, are valuable to them."[8] The time had passed when the followers of one religion could "stand and say, ours is the only true religion and all other are false." Hence co-existence and tolerance should be our guiding principle. He had chided Christian missionaries for their "irreligious gamble" for converts[9] and in South Africa be exhorted the Arya Samaj against undertaking any missionary activity in that country. He did not permit proselyting in his ashrams.[10] Contrary to it, he did convert Miss Slade to Hinduism and asked her that she would find everything good in the Bible which she found in Hinduism. Richard Greg, who wrote extensively on non-violence and stayed in Gandhi's Ashram was called Govind but never became a Hindu. Gandhi's "religion is not a religion of the prison-house".[11] He did not "believe in the exclusive divinity of the Vedas. I believe Bible, the Koran, and the Zend Avesta to be as much divinely inspired as the Vedas.[12] Religion to be religion of man should not be an exclusive. Gandhi "would not only not try to convert but would not even secretly pray that anyone should embrace my (his) faith."[13] Religion is a deeply personal matter, it touches the heart. Why should one change his religion because a doctor who professes some other religion has cured him of some disease. He did not believe that there is no such thing as conversion from one faith to another in the accepted term. It is highly personal matter for the individual and his God. "One should not have any design upon his neighbour as to his faith which one must honour as his own."[14] All prophets are equal. It is a horizontal plain. If we think in terms of Einstein's Relativity all are equal. But it is difficult to express that equality. That is why one should say that they are equally true and equally imperfect. One should not gloat over it and say mine is the superior one. "None is inferior to the other."[15] Fancis young Husband confronted the question "Are all mothers equally good? All mothers are not equally good, but each would think his own mother as the best in the world." But if we believe in the fundamental unity among all religions, this can be solved. Even if we regard our mother as best, it does not expect others to give up their own mothers and adopt ones own. Just as one's own mother is best for oneself, so is everyone's religion best, each for himself.[16]

To create fellowship of faiths, it is not only to treat all religions as true, indulge into the study of comparative religion but also "Fellowship in Prayer".

Universal Religion : Some Difficulties and Solutions

True the days of personal religion are over but religion is always and intensely a personal affair. But we can solve this paradox on the parlance of universal Man. Just as all individuals differ in colour, size, intelligence, power etc. but there is "an abstract humanity which is common to all," so it is with universal religion, which runs through all the various religions of the world in the form of God. God says "I am the thread that runs through, all these pearls" and each pearl is a religion or even a sect thereof.[18] Unity in diversity is the plan of the universe. The unity of sameness can come only when this universe is destroyed, otherwise such thing is impossible. Not only so, it would be dangerous to have it. We must not wish that all of us should think alike. It is the difference which is the soul of our progress, the soul of our thought.

So by a Universal Religion, we should not mean one Universal Philosophy or one mythology or any one universal ritual held alike by all. We have to recognize variation. We must learn that truth may be expressed in a manifold ways and each of these ways is true as far as it goes. The same Spirit is everywhere and this is the recognition of universality. Apart from this theoretical approach at working out harmony in religions, there are also practical ways. Firstly, we must have any plan which does not destroy the individuality of any man in religion and at the same time shows him a point of union with all others. Iconoclastic references do no good to the world. Then the second paradox is that in order to create religious harmony, it has been tried to bind them all down to a few doctrines, and so have produced more new sects, fighting, struggling, and pushing against each other.[19] This is again adding one more religion in the list of numerous religions that we have. 'Universal Religion', therefore is not a new religion destroying or rejecting the existing religions. All existing religions are different forces in the economy of God working for the good of mankind : and that not one can become dead, not one can be killed. Just as we cannot kill any force in nature, so we cannot kill any one of these spiritual forces. As the universal brotherhood of man is already existing, so also is universal religion. There should be no worry to find greater number of sicts, because they there is the more chance of people getting religion just like in a hotel where there are all sorts of food, everyone has a chance to get his appetite satisfied. That all these old religions are living today proves that they must have kept that mission intact, in spite of their mistakes and defects. They have not lost the great mission they came for. Islam has a great mission of brotherhood; with the Hindus they have the one national idea—spirituality; with the Christians, the central idea is purity and service. Hence "our watchword will be acceptance, and not exclusion."[20] Hence by Universal Religion, we should not think of a separate or independent religion envisaged by Akbar the great in the name of Din-a-elahi. It is artificial what is needed is to plead for the unity and equality of religions. Apart from the basic Scriptures, the saints, seers and Sufis etc. have strongly pleaded for the unity of man and unity of religions. Ramkrishna Paramhansa, the scriptural teacher of Swami Vivekanand had discovered and original dynamics of unity of religions. He did not only preach but shared in his own life the spiritual experiences of Islam, Christianity and Hinduism. I think this is by far the most exalted spiritual method of realizing Universal Religon. Tagore too advocated the "Religion of Man" rather than religion of sect or community.

Infact, the days of "sectarian religion" and "power-politics" are over. What is needed is a synthesis of science and spirituality. "Science is lame without religion, and religion is blind without science"—said Einstein. There are two kinds of reality or existence—the existence of our consciousness and the reality or existence of everything else. Cyril Hinshelwood therefore says "To deny the reality of the inner world is a flat negation of all that is immediate in existence, to minimize its significance is to depreciate the very purpose of living, and to explain it away as a product of natural selection is a plain fallacy." Faith in the pursuit and value of science goes beyond science and reason. It is akin to a religious feeling : it goes beyond science. Faith in science, faith in reason is not anti-reason but beyond reason.[21] If science in universal, religion is also bound to be so, otherwise it is to be brushed aside as subjective. The climax of the ordinary consciousness is Science. For the religious consciousness, this empirical world is not the final reality. Laws are for the mind's convenience but the process of supramental manifestation is different. This is through Yogic experience. Yoga is not subjective and personal it is as universal as science.

REFERENCES

1. *Isa Upanisad,* versions 6 and 7, *Bhagavad Gita,* 6.32, 6.30.
2. Mukherjee, R.K., *The Universal Principles of Forms of Civilizations,* Calcutta : R.K. Mission, 1961, p. 9.

3. Tagore, R.N., *Geetanjali*, London, Macmillan 1949, verse 1.
4. Gandhi, M.K., *Harijan*, 20.4.1934.
5. *Ibid., Harijan*, 20.4.1934.
6. *Ibid., Young India*, 11.8.27.
7. *Ibid., From Yerveda Mandir*, 55.
8. *Ibid.*, 11.8.27.
9. *Ibid.*, p. 13.
10. *Ibid.*, p. 13.
11. *Ibid., Young India*, 1.6.1923.
12. *Ibid., Young India*, 6.10.1921.
13. *Ibid., Young India*, 19.1.28.
14. *Ibid., Harijan*, 28.1.1935.
15. *Ibid., Harijan*, 13.3.37.
16. Gandhi, M.K., *Fellowship of Faiths and Unity of Religions*, Delhi : Gandhi Book House, p. 38.
17. *Fellowship of Prayer*, New Jersey, 1990, p. 2.
18. Vivekananda, *Universal Religion*, New Jersey, p. 13.
19. *Ibid.*, p. 16.
20. *Ibid.*, p. 45.
21. Kothari, D.S., *Some Thoughts on Science and Religion*, New Delhi, 1977, pp. 5-6.

8

Beyond All Frontiers : A Plea for World-Civilization

To be a little poetic at the outset :

Will you come with me across all the frontiers?
To a Brave New World Which knows not frontier?
Will you break with me heavy doors of our prisons?
Which are built in the name of security, which are guarded by the myth of society?
Will you shatter with me ancient walls of morality?
Which wants to shape our minds, which crave to cripple our lives?
Will you burn with me all scriptures and authority?
Which stifle human reason, which throttle holy passions?

Thesis : We need a world without war, a world without national frontier, a world without personalistic religion and a world-economy without private ownership and exploitation.

I. Logic and Logical Calculus

(A) Nation and Nation States : The concept of nation is very complex. Territory is but the body of a nation. The people who inhabit its hills and valleys, who share common joys and sorrows, constitute one common patrimony and inheritance, political, economic and cultural dreams and ambitions, constitute a nation. In place of the old local and national seclusion and self-sufficiency, we have intercourse and in every direction, universal interdependence of nations. The intellectual creations of individual nations become common property. But national one-sidedness and narrow-mindedness become more and more impossible and the concept of world-system becomes imperative. The vested interest or the bourgeoise put an end to all feudal, patriarchal and idyllic relations, drowned the most heavenly ecstacies of religious fervour, of chivalrous enthusiasm, of Philistine sentimentalism, in the icy water of egotistical calculations and money relations. It has built a world-market for more systematic, full-proof-exploitation, giving a cosmopolitan character. It compels all nations on pain of extinction, to adopt this mode of production, consumption and culture. It creates a world after its own image. It has its own Economy and Politics of its liking. Today, the I.M.F., World Bank and W.T.O. have become super-states dictating the national Governments to fall in line with their line in matters of agriculture, education and culture.

Capitalistic exploitation and subjugation under the leadership of the strongest States of the modern world, nacked aggressions take place turn by turn on false pretexts supported by their respective Parliaments in the name of nation and national interests. Right or wrong it is "my country", hence it must be supported. Apart from the capitalist brand of nationalism, the world has also witnessed the meteoric rise of national military fascism in Japan, Burma, Germany, Italy, some African countries and so on during the last fifty years unabated. It means that the so called "Nation" and "National States" are the holy-cows of modern politics at the altar of which human rights, individual freedom, minimum humanitarianism even world peace and human survival based on sustainable eco-development are sacrificed. Hence nationalism has become a narrow and dangerous tribalism.

(B) World Government : Therefore from Socrates to Marx and Gandhi, they have all decried narrow nationalism. Socrates rightly said "I am neither an Athenian nor a Greek but a citizen of the world." Similarly the ancient scripture of India treats the whole Earth as the Mother and ourselves as her children (*Veda*) and called the "entire universe as one family"

(*Vasudhaiva Kutumbkam*). So also the French philosopher Victor Hugo uttered a prophetic note in 1885, when the French Polity was in the midst of desperate experiments : "I represent a party which does not yet exist and what is that? 'Civilization'." Marx, who cannot be called as a Utopian or a mystic, has given an appropriate call : "Working men of all countries, unite", on the eve of the first Paris Revolution on 28-9-1864 and the First International Working Men's Association of glorious memory was formed. Professor Arnold Toynbee in his well-known book *A Study of History* expressed : "A fortiori, in our world-wide society in the present Atomic Age we shall not have assured the survival of the human race until we have established a world Government and have made the present national governments subordinate to it." Windel Wilkie in his book *One World,* 1941 and so also H.G. Wells advocated the establishment of a Federal World State. Harold Laski, in his famous book *A Grammar of Politics* wrote : "Either we create our world by a deliberate plan or we court disaster. It is a grim alternative." Mr. Clement Atlee, the then British Prime Minister of U.K. addressing the World Parliament Association at Oslo on 25-4-1959 said : "I would like to see a World Government grow out of the U.N." Another former British Prime Minister Harold Macmillan observed in the British Parliament in 1955 : "This is elevating the U.N. or whatever may be the authority into something like World Government; be it so, it is none the worse for that. In the long run, this is the only way out for mankind." The Prime Minister of India Pt. Jawahar Lal Nehru, while addressing the World Parliament Association firmly said : "I have no doubt in my mind that world federation must and will come, for there is no other remedy for world's sickness." Mahatma Gandhi, known as the Father of the Indian Nation said : "Nationalism is not the highest concept. The highest concept is "World Government". A great revolutionary and saint Sri Aurobindo in his book *The Ideal of Human Unity* said : "The creation of a world-state is the logical and inevitable outcome." Gandhi's disciple Vinoba has invented a beautiful phrase for mutual salutation as "Hail the humanity" : Jai Jagat.

(C) Political Imperatives of World Government : Nation States, today, there are intrigues, forcible occupation, geographical demarcations due to some historical circumstances. So it is rightly said : "God has made the world, man has made the nations for his vested interest." Emery Reves observes : "Wars between groups of men forming social units always take place when these units, tribes, dynasties, churches, cities, nations exercise unrestricted sovereign powers. Wars between these social units cease, the moment sovereign power is transformed from them to a larger or higher unit." In fact, nationalism is a tribalism writ large with all its irrationality. Hence a transformation of global political system through the instrumentalism of world government is thus the only remedy. In the name of nationalism, perhaps more than 60-70% wars have been fought. What to speak of capitalist systems, even Communistic system has become victim of wars among themselves.

It is said that the idea of World Government prescribes an apocalyptic leap into social order. But given chance and political will of the people of the whole world, it will succeed because it is necessarily a natural and inescapable product of the multi-state system. The World Government offers federalism as a proposition for political unity. Another objection is raised that a World Government will not be able to ensure law and order on the analogy that there is occasional national disorder under national governments. But World Government will be a true federation and hence the federating units will be responsible for the maintenance of law and order in their own areas and since there will be no national armies so there will be least scope of any confrontation and therefore, it will be solved soon and more effectively. It does not mean that global federalism does not and will not demand greater political wisdom and moderation of its participants. Nor we can be rash that there will be all smooth operation always. It demands proportionately a limited price. On the other hand, it gives in return a more precious thing—universal peace and economic prosperity.

To say that if we achieve disarmament and a dependable performance of the international obligation by the States, the U.N. may work well and there is no need of an artificial super structure called World Government, is fallacious argument. To say that if an Utopian idea as if we can not leave with adjustment within states, how can we talk of the world government. But it goes without saying that the problem of States and regions cannot be solved through a world government alone. As long as we have national frontiers, regional imbalances cannot be undone. And where there are regional imbalances national chauvinism will always provoke territorial conflict. A via media between national government and world government is half-hearted performance of the world bodies like the U.N. etc. but they only confirm the need of a fuller trial of the counterpart of the concept of World Government.

(D) Economic Compulsions of World Government : The population explosion is no less dangerous than the nuclear explosion, which is being polarised into dangerous divisions into two camps—the rich and the poor. There are 51% people numbering 1832 millions who have per capita income below $ 100, 18% or 672 millions with 100-500, 6% or 212 millions with 500-1000 and remaining 25% or 903 millions with above 1000 dollars. In 1970, per capita income of U.S.A. was 4000 dollars while in India it was only 90 dollars. Then there were parts in South Africa where 5% of the white people were ruling over 95% black ones. Then there is an awful gap between countryside and the cities. In the course of the next 20 years, 600 million urban population in poor countries is likely to increase by 500% to 3 billion. The poor countries are in fact not in a position to stabilize human population. The dimension will thus pose a stupendous problem.

(E) Compulsions of war for the World Government : Apart from the political and economic compulsions there is the compulsions of war expenditure for bringing the whole world under one government. The economic cost of armament is terrific. About 800 billion dollars are spent every year in the mad rush for armaments, while million of people die in hunger, thirst and disease. This vast amount of money can be utilised for alleviation of the suffering. Bertrand Russel said : "It seems indubitable that the scientific mass cannot long survive unless all the major weapons of war, and all the means of mass destruction are in the hands of a single authority, which in consequence of its monopoly would have irresistible power, and of challenged to war, could wipe out any rebellion within a few days without much damage except to the rebels"—Professor Arnold Toynbee also said : The warning of the father of the nuclear bomb, Albert Einstein is much more serious : "I do not know about the Third World War but in the Fourth World War they will fight with sticks and stones."

Peace is after all indivisible. There cannot be peace in one part of the world and war in another. Peace can be ensured in the world if a single government wields control over the armaments. In fact, no sacrifice would be too big to achieve world peace—be it a surrender of a part of the national sovereignty, or renunciation of the use of force in settling international disputes. And if humanity is to survive it will have to bring itself under the control of one authority and the sooner it is done the better it will be for its own sake.

(F) Educational challenges and World Government : At present the rich countries have an effective advanced system of education, whereas the two-fifths of the world's adults lack even literacy. While illiteracy is negligible in rich countries, at least half and in some cases three-fourths or more are illiterate in poor countries, mainly because the developed countries can afford to spend more on education. The educational and economic disparity can only be balanced by a redistribution of the world's resources. Hence there is an urgent need for internationalisation and rationalisation of the global production through dissemination of technology and redistribution of resources. Without restructuring the global economic, global communication, global transport system, we cannot achieve educational minimum.

(G) Conclusion : We can say that many internationalists of the world like Socrates, Lincoln and even Marx and Gandhi could not ignore national questions and national freedom movements. So far Gandhi is concerned, he was a great emancipator and liberator. But his nationalism, however fierce though it is, is not exclusive, not designed to harm any nation and individual. (Gandhi, M.K., *Young India,* 26-3-1941). He further said, "My notion of Poorna Swaraj (complete Independence) is not isolated independence but healthy and dignified interdependence." (*Ibid*). "Through Swaraj, we would serve the whole world." (Gandhi, M.K., *Ibid.,* 16-4-41). Therefore, he had addressed an impressive "Appeal To Every Japanese" (*Harijan,* 5-7-42) says "The end and aim of the movement for British withdrawal is to prepare India, by making her free for resisting all militarist and imperialist ambition, whether it is called British Imperialism, German Nazism, or your pattern. If we do not, we shall be ignoble spectators of the militarization of the world...." (*Harijan,* 5-7-42). In his historic letter addressed to Generalissimo Chiang-Kai-Shek on 14-6-1942, Gandhi had openly and stoutly denounced Japanese aggression against China. Expressing solidarity he said : "Very soon you shall have completed five years of war against Japanese aggression and invasion and all the sorrow and misery that these have brought to China. My heart goes out to the people of China in deep sympathy and in admiration for their heroic struggle and endless sacrifices in the name of their country's freedom. India and China will cooperate together in friendship and brotherhood for their own good and for the good of Asia and the world." (Gandhi's Correspondence with the Govt. 1942-44, A Ganeshan, Madras, 1930.) So Gandhi had also addressed a letter to Herr Hitler (*Harijan,* 9-9-1934) to prevent war. His advice to Czech People (6-10-1938) is a lesson in civilian defence. He issued an open letter to Every Briton to lay down arms and fight non-violently the Germans. He had written the U.S. President Roosevelt that there could be no living harmony on the basis of injustice, exploitation of the weak. He was neither a passive pacifist nor chauvinist nationalist. He had a global mind and according to him the principle of equality of all nations, non-exploitation and non-violence formed his fundamentals of a new world order. Gandhi frankly hints at some sort of world-federation : "The better mind of the world desires today not absolutely independent States warring one against another but a federation of friendly interdependent States." (*Young India,* 26-12-1924) and "one central governing body composed of representatives of the component parts." (*Harijan,* 8-6-47)

II. From Personal Religion to Universal Religion

Two attempts have been made in human history to social life—one of them on spirituality or transcendentalism, and the other one on materialism or realism. They work in wave-like motion following each other to fulfil. When the spiritually oriented civilization degenerates, it assumes the form of personal and sectarian religion, concentration of power and wealth in the hands of the vested interests. An unhealthy ego is developed in the mind and heart of every religionist that his or her religion is the best, most superior and the only way towards salvation, with the result that as our social struggles are represented amongst different nations, by different social organisations, so is man's spiritual struggle represented by various religious, and as different social organisations are constantly at war with each other, so these spiritual organisations have been constantly at war with each other, constantly quarreling. From a rough estimate nearly 86% of wars have been waged in the name of religions. Hence, Swami Vivekanand, the charismatic Indian delegate to the Parliament of World Religion at Chicago in 1893 rightly accused : "Though there is nothing that has brought to man more blessings than religion, yet at the same time, there is nothing that has brought more horror than religion......nothing has engendered fiercer hatred......nothing has bred more bitter enmity between man and man than religion...... nothing has brought the world with more blood than religion." (Vivekanand, *Jnana-Yoga,* Almora : Advait Ashram, 1948, 8th ed. pp., 372-73). If it were a fact that only one of these religions is true and all the rest false, by the time it would cover the whole ground. But this is not so; not one has gained all the ground. All religions sometimes advance, sometimes decline. Then sects are multiplying all the time in all religions. It means, that no particular scripture contains all the truth otherwise there would not have so many sects. In fact, any attempt to bring all humanity in one method of thinking in spiritual things has been a failure and always will be a failure. Besides, varieties of religions is not bad. It is the clash of thought, the deformation of thought, that awakes thought. If we all have thought alike we would be like Egyptian mummies in a museum looking vacantly at one another's faces. Whirls and eddies occur in a rushing living stream. There are no whirlpools in stagnant dead water. When religions are dead, there will be no more sects; it will be the perfect peace of the grave. But when religious preachers behave like invaders talking of crusades, Jehads etc. they appear as blood-thirsty as the tiger, the cannibal, the savage.

In fact, all these religions are different forces in the economic of nature. Differences are not due to fundamental differences but due to different standpoints. Truth has many dimensions. If we can synthesize these different viewpoints, we have a richer world. Our watchword, therefore should be acceptance, and not exclusion or toleration. So called toleration is often blasphemy. It only means that "I think that you are wrong and I am just allowing you to live." Hence, we must go forward and say that all religions that were in the past or present are like our own. We can worship with everyone of them in whatever form they worship. There is no harm, if we salute all the prophets of the past and present.

There are three parts in every religion—its philosophy, mythology and ritual. There is no one universal philosophy of religion or mythology or ritual. How is it possible to have a universal form of religion? We all hear and talk about "universal brotherhood" but one who does not belong to our religion, this brotherhood does not apply. But we should note that there is an "abstract humanity" which is common to us all. Unity in variety is the plan of the universe. We are all men and women, and yet we are all distinct from one another. As a

part of humanity, I am one with you, and as a Hindu, Buddhist, Confusian, Muslim or Christian, I am different from you. Further as a man/woman, we are separate from animal, birds or plant but as living beings we are all one; and as existence, we are one with the whole of universe. This universal existence is the common denominator, the L.C.M./G.C.M. No one set of ideas or doctrines can be believed in by all mankind, because variety is the plan of universe. There can not be one single philosophy of religion or single mythology or one set of rituals. If it ever did, the world would be destroyed because variety is the first principle of life. Perfect uniformity or total balance would be our destruction. The unity of sameness can come only when this universe is destroyed, as it is sheer impossible and also extremely dangerous to have it. Hence universal religion does not mean any one particular philosophy, mythology and ritual held alike by all. The world must go on working, wheel within wheel. What we can do is to try to make it as smooth as possible by recognizing natural necessity. The ideal which every religion represents is never lost and so the universal religion already exists as universal brotherhood. But as soon as make a 'Muslim brotherhood', or a 'Christian brotherhood', or a 'Hindu brotherhood', a throat cut competition starts between one brotherhood and another brotherhood.

People may say that all religions come in love but they have all failed. This is because they have not adopted any practical plan.

To start with we must recognise : "Do not destroy". Iconoclastic reformers do no good to the world. If we cannot build a temple or mosque, school or hospital, let us not pull them down. If we cannot provide even a first-aid, let us not inflict any injury to any one. Secondly, take man where he stands and from there give him a helping hand. True divinity lies in true humanity. Thirdly, we should not behave as the sole possessor of truth and the rest in the clutches of devils. None is omniscient, hence any absolutism in thought, word and deed is violation of the truth. Truth may be expressed in a hundred ways, and that each of these ways is true as far as it goes. The same truth can be viewed in a hundred standpoints, and yet be the same thing. Reality is complex and human knowledge is limited hence it is arrogance to claim sole monopoly of truth, which generates violence in words and deed.

Religion needs to be free from this absolutism or egoism. We must not extol 'my religion', 'my prophet', 'my scripture', 'my faith and fellowship', just like we say 'my house', 'my property' etc. This is vulgar display of individualism or egotism. In fact, this 'self-sense' is anti-thetical to spiritual freedom. Personal freedom is unspiritual. Individual salvation is imperfection. Hence we should think of synthesis between spirituality and social service, between religion and scientific social change.

The concept of Essential Unity of All Religions (Bhagawan Das & Theosophy) is good but not enough; similarly the concept of "Equal Respects for All Religions" (Gandhi) is much better but not fully practical. Hence we should try to adopt and concretise the idea of "Universal Religion" (Swami Vivekanand) or "Religion of Man" (Tagore). As a matter of fact, universal religion has been already existing. For example, the mission of Islam is to make its followers "all equal" through practical brotherhood. With the Hindus there is one national idea—spirituality and the other is renunciation, while the central idea of the Christians is self-purification and service. These different ideas of different religions do not contradict but supplement each other. So far mythologies and rituals of the respective religions are concerned, the followers are free to follow their own. The only caution has to be kept in mind that willy-nilly, we have to accept religious pluralism as an imperative. When religions are dead, there will be no more sects. Variation is the sign of life. If it were a fact that only one of these religions is true and all the rest false, by this time it would have covered the whole ground. But this is not so, not one has gained all the ground. All religions are living with sometimes advancing, sometimes declining. If the claims of a religion, that it has all the truth were true, why are there so many sects. Hence, it is nature's plan that religious organizations have come into existence for awakening the awareness of all permeating Divinity and Humanity.

However, that sole responsibility was betrayed by practically every religious organizations. Sectarianism overpowered the initial motivation instead of uniting humanity and inspiring it to launch the pilgrimage towards Truth and Reality, they divided the human beings, just like feudalism and primitive capitalism converted human beings into slaves and disposable means. As a result philosophy of Humanism, Human Rights, Socialist and Communist Philosophy, and Secularism had emerged. At present, variety of religious fundamentalism and the cult of violence have come up. But they cannot be eliminated by chanting the slogans of Secularism, Rationalism and Humanism. We have to review our perspective of life, in the light of nuclear physics, molecular biology, ever advancing electronic technology as well as metaphysics, the science of non-material energy or energy of consciousness. It is only through the synthesis of science and spirituality. The divided and disunited humanity is a menace for all civilizations. A new radical perspective and transformed approach towards individual and collective life are necessary. Peace is the path, mutual love and respect is the light and sharing the planet will bring about the ending of misery and suffering. "There is no religion higher than Truth and Righteousness"—said Gandhi (*Ethical Religion,* p. 49). True religion and true morality are inseparably bound up with each other. Religion is to morality what water is to the seed that is sown in the soil. Religion is never 'No' to life. Hence according to Gandhi, a Religion which takes no account of practical affairs and does not help to solve them is no religion. (*Harijan,* 7-5-25). In his *Autobiography,* he admits that so long as there are different religions, every one of them may need some distinctive symbol. But when symbol is made into a fetish and an instrument of proving superiority of one's religion over others, it is fit to be discarded. (*Autobiography,* p. 480). Gandhi came to the conclusion that *(a)* all religions are true *(b)* all religions have some error in them *(c)* all religions are almost as dear to me as my own Hinduism.... all human beings should be as dear to one as one's own close relatives. "My own veneration for other faiths is the same as that for my own faith, therefore no thought of conversion is possible. "Instead of conversion, we should develop fellowship to help a Hindu to become a better Hindu, a Mussalman to become a better Mussalman, and a Christian to become a better Christian." (Report of the 1st Annual General Meeting of the International Fellowships, held at Satyagraha Ashram, Sabarmati, Jan. 13 to 15th, 1928.)

The challenge before the 21th Century is to demolish these modern superstitions and verbalize a new perspective of Global as well as Cosmic Life. Life is for living. The act of living is the means of Liberation; if at all the word liberation has to be used. When one moves through relationships in the utter simplicity and spontaneity, the concept of space and time disappears. Drenched in the sense of timelessness a person can remain physically ever fresh and psychologically ever alert and attentive.

III. The Cult of Economic Imperialism and Globalisation

In the ancient past during feudalism and primitive capitalism, human beings were converted into slaves and disposable means, to grab land, money and political power. Every kind of respect, honour and dignified livelihood was denied to them. The philosophy of Humanism upheld that all human beings are equal and had a right to a decent social life. The emphasis on Human Rights was the highlight of Socialist and Communist Philosophy. Religion, no doubt upheld the spiritual equality of all men and women, they also denounced the system of private property as the root of worldly attachment but no solid social structural framework was evolved. As a result, capitalism engulfed the entire except to some extent in old Soviet land and partly in China, where private capitalism was replaced by State ownership. On the whole, capitalism has overpowered practically the whole world under the banner of International Monetary Fund (I.M.F.), World Bank and now World Trade

Organization (W.T.O.), taking away national economic sovereignty into the hands of a few most developed industrialized States backed by strong economic and military power in the nuclear age. In the name of development, blind urbanisation, mechanisation, automation and centralisation have become the characteristic features of the New Economic World Order with its own ingredients of liberalisation, privatisation and globalization (L.P.G.)

To start with "globalization", we have to distinguish between "true globalization" and "pseudo-globalization". There was the idea of globalization in the past but this was not possible then. Now science are brought it on our doorsteps. The problem is how to synthesise the imperatives of physical sciences or study of nature and the science of values. Richard Dawkins in his *The Selfish Gene,* emphasizes that this little genetic system is essentially selfish. It is incapable of communicating with or serving others, understanding compassion, love, maturity etc. This science of values, is unfortunately neglected all over the world. Hence globalization has become without human face or compassion. Hence there is poverty amidst plenty, ambition for peace but preparation of war, talk of universal brotherhood but ruthless exploitation in action. Hence Schoringder reminds in the Upanisadic spirit to us that we are not puny genetic system but pure consciousness. That is why this process of silent, surreptitious exploitation is more than evident in the present process of globalization. No doubt people have come closer but this coming closer to each other is only for the rich and not for the 40 or 50% poor of the world, who still remain isolated, inalienated and marginalized. The globe remains sharply divided between the North and South, the developed, the developing or underdeveloped countries. The disparities are so vast that there does not appear any meeting point between the two except probably in the relation of the exploiter and the exploited, the privileged and the deprived. It is why the Council of Europe, with 40 member States, recently launched "Globalization without Poverty". Extreme poverty and social exclusion are a denial of human rights. Another initiative, the Global Forum of Poverty Eradication has been inspired by the work of the Forum of the Poor in Thailand. The campaign message is : "Europe is not a planet, but part of our world, and that creates both opportunities and responsibilities." (U.N.D.P. Report, 1999).

Conceptually, globalization is a process of unification, unity and uniformity and one of the major reservations against it rightly voiced by various thinkers and scholars, is its tendency to destroy variety and diversity. Absolute uniformity would mean death. Globalization is threatening to destroy diversity but establish differences to privileges based upon economic disparities and power acquired by knowledge.

In recent times due to the spurt in globalization, AIDS and other new and mysterious diseases have globalized and far and wide in every corner of the east. The root cause of this problem is, however, not the globalization of a virus, but the globalization of a life-style. Indiscriminate and uninhibited sexual behaviour is the main cause for the spread of AIDS. Another danger from globalization may prove to be more dangerous in the long run in intensification of consumerism causing unnecessary luxury-cruze and distortion in our life-styles, marked rise in the stress and strain of our daily life. Life is becoming too complicated for the common man. Devaluation of indigenous method of healing which are cheap, simple and available is being virtually demolished by multi-national drug corporations with professional degradation due to unrestricted cascade of global consumerism. "Nature has enough to meet our needs but not our greed"—said Gandhi.

There are a few myths which have been used to immunise us about globalization. The first claim is that it is natural. In fact it is probably the most coercively and most secretively worked out system. The second myth that it has novelty is also wrong as it is not happening for the first time because in 1711 the British East India Company, the first Corporation in the World, came to India to trade. The third myth that globalization has made the State weaker and citizens have become freer, the result is just the fast disappearance of citizen democracy and citizens freedom because of Multilateral Agreement on Investment (M.A.I.) which will go beyond GATT and W.T.O. Fourthly, it is a misnomer that Multi-National Corporations (MNCs) are creating the wealth of the world. In fact, nature has given it, and we build on it. We have been under extraordinary pressure of corporate rule.

The advantages of globalization would reach the masses only when the economic system is efficient. The weak will suffer—so the survival of the fittest is the rule. Hence globalization has on the one hand increased the global economy from an annual output of 2300 billion dollars in 1900 to 39000 billion in 1998, average grain yield per hectare from 1.06 tons in 1950 to 2.7 tons in 1998. Global ownership of cars grew tenfold between 1950 and today and in bio-technology man is playing God by successful cloning exercises, but growing disparity in income among countries and within countries. An estimated 841 million people are undernourished and underweight, 1.2 billion do not have access to safe water, 1.6 billion are illiterate, 2 billion have no access to electricity. The weapon technologies have taken quantum jump, the two world wars have killed 26 millions and 53 million people respectively surpassing the war casualty figure from the beginning of civilization until 1900. The increasing pressures on the earth's eco-systems usher in, among other things, a new period of climate instability, with indeterminate adverse consequences.

Hence, we should have a fresh look at globalization as it stands today. "The world is an indivisible whole. Its parts are interrelated and interdependent, so that what happens to one part ultimately affects the whole. So progress in one part cannot succeed unless it ultimately spells progress for the whole. Humanity, therefore, tends to be a unity in all its aspects and activities." (*School of World Civilization,* Swami Nityaswarupananda, Ministry of Education, Govt. of India, New Delhi, 1967, p. 19) So also Alfred Toynbee in his introduction to the book said : "I feel confident that the tradition of the past is also the wave of the future." We are moving in a chapter of human history in which our choice is growing to be, not between a whole world and a shredded-up world, but between one and no world." In the 21st century, human life is going to be a unity again in all its aspects and activities." (*Ibid.*, p. 17) The quest for a unified world order has always fascinated the thinking minds of India and abroad. Pseudo-globalization is the outcome of scientific and technological advancement and the result of industrial civilization and commercialisation. It is in its nature materialistic and consumeristic. If motivating force is self-interest, profiteering and its success depends upon exploitation of man, nations and nature. There is very little ethical or moral consideration in its working. Naturally it is bound to lead to struggle, competition and ultimate destruction. True globalization, called Vasudhaiva Kutumbkam in Indian classical language is essentially a cultural and spiritual concept. It looks upon the whole world as one's own and 'mutual aid' and cooperation are the basic ingredients, as in a family. Unlimited consumerism is ruled out otherwise everyone has to be provided with the basic minimum. At present U.S.A. with a total world population of 6.5% consumes nearly 40% of things. Hence an ethical idea of simple living and high thinking should be our ideal. Our approach should be integral rather than dialectical, sustainable rather than temporary, inclusive rather than exclusive, holistic and theological rather than materialistic and mechanistic. Every idea has to become broad till it covers the whole world. One atom in the universe cannot move without dragging the whole world along with it. There cannot be any progress without taking the whole world. Any national, racial or narrow approach will be suicidal.

IV. Finale

We need a breakthrough in the traditional conceptual thinking especially after the new interpretation of the world by Einstein along with new sociological theses and social space-time ideas. The borders between science and spirituality are becoming fuzzy. We have to start from calling ourselves as 'Global Citizen' and adopt 'global village' as our habitation. We have not to bother about clash of civilization, or East-West divide. Every nation or religion has a national mission. The present trend towards globalization will free us from our narrow cobwebs and provide necessary infrastructure to interact with each other for mutual benefit, and harmonious process of give and take. "There is no limit to extending our services to our neighbours across State-made frontiers. God never made those frontiers." (Gandhi, *Young India,* 31-12-31). While fighting his battle for freedom, Gandhi remained an ardent internationalist when he said : "My love for nationalism, or my idea of nationalism, is that my country may become free, that if need be, the whole country may die, so that the human race may live." (M. Desai, *Gandhiji in Indian Village,* Madras, 1927, p. 170). His religion was also global—"My religion has no geographical limits." (Gandhi, *Young India,* 11-8-20). He derived his economic ideals from Ruskin's *Unto This Last :* "That the good of the individual is contained in the good of all." This is faith in globalism par excellence.

9

A Resolution of Indo-Pak Conflict : A Gandhian Approach

Swami Vivekanand had predicted in 1898 "India will have to play the role of a Friend, Guide and Philosopher to the World". So also Mahatma Gandhi had visualised India to take up a role towards a world, free from hatred and war. But unfortunately Indo-Pak conflict even after half a century has developed into the greatest potentiality of nuclear holocaust. During the last Kargil conflict, the Pakistani army was almost prepared to strike India with nuclear devices if the Indian army dared to cross the boarders. Even now we have reports that Pakistan is strengthening its nuclear capabilities through many clandistine methods. So also Indian Defence Minister openly vows to annihilate Pakistan if it dares to attack India. The most unfortunate thing, what to speak of the politicians even the mind set of the so called intelligensia and to a great extent of the youth has been undergoing a war-posychosis with anti-India or anti-Pak hatred due to political communalisation, ushering in Jehad or Dharma-Yudha. A new aggressive political culture is being adopted instead of opening a door for dialogue. War seems to be the only solution. Thanks to the continuing cross boarder terroristic overtures from the fundamentalists from Pakistan and the role played by state sponsored media, the mind of the common people in India has been more anti-Pakistan and consequently more anti-Muslim. The situation in the sub-continent is of total turmoil and perenial tension. Domestically the danger of communal riots to win votes in elections cannot be brushed aside as it does pay its dividends.

The clouds of mutual fear and distrust have darkened the horizons both in India and Pakistan. The political communal militants in both the countries are bent upon destroying the efforts for harmony between the Hindus and Muslims as well as between India and Pakistan. President Mushraf, inspite of his obvert advocacy for peace, cannot declare Kashmir as a problem non-grata for Pakistan nor no Indian Prime Minister is in a position to surrender Kashmir to Pakistan. This total incompatibility of claims over Kashmir has been so much hardened that resolution of conflict seems beyond the grasp.

Under this complete and complicated situation and compulsions any resolution of conflict seems to be unthinkable and impossible. But this does not mean that it will be so far ever. We should not think that in this Imbriglo there are two parties *i.e.* India and Pakistan. It is not an isolated world. Both the countries are under severe strain and considerable pressure from their friends and neighbours and international powers. They will certainly do what they can to avert a confrontation between India and Pakistan. Secondly, saner elements in both the countries will try their best to persuade the rulers to avoid war. Then there are anti-war forces and NGOs, who will try their best to stop war. The cost of war is so much high that it is simply unbearable for both these countries. As Pakistan has support from U.S.A. and some Muslim countries, so India too has same powerful Islamic countries as friends like P.L.O., Iran, Egypt, Iraq, Indonesia which would restrain both the countries. Even Russia will not encourage India to go to War. Even China will not openly displease India by openly siding with Pakistan. This also is known to Pakistan.

But all these and any more arguments against the possibility of Indo-Pakistan war may not hold good for establishing a tension-free or conflict-free relations between India and Pakistan. We have to prepare the background for unity between India and Pakistan.

The most crucial problem for a good relations between the two countries is to improve the Hindu-Muslim communal relations, in India because India constitutes the second largest population of Muslims in the World. Besides no where in the World there is such a mixed population of Hindus, Muslims and other religious groups than India. Hence to search for a behavioural dynamics and a balanced social ethics is our greatest problem. To think that we can substitute the religious cultural model with citizen-nation model is more artificial and unrealistic, because we are a deeply religion oriented people. The second method to dissolve the antagonism between the two communities, the Indian experiment of "Democratic Ruralism" and decentralisation of powers, under common institutions like the local grass-root democracies called the Panchayati Raj in the educational and other fields. Thirdly, there should be an effort to prepare both the communities to review the rigid distinctive features of their respective identities and accept changes to bring them into a synthetic frame. Secular character of the state and education with a guarantee for non-discrimination will be a must for ensuring and generating a common outlook, shared ethical values, common cultural patterns, and secular character of state administration are likely to improve Hindu-Muslim relations. However, care should be taken that pluralict norms should be respected and there should not be any suppression of smaller or minority entities under dominant and the majority in the name of bringing them into the main stream. Variety should not be suppressed in the name of uniformity. The lack of trust undermines all efforts towards harmonious community relations. Hence the Hindus should not suffer from self rightousness and Muslims should not be treated as alien or suspects. On the other hand the Muslims should review the features of their identity so as to achieve maximum accommodation and adjustment. There should be an open dialogue between Hindus and Muslims on the controversial problems like common civil code, polygamy, control of population rise, use of Urdu, visit to Macca, etc. with free mind. Differences of opinion should be respected and a permanent free forum be framed to find out conciliatory positions acceptable to both. Such organisations like the South Asian Fraternity, the Association of Assian People etc. be requested to coordinate their activities towards informal contacts, fraternity camps, tours, exchange programmes, sports, cultural festivals in both the countries. Since there is common history and common geography, common art, music and culture, there will be less difficulty in forging a unity of mind and emotions between the people on both sides. We should also encourage inter-communal or inter-country marriages. In short, all sortes of modes be explored to encourage interaction, contact, and living before we can conceive of an amity and rapproachment on the national levels of both the countries. This does not mean that we should not attempt reconciliation at the apex level but unless we work on the ground level, our success above will be limited.

Some Models for Indo-Pak Conflict Resolution

There are ways to approach reconciliation between India and Pakistan :

1. Firstly, we can approach the two governments to start meaningful dialogue first on the non-official or non-formal level if there is inhibition to go on the formal level. This should be without any condition. Talks on second level diplomatic channels have already been going on. I think that the Ex-Prime Minister Sri I.K. Gujral, and perhaps Sri V.P. Singh can take the initiative in this direction. If not some impartial respectable foreign personalities like Nelson Mandela, Arc Bishop Tutu, Aung Swi the Dalai Lama or any other be involved in bringing the two Prime Ministers on the talking table as the Norwagion peace negotiation team have done in the case of Sri Lankan Imbriglo. We can made a more comprehensive list of such personalities including that from the U.N.O. and Nobel Peace laurets or peace personalities.

2. **Proposal for Indo-Pak conflict Mediation :** We should try to explore the possibility of an impartial mediation or arbitration. Before we talk to the Govt. leaders, we should prepare the background through people's education through publishing feature articles, letter to the editors etc. by respectable persons and journalists, so that we can know the

reaction of the people and also avail of their suggestions. I know that mediation is difficult but in view of heavy public expenditure involved in defence budgets, we can persuade the people to our side. We have already fought three wars and the last Kargil proved inconclusive. Now both India and Pakistan have acquired nuclear weapons. Hence any war will be suicidal for both the countries. True, there are difficulties in choosing impartial mediators but if we try we can find some people who will be both impartial and just. The world is not devoid of such people. If we cannot agree to mediation, it means either our case is weak or the whole world is our enemy. Let India float a few names. If Pakistan agrees to it, it is alright if not let Pakistan come forward with its own proposal. I am sure that we can find some sensible and impartial persons for this work. During partition we had agreed to Radcliff award when passions had risen high. Mediation is neither against our self-respect nor against self-interest, especially whenever bilateral dialogue is not being agreed upon from our side. If we put conditions we can take up them while discussing the thorny problems. Such hardened attitude towards any dialogue puts ourselves on the dock in the eyes of international opinion and we unnecessarily loose other's goodwill. On the other hand, we should be always ready for dialogue to earn the goodwill of the international community.

3. **People to People Relations :** Prior to any formal rapproachment on the government level, we should try to establish people to people relationship through larger exchange programme, free visits, friendship camps, inter-country conferences in music, art, literature, development and other problems. This will normalise our relations and will go a long way in reducing tensions. We should remember that though politically, we are two countries or two nation states, but we have a long common history, common tradition, common art, music etc. We have almost the same heritage. Hence, this will be a most welcome and useful proposal towards normalisation of relations between the two relations. We have almost the same food habits, same dress and same view of life. There might be

many more devices to boost up social and cultural contacts between the peoples. We can coordinate and cooperate with each other in trade and commerce, scientific and literacy ventures. Both countries have strong bias for agriculture and religion in life. We share almost the same set of moral and spiritual values. Hence such camps arranged by South Asian Fraternity have been a great success. True, there are some differences, but there are also many kinds of differences in our own country. We have extreme diversities. We have differences in our languages, dress, food habits, etc., but these differences do not come in the way of unity. It means that there is unity in diversity. This is our culture. Hence, we can reconcile with whatever differences we have.

4. **Loose Political Models :** With such bitterness, it is difficult to establish a political unification at once. This is also not desirable. India is a big country, so is Pakistan. Bigness come in our way of efficient administration. Decentralisation of administration is a prudent policy. There is more scope for corruption, misuse of powers, criminalisation in big political structure. "Small is beautiful", says Schumacher. Centralisation of power has violence ingrained in it. Hence today, decentralisation has become a political creed. In India, we insist on grass-root democracy of the Panchayats. Therefore, we should have craze for unified unit òf India and Pakistan. A loóse political model of federation or confederation should be attempted where we have both autonomy and security. Dr. Ram Manohar Lohia and Jaya Prakash Narain have advocated such a loose federation between the two countries with maximum powers to the units and minimal power to the centre. In Eastern Europe, there is a union of about 20 countries with Common Market, Common Parliament, Common Currency, and Common Visa. In this way, identity of each unit is preserved and when they unite together they acquire greater strength. If India and Pakistan unite even loosely on this pattern, there will be a much less strain on army and economy. At political level we will have greater bargaining powers with super powers and a possibility for becoming a permanent

member of the Security Council. We can defend our boarders better and we can gear-up our economy more efficiently. One World is a far cry at present, but loose federation between India and Pakistan will certainly pave the wave for World Government and World Peace. The communal tension in both our neighbouring countries will also subside. Even vexatious problem of Kashmir might be solved. Vinobaji in his most original way has projected a solution for establishing a political triangle with Afganisthan "A", Berma "B" and Ceylon "C" called ABC as a triangle. We know that all countries within this geographical triangle have become victims of poverty, unemployment, illiteracy and ill health, but their worst malady is internal and fraternal strife leading to occasional wars and foreign exploitation and intervention. We have a similar political framework called the SAARC though it has not been very effective. But such models in Atomic age are going to have more survival value. Socrates had said "l am neither an Athenian nor a Greek but the citizen of the World". Our scripture also proclaims that the whole world in one family—Vasudev Kutumbkham. We need a world citizenship and world without frontier. Nationalism today has become and outdated ideology. It has generated enough haltered and has resulted in thousands of wars. Even today humanity is in danger due to narrow nationalism. Let India and Pakistan lead the World towards World Government and World Citizenship.

10

Freedom Through Non-violence

Believe me, I have no claim to inflict upon you a lecture on Freedom or Non-violence, but as a humble Freedom Fighter myself under Mahatma Gandhi, please remit me to convey the greetings and solidarity of 1000 million Indian people to you at this hour of crisis as well moment of jubilation. Freedom is indivisible hence to me Korean Independence is as precious as our Indian Independence. Therefore, the Indian Nobel Laureate Rabindra Nath Tagore, though he could not visit Korea in 1824, he having deeply moved by the invitation, found expression in the poem :

"In the golden age of Asia, Korea was one of its lamp-bearers.

And that lamp is waiting to be lighted again, for the illumination of the East."

Not only this, the Poet had supported the Korean cause of freedom then in front of a crowd in Japan in 1924, notwithstanding the protocol.

Even earlier, just as the Japanese ruthlessly attempted to suppress the Korean nationalistic fervour, through oppression and suppression when thousands people were killed and imprisoned, an armed revolt called the First War of Indian Independence was started in 1857 against the British colonialism. However, when Gandhi assumed the leadership of Indian Freedom Movement, it assumed a peaceful but powerful mass-character. Similarly, as on March 1st, 1919, a

Proclamation of Korean people in India, such a Proclamation of Complete Independence was made on 26th January, 1930 under the leadership of the Mahatma, Nehru and others. Incidentally, 26th January is celebrated as our Republic Day. In the small beautiful country of Korea, about 50000 people took part in Peaceful protest demonstrations. According to Japanese military reports, during this non-violent movement for two months, 533 Koreans were killed, 1409 wounded and 19054 imprisoned. But the Korean spirit could not be subdued and Free Korean Govt. in evil and missions were set up at Sanghai, Siberia, Manchuria and U.S.A. Similarly Indian patriots tried to mobilize world opinion in favour of India's independence. It was Gandhi's magic power that he could enlist active support of world leaders including many eminent British politicians in his "battle of right against might", although Raja Mahendra Pratap and later Subhas Chandra Bose formed full-fledged Free India Govt. outside India. Mr. Bose even set up a full-fledged Indian National Army.

However, the mainstream of Indian Freedom struggle remained peaceful under the Mahatma, so it was in Korea under the great leader Han-Yong-Un. Perhaps, there is the Buddhist legacy of compassion, loving kindness, friendliness and equanimity and the doctrine of Five Precepts (Panch-Ṣhila). But non-violence or compassion of Lord Buddha or Gandhi did not mean that it is a weapon of the weak and submission to injustice. Did not Buddha fearlessly carried the war into enemy's camp and brought down on its knees an arrogant priesthood. But like Buddha Gandhi showed unmistakable love and gentleness even when he indulged in intense direct action. Hence, non-violent method of resistance is morally and spiritually superior.

Gandhi rejected the method of violence also for practical reasons. India was an unarmed country and to arm India like the British would be time consuming as well as impractical. This was also against Indian civilization required a different higher weapon of self-protection. The world is weary of hate and violence. So he thought that let it be privilege of India to turn a new leaf and act as a becon to the world. He went to assert that he will not purchase his country's freedom at the cost of non-violence. People might applaud the examples of Mustafa Kamal Pasha, De Valera or Lenin. But his accumulated experience of more than 50 years in South Africa and India filled him with the greatest hope that in the adoption of non-violence, lies the future of India and also the world. Violence leads to counter-violence and civil wars which never endo. Besides, through a violent revolution, the power seldom comes to the people. In French Revolution, after the murder of Emperor Loius, we had Napolean; in England after liquidation of Charles I, we had Cromwell, after the killing of a spineless monarch like the Czar in Russia, we had Stalin, in recent history and in our neighbourhood, after the massacre murder of the entire family members of Muzibur Rahman in Bangladesh, we had one dictator after the other violence may destroy one or more rulers but like Ravan's Leads others will prop up in their places. We should also remembers that in the modern age of science and technology, the State has become more powerful than the Leviathan and in a violent struggle even the legitimate participation is not possible while in Gandhi's non-violent movement, even old men, women participated effectively.

Gandhi's mission was more than achieving India's Independence. That is to focus that non-violence is the law of our species as violence is the law of the brute. True democracy can never come through untruthful and violent means. However, Gandhi's non-violence was not a passive spirituality that spends itself in idle meditation but it presupposes to ability to strike. It has no room either for cowardice or vengeance. Non-violence and cowardice go ill together. Hence, he said : "Where there is a choice between cowardice and violence, I would advice violence"... I would risk violence a thousand times than the emasculation of whole race.

Korean and Indian non-violent Freedom struggles have partially refuted the belief that no non-violent freedom struggle has been known to history. During mid 19th century (1860-67), when Emperor Franz Josef attempted to subjugate Hungry to the then Austrian power and when moderates felt helpless, a Catholic landowner Ferone Deak not only protested but also organized independent Hungarian education, agriculture and also the boycott of Austrian Jails and Parliament.

There was also non-violent resistance against military action and finally the Emperor had to give Hungry her constitution. In Denmark in 1940, Danish people organized non-violent resistance against the Nazis, so also in Norway in 1940, non-violent resistance was organized in which athletic clubs, judges of the Supreme Court etc. participated. Recent example of non-violent resistance movement against racial segregation in U.S.A. under Martin Luther King is well known. More recent and vivid example in non-violent mass-action against Martial Law regime in Poland under Lek Walese and latter in U.S.S.R. in getting back Gorbochev from the clutches of military junta are before our eyes. Not to speak of many non-violent Non-cooperation and Civil Disobedience movement during Gandhi's time at Champaran (1917), Vykom (1925), Kotagarh (1921), Bardoli (1928), Ahmedabad (1917), Kheda (1926-27), Borsad (1923), Nagpur (1927), Salt Satyagraha (1930) and major three All India movements like Non-cooperation (1921-22), Civil Disobedience (1929-30), and Quit India (1942), India has witnessed many smaller non-violent movements and one nature in 1974-75 against imposition of Emergency to curtail individual freedom.

In short, violence has lost its dynamics. It has become an out-dated weapon. We must explore the moral equivalent of violence whose final culmination lies in nuclear terrorism. Hence, either we learn and perfect non-violent resistance or face total extinction of the human race. The West has given us the curse of Hiroshima and Nagashaki, let the East repreat the Gospel of Lord Buddha : from anger, anger is not satiated.

11

Puzzules and Paradoxes in the Contemporary Sarvodaya Movement

After Gandhi left this world on 30th January 1948, with a significant note regarding the future guidelines for Gandhian institutions and work known as his last testament, it was under the charismatic and unifying leadership of Acharya Vinoba Bhave that Gandhian movement achieved extraordinary height through land-gift mission, which was remain scent of the days of non-cooperation movement only on a little lower scale. From the President and the Prime Minister to the smaller people paid lip services to Gandhian ideas but it was Vinoba who provided Gandhism a new definition and a new strategy through his multi-dimensional gift-missions. When consumerism and materialism were touching the new high in the name of development and modernity Vinoba silently walked on foot almost the whole of India preparing the common mass for a peaceful solution for the vexed land problem, which has been defying all solutions even after blood bath in the Telagana region of Andhra Pradesh : According to Hindi Swaraj (1909), the Bible of Gandhism, the real enemy of India's downfall are our materialistic aspirations and moral degradation Gandhi would refuse to submit to million copies selling modern Bibles of Elvin Toffler that "power, wealth and sex" are the dominating tools of human motivation. He provided negative ideas of service, voluntary poverty simplicity and self-control.

Vinobaji true to his genius, provided a new life-style and a new strategy of social action, much different from prevalent political culture rooted in power-politics and party politics. It was a great ingenuity to invent a special organisational engineering through twin apparatus of **Sarva-Seva-Sangh** and **Sarvoday-Samaj** to take up the guidelines contained in the **Last testament** of Gandhi. At the crucial moment of transition from the long freedom struggle to independent Sovereign Democratic Republic, India needed a democratic polity. Politics has not been an untouchable thing politics in like the coil of snake which we cannot escape. Hence we have to wrote with it. But Gandhi was fully aware of the defects of the prevailing Westminister model of parliamentary democracy based on party system and power-politics. Party is a part of society and hence it cannot do proper justice to the whole of society. Party system is bound to create partisanship mindset besides generating spoil-system, corruption, criminalisation etc., in the name of party. Structurally, party system is rooted into oligarchical functioning. Parties are controlled by party bosses and party cancuses. Hence individual freedom is curtailed and the party members have to be like mere power downs of the party-leaders. In short, parliamentary democracy neither reflects the conscience of the people nor of the entire parliament. Hence it is not also purely representative. Hardly 40-45% people caste their votes in elections which are manipulated through purchased media and propaganda machinery. There were division of votes resulting in the formation of a government with even 1/3rd of the percentage of electorates voting in the election. Hence Gandhi was dead against his sort of parliamentary system which was neither representative nor democratic in spirit and structure. He had visualised a real democracy based on the grass-root level on the pattern up oceanic circle.

However, Gandhi being a practical idealist thought that unless people are properly educated and worker are trained at the grass root level, this will clude the grasp of the people. So as a long term plan, he placed the blue-print of a non-violent people's organisation having no truck with power-politics and party-politics. By remaining in a party or working for a particular party, one cannot work like a fire agent. Hence there is a tussle between the loyalty to a party and loyalty to the people. In a parliamentary system, party interests often prevail and parties are indirectly or directly controlled by monied people to safeguard their interests. Hence Gandhi, Vinoba and J.P. tried to evolve "people's democracy" or **Lok-Swarajya** or **Gram Swarajya**, for a real democracy.

Gandhi floated the apparatus of **Lok-Sevak Sangh** whose member will not be attached to any political party or power politics for three simple reasons. **Firstly**, being a party-man, his views become party oriented and he has to abide by party mandate and party discipline. He cannot take up an independent stand. **Secondly**, parties do not allow a government 'by the people' or 'of the people'. It becomes a party government. Thirdly, there is a decision by majority. In the name of democracy, a simple majority of 51% wins and 49% is defeated. This creates a social division and permanent discontent. Gandhi and Vinoba, therefore wanted to make decision making process more democratic on the basis of unanimity (Sarva Samiti or Saravanumati) or through consensus so that all sections of society feel involved in the decision making.

The contemporary Sarvodaya movement had been trying to strengthen itself on the one hand through grass root democracies of gramedan or Gram Sabhas and on the other hand spearheading many organs of non-violent social change to build non-violent people's power such in Santi Sena (Peace Army). Acharaya Kula (Teachers Fraternity), Female Power (Stri-Shakti), village oriented non-governmental Khadi (Gramabhimukh Khadi) the intensive Gramdan areas (Saghan Ksetra), Cow-Protection movement (Go-hatya-bandi) etc. All these required long ardous and sustained and dedicated effort for which one-pointed devotion of a Servant of the People (LOK SEVAK) is essential.

However, there were certain organisational and strategic compulsions which led the Sarvodaya movement to re-consider its stratigin and priorities. Firstly, the Bhoodan-Gramdam movement developed some structural and functional defects. Since it became a massive unwieldy movement without developing appropriate and adequate organisational apparatus and trained man-power, it could not withstand the populist craze for fulfilling the unimaginable targets. Like an invading army, the chariot of Bhoodan like the victorious horse of Asvamedha went on marching and conquering one district after another caring nothing about consolidation of its gains. The victory was so quick, unorganised, unplanned and spontaneous and the follow up so weak spurious and without man-power, that it became etherial and evaporous. Vinobaji perhaps knew it but he might have thought that let us create a favourable climate first and obtain people's consent, then it will he easier for the worker to follow up in details. But this could not happen and all efforts dissipated into nothingness because of lack of proper planning. The open declaration of the land of entire Bihar State in 1969, is an example of the greatest hoax of the Bhoodan history so much so that Vinoba had to admit that he is bogus so his Bihar dan is bogus. After achieving a land gift of about 65 lakhs of acrus in Bhoodan for the landless people in whole of India and having declaration of offering of about 10,000 village gift (gramdan), Bhoodam movement has achieved a grandeur and splendour no less than the Non-Cooperation movement of 1921-22 but it was a tragedy to see it anticlimax so soon. However in terms of qualitative achievement, it was indeed no mean an achievement to collect 60 lacs acres of land and distribute about 15 lacs acres to one million landless farmers. All land-movement either of the Naxalites or of the Kisan Sabhas or of the Land Reform measures of the different State Governments taken together could not touch even the half of this magic figure of distributed Bhoodan land. Hence, Bhoodan movement must be viewed in balanced perspective. Ideologically also it achieved the Himalayan height but it also failed to develop appropriate organisational apparatus, which was it Himalayan blunder.

Then came a period of fatigue and rest which is usual after

such a mega-event. Vinobaji had become too old after two decades of penance. Besides these was his spiritual demand for proceeding "from the gross to the subtle, political to the spiritual, attachment to the non-attachment. He thus preferred gradually to cut off himself from day to day gross work of Bhoodan and guide them spiritually. This was a sort of chamber practice or chamber consultancy. Instead of moving from place to place, he stayed for quite sometime at one place where worker came to him to get his guidance and inspiration. There were other Bhoodan stalwarts like Jaganthanji in Tamilnadu, Anna Saheb Sahasra Buddha in Orissa, Kellapan in Kerala, Manmohanbhai in Orrisa, and many small workers here and there.

To prize them all, the great J. P. with a mind of a true social scientist concentrated himself in a Naxal infested rural area in Muzaffarpur (Bihar) for months together like the peace voyage in Noakhali braving all dangers. He visited village to village and house to house, tried to organise them on the lines of Grandam-Gram Sabha. He was sitting not on an ivory-tower but was 'face to face' with the people. He tried to see the gusto of the movement and also of its dynamism. He was impressed by the spontanow enthusiasm, initiative, and community-feeling among the rural folk but he also found conservative outlook, indulging in small fueds, casteism etc. Illitrary and lack of awakening were the causes. Many outdated customs and social evils have stunted their dynamism. Economically, they have no occupation except agriculture and some animal husbandry. Indian politics had been totally unsympathetic towards rural people. Good roads, good schools, good hospitals, clubs are not meant for them. Anyway, regeneration of Sarvodaya scheme of things, require a massive sustained effort. It is why Vinobaji tried to obtain the moral power and achieve support of the good and the different political parties at a national convention held at Yelwal in Karnatak in 1957. Vinobaji was by temperament not a confrontationist Sarvodaya too does not believe either in class conflict or confrontation. This was because of following the policy of collaboration, cooperation and mutual-aid class-struggle might work where there are two distinct polarised classes of "haves" and "have-nots" but where there are multi-heirarachial order, it is practically difficult to organise any struggle on the basis of permanent class-conflict. Hence, in the Indian context, Sarvodaya strategy is much more appropriate. But then Sarvodaya movement was weak because it lacked dynamission and lacking in resistance to injustices as we find in Gandhi. Gandhi never adopted violence but he never hesitated to tolerate injustice. This was Satyagraha. Unfortunately, during contemporary Sarvodaya movement this element of Satyagraha has been totally absent. To tolerate injustice is worse then to commit injustice. But this was ignored by Vinobaji's leadership. On the other hand, he propounded a theory of practicing "mutual assistance" rather than indulging into "resistance". Whatever be the spiritual significance of this theory of Vinobaji, the people in general and Sarvodaya workers in particular gave up their mindset to fight out injustice or practice Satyagraha. Vinobaji might have other reasons not to ask the worker to take up Satyagrahas. He felt that in a scheme of self-government with democratic set up and regular election, fundamental rights, court as custodian free press and multi-party system, any confrontation at their delicate period of newly attained independent will weaken our nation.

It lacked vitality to resist growing corruption violence, Poverty and unemployment in the country. It was a paradox that while number of Gramdans were gained beyond then thousands and Bhoodan gift land rose over six million acres, there was an awful increase in the rural and urban violence in the country. Unemployment was on the increase and worst of all there was extreme erosion of democracy in the country. Intra-party democracy in the Congress was almost finished and there appeared a dreadful authoritarian and despotic rule. J.P. as foremost freedom-fighter and an ardent devote of individual liberty could not tolerate it. He was constrained to give support to the youth movement against the misrule of the Congress Vinobaji, as was his nature, was not in favour of such confrontation but J.P. thought his moral responsibility to take up it as a national cause against suppression of dissent, Indiraji came into her true dictational colours and imposed emergency suspending all fundamental rights and putting thousand of persons behind the prison. J.P. tried to follow the Gandhian path of truth and non-violence in his fight for freedom. It was his genius that he led the vast mass of students and youth and kept them peaceful and also orderly. He himself suffered to the point of death and lost his kidneys in jail. The nation which had been stunned during emergency gave a fitting reply to Indira Gandhi and dumped the Congress into the dustbins of history. But true to the Gandhian ideal of having no lust for power, J.P. being at the helm of affairs did not aspire for any post and throughout tried to guide the youngmen and women on the pathway of truthfulness and peaceful means.

However, this led to vertical division among the followers of Sarvodaya but about 90% were with J.P. Credit goes to Vinobaji, he saved the formal division of Sarva Seva Sangh by allowing freedom to worker to join or not to join the J.P. led movement and yet remain in the Sarvodaya organisation. But this internal division left a chasm which has not been as yet healed up. A very dynamic dedicated enlightened lady, well trained in the spiritual centre at Vinoba's Ashram at Paunar Miss Nirmala Deshpande led an open revolt against the official line of Sarva Seva Sangh and she began to moblise Sarvodaya workers all over the country with extraordinary courage, sense of organisation and gusto. As J.P. was convinced that Congress rule was a menace to India, Nirmala Didi, as she is affectionately called, was convinced that it was the Congress rule that can save India's freedom and integrity. So sometimes at a distance and sometimes being closely associated, she stood along Indira Gandhi and Late with Rajiv Gandhi and the Congress to support their policy but maintaining her independence as a Gandhian activist. She was also offered a seat in the Rajya Sabha for sometime and she continued to maintain close relations with the Congress High command with grace and gave her suggestions and recommendations not only with regard to formulation of policies but in terms of electoral strategy even to the extent of selection of candidates. However, her herculean voyage for Indo-Pak friendship is her best contribution, which has new come to bear fruit.

After three decades of this informal-formal division within the Sarvodaya field, the scars are there although much of personal agarandisement has been over. This is because the two factions of Sarvodaya workers are united against the communal and racial facism of R.S.S.-B.J.P. combine. Both of them feel that R.S.S.-B.J.P. has become the greatest threat to the very survival of our nation with a composite culture.

Both of them feel that that dictatorship or facism has been ingrained in the long structure of R.S.S. and like Hitler or Mussolini they might overtake the destiny of the nation and turn India into a nation of Taliban-type racial facism of Hindu Rastra. The second point of agreement is that both feel that the so-called cult of liberalisation, privatisation and globalisation has been not only anti-Gandhian but also anti-Nehruvism and anti-socialism. However, if it is not clear how far Nirmalaji with her pro-Congress bias will be able to go with the Sarva Seva Sangh, since it is the Congress under Dr. Narsing Rao and Dr. Manmohan Singh which had initiated the so called New Economic Policy in 1986 and B.J.P. with its traditional rightist large-scale retreachment and devastating disinvestment policy with coming closer to U.S. policy as dictated by the I.M.F and World Bank are almost alike. On this issue, the stand of Sarva Seva Sangh in unambigous, clear and more radical but Nirmalaji has yet to make up her position clear visa, visa the Congress policy.

There is also a third point of understanding between these two factions that they want to keep up a united stand against the systematic and concerted attack by R.S.S. power-lords either to weaken or liquidate Gandhian organisations and institutions or to overtake them for gaining prestige. Gandhian workers, by no stretch of imagination, temptation or torture can submit to the false doctrine of "our nation and nationhood defined" or the very concept of Hindu Rastra. Many Gandhian institutions throughout the country have been under great stress and strain, their grants stopped, their registration charter cancelled and at some places there has been effective inflitration in their organisation. It was not a shock and surprise to listen to the present Gujarat Chief Minister during the course of a privati conversation that after Pak I.S.I. and the Marxists, Gandhians are their enemies. It is also because the Sarva Seva Sangh with his small contingent of Rastriya Yuva Sangathan volunteers and some activists had plunged into Gujarat election against the B.J.P. Even Nirmala was not far behind and had visited Gujarat to lend her moral and material support against Modi.

On this point, I have some doubts as to the fundamental credibility of Sarvodaya movement to take sides in an electoral battle openly or indirectly. Is it not against the fundamental pledge of the Lok Sevak which is required to be signed by every Sarvodaya worker? Is it not against the conditions laid down in the pledge prepared by the Mahatma in his Last Testament? Danger was of facism Gujarat in the wake of the worst communal holocqast. Then came elections in Himachal then and some other states. Then we had the same political polarisation in M.P, Rajasthan, Delhi. And now Lok Sabha and some Vidhan Sabha elections are knocking at our door? The same clear cut political poliarsation is before us as secular vs. the non-secular.

It is a dilemma, whether the Sarvodaya workers and institutions in face of the dangers of racial facism should opt for anti-B.J.P. front either under a corrupt Pro R.S.S. Sankar Singh Baghela or a corrupt, castist and inefficient Laloo Yadav with dynastic rule in Bihar or sit like a silent spectator? It is a pity that an avowed anti-R.S.S. George and Sharad, the Solialists, a valiant high profile Tribal Sargama and many other have joined the bandwagon of N.D.A while the Congress-C.P.I.M. are trying hard for even a patch work united front, there are more puzzles and paradoxes before the Sarvodyist for both theoretical and practical reasons. If they adhere to the pledge of a Lok Sevak, they have no option but to limit themselves to perform voters education duties as clearly mentioned in the Last Testament of the Mahatma Gandhi. But if the situation becomes untolerable and they wish to plunge into electoral politics in the name of "political intervention", they should immediately either form a political party of their own or join such a fraternal party as Jan-Samajvadi party or anyone else. To work as election agents or propagandist of any party for or against is to play badly with Sarvodaya pledge, and dabble into party politics and power politics. Unfortunately some of the grandmasters and most credible leaders of Sarva Seva Sangh have been itching since long to convert Sarva Seva Sangh into a political forum called *Swaraj Savagram.* However, it could not materialise then. Recently a theory of "political intervation" has been updated around real phobia of R.S.S.-B.J.P. terror. But I feel that by playing the role of a party propagandist, the Sarvodaya workers will not only violate its sacred pledge but will loose its all-party or no-party identity in society. On practical front, they are so resourceless and unskilled that they can hardly influence any important segment of society. We shall have to accept Congress as the alternative whom ourselves and the nation have already rejected. So far the crucial secular credit of the Congress, it is under cloud. Did not the great Rajiv Gandhi manipulated to open the lock in Ayodhya for Hindu votes? Did not the same Rajiv usurped and insulted the supreme court of India and inflicted a communal decision in Shah Banu's case for Muslim vote? It will be a moral dilemma in Bihar whether to vote for a corrupt, dynasty ruler, inefficient R.J.D. rule or opt for a racial facist? I do think that the choice before the Sarvodaya worker is not easy and simple but any alignment is theoretically against our pledge and principle and practically counter productive.

We should limit ourselves to set as honest frank and enlightened voters education till we are in a position to set up people's candidates but not a caricature in a manner hurriedly and hastily done at Wardha to become a langhing stock of all. Only in an intensive area for atleast five years hard work will entitle us to think about settling up peoples candidate including following other conditions.

We shall overcome someday. The mighty Mahatma with massive number of dedicated workers had to toil for half a century and even then he could get a divided India. India has an extraordinary resilence power of its own. It has changed the face of Communism here so it will change the thinking of communalism too. Did not Atalji has stolen a march over all the past Prime Minister of India, including the great Jawahar Lal Nehru in matters of Indo-Pak solutions? Let us hope, we shall overcome.

12

Good Government and Good Governance

I

"Government is no doubt an essential feature of the State but the term government has varied and even contradictory meanings, depending on its respective philosophy. In the old and primary sense, 'governance' implies a guarantee of safety and security of life, property and honour of the citizens from external invasion and internal disorder. But gradually, this conception has been substantially enlarged to include many social welfare functions so much so that the modern state is regarded not only a law and order maintaining machinery but it is a 'Welfare State'. But when the State tried to usurp the basic human rights of the citizens in the name of 'governance', there has been a swing towards the other pole. Hence, David Thoreau's maxim is often quoted : "That Government is the best which governs the least". Even an advocate of dictatorship of the proletariat like Marx and Engels are constrained to plead for "the withering away of the State" in the final phase of Communism. Gandhi goes ahead and prescribes structural erosion of the power of the State through gradual and maximum decentralisation from top to bottom. He would not tolerate even so-called transitional dictatorship because a dictator does not like to abdicate the absolute power and privilege unless compelled to do it. To him, "political power is not an end but one of the means enabling people to better the condition in every department of life".[1] To him, "State represents violence in a concentrated and organised form."[2] But this is a necessary evil. Hence Gandhi as a practical idealist advocates the "least government". Emerson also thinks exactly like this : "Less government we have, the better, fewer the laws, the less confided power."[3] So Goethe also supports this idea by saying that "the best of all government is that which teaches us to govern ourselves." Gandhi gives the guidclines : "Under my plan, the State will be there to carry out the will of the people, not to dictate to them or force them to do its will".[4]

Discarding the notion that it is only under some sort of dictatorship, efficiency in governance can be achieved. Gandhi counters, "For administration to be efficient, it must always be in the hands of the fittest. There should be certainly no favouritism". Gandhi's second argument against the so-called autocracy is moral and sanctity of individuality. He looked "Upon an increase in the power of the State with the greatest fear, because although while apparently doing good by minimizing exploitation, it does the greatest harm by destroying individuality, which lies at the root of all progress".[5] Government is only a necessary evil like our go-carts and crutches. All over much governance kills the self-help and energy of the governed. The third argument against the 'governance' theory is that of corruption. It is a wrong belief that there is lesser corruption under dictatorship. It may not be visible but it is much more in an autocratic rule. Only, the rate of corruption, bribery or slush money is being high, The dictator has no fear for using unfettered corrupt devices. We have seen cases of the highest degree of corruption, favouritism and dynastic rule during Pol Pot, Ayub, Idi Amin etc. Power corrupts man and absolute power corrupts absolutely.

Hence we come to the conclusion that no doubt "a good government is a government of the people, by the people and for the people" as Lincoln said, but it should be also decentralised democracy with the least power to the centre. Man is the supreme consideration. State or government is for man not man for the government.

II

No body should have any objection against "good governance". But "good governance" without a "good government" is an illusion. There can be 'good governance' in the sense of a strict law and order situation as it generally happens during an autocratic rule equipped with full police and military power and no responsibility or fear of victory or defeat in any election, no fear of any stricture from the Lok Pal or the judicial court. But it is very short lived. As soon as the dictator retires, the law and order or the governance degenerates into full fledged anarchy. There might be defects and flaws in a democracy; we can change the 'representative democracy' into a 'participatory democracy', or have better electoral reforms, or introduce grass-root democracy, greater control of the electorate in the form of Referendum, Plebiscite etc. but there is no alternative to democracy. If there is any alternative, it is to find out more vigorous and refined one. At present, unfortunately, there has been a conflict between 'good governance' and 'good government'. This is because of new thrust in international organisations, mainly World Bank, International Monetary Fund and now World Trade Organizations. However, their chief aim is "to make economic policy decisions more transparent, to make available maximum of information regarding public finances, to standardise procedure and to combat the financing of terrorism." According to the World Bank, the governance of "client countries" should go beyond dysfunctioning of the public resource allocation mechanisms, "institutional development of the State, the process of formulation, choice and implementation of policies, and the relatives between citizens and their governments".

Hence, the concept of "good governance'" differs from the varied economic interests of each international organisations. For example, for UNDP, good governance means "sustainable human development", for the Asian Development Bank (ADB) it means "private sector participation", for Inter American Bank (IAB), it means the "strengthening the Civil Society", for the Organization for Economic Cooperation and

Development (OECD) it means "accountability, transparency, efficiency and effectiveness, economic forecasting and primacy of loyalty and for the European Bank for Reconstruction (EBRD) good governance means "human rights and democratic principles".

But in spite of varied interpretation, there is one thing common, "the shaping of states" policies to create these institutional environment most favourable to the opening up of the countries of the South to globalized financial markets. The official line is that of the IMF for which "good governance" consists of deregulating the exchange, trade and price systems", "limiting of adhoc decisions and making preferential treatment of individuals and organizations and of "eliminating direct credit allocation" by the State". To attain this is almost indissociable from pursuing the neo-liberal economic policies and also the social model, which is the ultimate motivation behind the strategy. This has been found in majority of countries, in every domain and in every continent. Hence we can say that neo-liberalism is not a development model, but truly a domination model. Its social disaster, its human *trasadi* (त्रासदी) are open and clear. Its new ideological slogans of anti-State dogma, 'good governance', can thus only be seen as an inversion of 'good government'. Its aim is not democratic participation in the process of development but state-sponsored market deregulation, in other words, regulation by the brute force of the capital on a worldwide scale. Confronted by the dilemma of the impossibility of managing of this world system and the refusal of international organizations like the IMF, WB, WTO etc. to acknowledge the urgency of finding an alternative development model, it might capitalise dynamics of expansion limits independent of its drive for profit maximization, the slogan for "good governance" can only intensify its criticism of '"State failures". They may not only accuse the 'public enterprises', and 'civil servants' to manage public affairs, they have in store ultra-liberal remedies of proposing "national defence", for privatisation a "foreign currency" for the "national currency", privatization of tax-collection etc. for "good governance". This is the strategy or conspiracy to manage the state apparatus of the South directly from the centre of the world system while neutralizing their State power by striping of their minimum prerogatives (defence, currency, diplomacy) and maneuverability in the name of "ideal governance". Hence the slogan for privatisation, liberalisation and globalisation by the neo-imperialist nations is to diffuse their sovereignty and to secure the non-renewable resources for their own nationals, and pushing the others into the quagmire of non-development.

India is also a victim of this conspiracy. If it has to get out of this syndrome, Gandhian model of Swadeshi and political and economic decentralisation called *Swaraj* is the only way out. If we are convinced of our goal, we again can trust the Gandhian method of non-violent struggle *i.e.* Non-cooperation Civil Disobedience and Satyagraha. Congress and B.J.P. have almost accepted the LPG model, we can fight only with non-violent "people's power" this neo-imperialism. We have the experience of successfully fighting out the biggest empire with first grade military-power and won our independence. We have experience of triple-boycott—foreign goods, foreign courts and foreign system of education. We can organise the people on the line of Salt Satyagraha. Time is more favourable today. We should not waste our precious energy in the change of party-governments. With regard to LPG, they have almost the same commitment. As J.P. would say, they are two sides of the same coin. When the people become conscious about the neo-liberal model of development which hardly cares for 10% of the total population as beneficiaries of the liberal model. If we can awaken this vast mass of 90% in the name of the "people's development model", we are sure to compel any government to cast off this lethargy in overthrowing the yoke of slavery of the new world imperialism which is a dependent, techno-cultural invasion on India. Thus this is not only an economic but also political and cultural challenge.

REFERENCES

1. Gandhi, M.K., *Young India,* 2.7.1931.
2. Gandhi, M.K., *Modern Review,* MCR, 1935, p. 412.
3. Singh, R., Gandhi and the Modern World, Delhi : Classical Publishing, Ch. VI.
4. Tendulkar, D.G., *Mahatma,* Vol. VII, p. 48.
5. Gandhi, M.K., *Modern Review,* Oct., 1935, p. 412.

13

J.P.—A Practical Idealist

J.P. has been widely respected but often misunderstood. Some of us feel that he was simply a dreamer of dreams, while to the less sympathetic, he is a carrier of "Missed Opportunities" and his Gandhian—Bhoodan Mission is mostly an escape from active politics. These are also those critics who do not hesitate to brand him as political opportunist and too much vacillating in his ideological framework and action-strategy. He is said to have changed his horses too often in a most unpredictable manner.

Taking his whole life into consideration, he can be atleast called a visionary or idealist but not an utopian. He was, no doubt a saint among politicians scrupulously following the path of "Goodness Politics", akin to the Gandhian concept of "Spiritualisation of Politics". For J.P. politics has never been an untouchable thing as it was also not to Gandhi, because "Politics is the coil of a snake which he cannot escape therefore he must wrestle with it." J.P. like Gandhi, Vinoba and M.N. Roy did believe in partyless democracy but he did not overlook the transitional steps in strengthening the parliamentary democracy including "Opposition Unity" or openly, fighting emergency and personal dictatorship. Hence he was both a saint and a warrior, a Moralist as well as a Realist. Like Wordsworth's Skylark, J.P. was true to the kindred points of heaven and home. He was, a master of ideas as well as a man of mission. Apart from his refreshing ideas and action, he had introduced a third dimension motivation and inspiration into his strategy of social action which made him a hero for all times.

He never lived in the past but in the present as well as in the future through his perspectival vision and word-view. Hence we find him a romantic Robbinhood during Pre-Independence freedom struggle as well a charismatic hero at his advance age of 74 years during Bihar movement in 1974-75. Even during Bhoodan movement under Acharya Vinobha Bhave, J.P. struggled like a legendary Abhimanyu taking all his political ambitions by offering the supreme gift of his whole life of dedication called Jevandan. This was heroism par excellence. Thus he galvanized very dimension of his social and political enterprises, whether it was his Kisan struggle or his All India Labour Movements, Grass Root Panchayat Democracy, or interlocking voluntary organization (AVARD), his peace missions in Nagaland, Kashmir and elsewhere. He worked like angel during communal carnages in Jamshedpur, Rourkela, Ranchi, Ahmedabad etc. He could not remain a silent spectator during liberation movements of Goa or Bangladesh, Tibet, Czechoslovokia or Hungry. He was versatile and a social scientist genius and a sophisticated intellectual but he was not an arm-chair drawing-room-politician. His nature was such that he never shirked to take risks or accept challenges with the greatest humility and sincerity of which he was capable of, whether it was during chivalrous escape from prisons from Nepal and Hazaribagh during Freedom Struggle, Naxal threat to the lives of his humble Sarvodaya workers in Muzaffurpur. Infact he was more an inspirer like Sardar Bhagat Singh, Netaji Subhas Chandra Bose rather than a professional politician or statesman. Hence we recognize J.P. not only as a hero of the past but a hero-eternal. J.P and heroism sound like identical terms. This was indeed his Gandhian cum revolutionary legacy. His was a life of long and continuous fight against injustices. Had he been alive today, J.P. would not have remained an onlooker to the engulfing corruption, collapse of civil society and worst criminalisation of politics. This revolutionary adventures were not a gift given to J.P. by anyone, it was in-built in his being. Hence his contribution is not only intellectual and actional but also emotional.

For the constraint of time and space, I wish to analyse the niche of his instrument of social change through youth-power about which he has written in his Prison Diary known as his last testament. J.P. was a great inspirer of youth and he was convinced that for a total revolution, it is the power of youth which can bring tangible results. He visualized a prophetic vital urgency in youth power without which we cannot achieve revolutionary change bereft of vested interest. Revolution needs an asceticism and no vested interests. J.P. had tried and tested all agencies for social change. He had launched a new political forum and latter a new political party called Socialist Party to achieve social and economic justice and take the place of the Congress Party, which had almost completed its historical role of providing a common platform for freedom movement. Even Gandhi is his last testament had asked the Indian National Congress to wind it up so that when India gets freedom, people should choose its own political framework for the reconstruction of the nation. During 1952 general election J.P.'s Socialist Party appeared like the most viable alternative to the Congress. But after the great debacle in the election, J.P. had a taste of the same moral degeneration, unhealthy cut throat competition and lack of missionary zeal in politics. All these are cross materialism which can offer no incentive to goodness. To him politics without morality was a death trap and it cannot yield any real revolution. Besides, the parliamentary politics is rooted in a structure, which has its own limitations. A party looks to a part of society only hence it cannot do justice to the whole society. The western democracy based on the West minister model is only so called. It is diluted Fascism and Nazism. Party bosses and caucuses usurp the power of the ordinary party members and rule through forming eliques and groups.

All decision making jobs are in the hands of only a small party oligarchy who select candidates for election, provide funds, create groups, distributes rewards and spoils. Hence the representative democracy of today is neither representative in character or in functioning. There is no participatory and no grass-root democracy. Hence parliamentary democracy ceases to be "of the people" or "by the people" and hence it can never work "for the people". It is not "Peoples democracy" which J.P. had in mind. It falls short of its Jefforsonian Linconian ideal but as an instrument of making peoples republic and degenerate into a craftsmanship of power politics based on materialistic consideration of self-interest. Hence, this is most deficient in its structure.

Party system tends to turn the whole political system as anti-people as well as anti-democratic. Hence, J.P. left traditional politics of power and party and instead tried to develop people's politics through grass-root work. He tried his best to set up a communitarian non-party village governments in Mushari block in Muzaffarpur. Like a true social scientist, J.P. had his mind open about the Gramdan republics and he tried his best to find out its potentiality for a new dispensation. But he could not find adequate response and dynamism in Gramdan experiment too. The Bhoodan Gramdan movement also suffered from some organizational and structural defects. There was an ugly pressure to complete the target of gramdan villages resulting in a mega hoax of Bihardan. This was anti climax. Had Gramdan experiment been executed in a scientific systematic and dynamic manner, perhaps it would have yielded some tangible results. But Vinobaji being the Field-Marshall of Bhoodan-Gramdan movement, J.P. could neither openly disassociate with it nor conceal his disillusionment and reservations its in pathway of real social revolution. He was always in search of a tool or agent which could further this cause. Earlier he had tried Kisan Movements and fought with feudal and conservative power. But it was not enough for an upheaval in the whole society. Similarly, he tried to organize the labour-force and was president of such powerful associations like the Railway Men's Federation. A. 1 Post and Telegraph Employees Union, A. 1 Dock Workers Union but J.P. discovered a serious moral flaw in these organizations. They had, no doubt the zeal for struggle against their employers and a militant fighting spirit but they became more interested in their pay, pension, promotions and pirks rather than ushering the total revolution. They themselves are in the habit of developing their vested interests. For example, the three day total bundh call given by J.P. during crucial struggle of Bihar Movement, he was disillusioned to find that the industrial workers in Bihar could not try to go for even a one day sympathetic bundh at their own places, where as youth in Bihar gave up their studies, examinations, carrier-courses etc. to make the call a complete success.

All these evidences led J.P. to think that the youth force is the most appropriate and effective revolutionary instrument of change. There are both psychological and sociological reasons for this inherent revolutionary urge in the youth power for ushering total revolution. The reasons are as follows :

Firstly, the youth power has the least vested interest both structurally as well as emotionally. They do not have any pay, promotion or pension interests. Then the youth power has an additional advantage of having the surplus energy also. They have both desire and energy to work day and night for any social-political upheaval. A grown up or an elderly man with settled life needs comforts leisure and rest but the youth because of their inherent surplus energy can work with greater guoto and strength. A revolutionary situation does need greater time, energy and speed of action. Revolutionary work demands a madness, an untiring effort, for which the youth-power is greatly inclined. A youth is generally a dynamo of energy.

They are more free agents of social changes. A Govt. employee or factory servant, an officer or a teacher, a doctor or a businessman has liabilities enough which find them to their vested interests but student and youth have no specific responsibility to take care of except his studies and future career about which only an uncertainty looms large.

So, the youth power can shoulder more risks. Any person with a job or business will think thrice in order to plunge into the vertex of revolutionary movement because he has to loose them but the youth has no such mental constraints except a distant one. So he can take greater risks and adventure. By nature youth-power is sensitive and also romantic. Revolution demands sensitivity to the suffering of the people. Those who do not possess a kind and sensitive heart cannot be a sincere partner in the process of social revolution.

The suitability of youth power for being a favourable agent of a major social change is also due to the fact that even numerically they form a big chunk of society. If any problem catches their attention, they can mobilize a greater number of their friends and comrades. From the age group of 12 to 40 years, the youth force form the most formidable wand wagon of social change. Besides they can mobilize the other sections of society, with the result that they have the capacity to shake up the entire social fabric.

History also provides the evidences that the youth power when arises and awakes humble the mightiest politicians and power brokers on the earth. Greatest rules of our time like General Dr. Gaulle, Ayub Khan, Soekarno and Indira Gandhi were humbled when the students and youth power became the vanguard of the revolutionary change. Even in India during 1942, it was the youth force which kept the flame of Quit India Movement burning when all the elderly leaders were put behind the prison bars. Even during the Bihar movement of 1974-75, it was the youth power which worked predominantly as its vanguard.

Besides, we can attribute a spiritual factor also for the greater suitability of youth force for being the true agent of revolution. It is generally believed that the young mind is generally free from all prejudices and evil thoughts. Child is supposed to be nearer to God so youth power is likely to have more purity, and stranger moral fibre than the grown up people who develop many complexes and vested interests.

14

Potentials of Gandhian Initiative in Bihar Retrospect and Prospect

When we eulogize or condemn Bihar, we suffer under a fallacy of illicit particularization or false generalization. Bihar is very much a part of Indian socio-cultural fabric and an interdependent political phenomenon. Hence, no impartial study about Bihar is possible without a national perspective.

Without going too far into the ancient history of Bihar during the Vratyas or the Licehvees experiments about democracy in Bihar we can say that the very idea of the Nation and Nationhood into the Indian psyche seem to be introduced partly during the British regime and partly during the freedom struggle led by the Indian revolutionaries on the one hand in a sporadic manner but in a systematic and organized manner under the banner of the Indian National Congress and the leadership of Tilak and Mahatma Gandhi. When the Britishers disappeared from the Indian scene, a degeneration in national life stealthily set in because of the cult of sub-nationalism ingrained in us. Unfortunately, Gandhi, the symbol of non-party, non-political people's power was removed away from the national scene and there was a halt to post-independent moral and spiritual renaissance. Gradually, we became communal minded and inherited a worn out caste ridden psyche. It is no denying the fact that even after 56 years of political freedom, we are not free from this psychological inhibition. The democratic framework of voting and gradual consciousness of the under privileged backward classes of people under the 'socialist slogan' of social justice with its castiest perversity have taken over on all India dimension.

The economic content to this socio-political resurgence had a legacy in the system of Permanent Settlement in granting big chunks of land to the mostly upper caste feudal land-lords during the regime of Lord Cornwallis to derive their political support for the safety of the British Crown and use it as a class-divide mostly based on caste divide. The feudal landlords called the Zamindars mostly belonged to the upper caste people. In this background, Gandhi's crusade in Champaran, Kheda, Bardoli etc. and the Congress Commitment for abolition of the Zamindari system, Vinobha's insight into launching a Gandhian technique of securing surplus land to be distributed to the landless peasantry (Bhoodan-Gramdan) and J.P.'s insistence on "Land reform measures" through S.V.D. and Janta Governments should be borne in mind. Thus the present socio-political phenomenon of Bihar is a logical conclusion of its feudal Permanent. Settlement and to the legacy of caste system of the age-old Hindu-Brahamnical orthodoxy. People with feudalist structural, exploitative aspirations, authoritarian habits and a new social force for freedom from the age-old shackles of caste hierarchical system living in utter poverty and starvation generated unbridled passion for liberation through their voting power those who had suffered for long from social inequality on account of caste system based on the vested interest of a minority section of society. It was a tragedy that these backward classes of people constituted the working force of India's social system but they simultaneously suffered from economic, educational and political backwardness. Only a handful of upper caste feudal elites controlled the entire polity as well as the bureaucracy of the state. The upper caste lobby was so powerful in India that the Report of first Backward Classes Commission prepared under the Chairmanship of late Kaka Kalelkar could not even see its presentation to the Parliament and died its natural death. But thanks to the political consciousness and wide spread upheaval in Bihar, that led to setting up second Backward Classes Commission under the chairmanship of Sri B.P. Mandal, which gave great impetus for enacting laws in almost all the states for reservation of jobs in Government Services. This had also influenced in selecting candidates in the Assemblies and Parliament. Soon the political structure was changed. There were more backward caste people among Chief Ministers, Central Ministers and other high posts. It provided a qualitative psychological change. No doubt, this became an all India phenomenon but it was the backward classes youth and their leaders in Bihar that defeated the unholy conspiracy of the vested interests. It is a fact that after independence, there has been a considerable reduction in the number of big land lords and their influences upon society has also considerably avoided and these has been most rapid growth in educational field of the backward people in Bihar. These has been reduction in torture and suppression, open insult, and abuse of the backward classes people. They have learnt to resist such un-welcome ignominious insults which were earlier common feature in Bihar. It is one of the reasons that knowing full well that there is vast corruption, inefficiency, lack of development thrusts in Bihar and many other negative factors in administration, the majority of backwards classes people continue to support even his puppet Chief Minister as she symbolizes the self respect of the backward classes people as she belonged to their class-caste.

Even earlier, Bihar has been in the fore-front in its fight against feudalistic hegemony of the landlords having deep roots of Kisan Sabhas organizations and their fierce struggles. Even the Indian National Congress during the period of freedom struggle had very powerful farmer's organizations in Bihar led by Swami Sahjhanand Saraswati and others. The Socialists were known as the most valient fighters for the rights of the tillers on the land, so were the Communists. Swamiji was the first to set up Kisan Sabha on all India bases and he draw vast crowd outside Bihar even in the south. He was the pioneer in defeating the Raja of Hathwa, a candidate on behalf of the landlords through a Congress candidate, who belonged to scheduled caste. Some people wrongly brand him as protagonist of a particular caste called Bhumihar but this charge is contradicted by his action. Though there were a very large number of Bhumihars among the Zamindars, Swamiji was an uncompromising fighter against the Zamindari system. Even in case of Hathwa Raja, who was himself a Bhumihar, Swamiji did wage a relentless fight against him and succeeded in getting victory for the Congress candidate, who belonged to a S.C.

Bihar has also shown its leadership in the non-violent movement of land gift mission launched by Acharya Vinobha Bhave. In the 60 lakhs of acres of land collected throughout the country, Bihar alone provided a lion's share of 21 lakhs of acres of land. The Congress, Specialists, the Communists forgot their party affiliations and participated in the collection of land gift movement. The Chief Minister of Bihar and the Bihar Pradesh Congress Committee had formally resolved to collect 32 lakhs of acres of land as per wishes of Vinoba Bhave. We cannot underestimate the importance of Bhoodan-Gramdan movement in the field of peasault revolution, as neither through bloodshed in Telegana or Naxal movements here and there, nor through Kisan Sabha movements nor through government measures for land reforms, ceiling acts, sharing of crops etc., taken together can equal to the amount of land collected and distributed through Bhoodan. Even today more than 5 lakhs of families are the direct beneficiaries from Bhoodan lands.

Even today when the Naxal Movement in Bengal has taken a back seat and they are only in sporadic presence in some states, Bihar has a formidable force of P.W.G, M.C.C., and M.L. grass root organizations. This shows that there is natural urge in Bihar to side with the underdogs and fight out injustice. Here I have already explained, why the people of Bihar including the backward classes are constrained to support the most corrupt, caste-oriented, inefficient and keeping people on false promises because the majority of the backward classes people feel that even the leaders belonging to the high castes have been corrupt and inefficient etc. but they do not belong to their community hence, they fail to share their owes and sorrows.

However, Laloo Yadav with all his defects, has been able to provide self respect and prove that a man born in such a low caste family can rule over Bihar. Because of him, many backward classes officers have got postings at crucially high positions. Statistics can prove this fact that what the B.C. people could not achieve during the last 56 years in Govt. jobs have got in during the last 13 years of Laloo's rule.

Apart from this, Bihar should be credited with pioneering many of the peoples movements during the last 3-4 decades apart from the total revolution led by Jaya Prakash Narayana, like Ganga Mukti Andolan, Bodha struggle against the holding of excess lands in possession of the Head-Preast of Booh Gaya Math, movement against the non-payment of fair prices to the sugarcane growers in North Bihar and so on. Then there are a good number of N.G.O's who are a little different from usual N.G.O's working as relief agencies. On the other hand, I can personally testify that there are a good number of N.G.O's who have taken up programmes relating to the under privileged, weaker sections of the society, gender equality, social and political awareness, communal harmony, peace action, santi sena etc. The reason of such an interest in revolutionary programme in these many young men and women who had joined J.P. movement in 1974, hence set up such N.G.O's to meet both ends and keep them on their own feet. It is why many N.G.O's in Bihar are very close to the current of total revolution and social change. They maintain the same old fervour of carrying the torch of total revolution. If their work can coordinated, they can prove to be effective instruments of social change. Mostly, these N.G.O's aim at revolution rather than relief.

It has been a common charge that Biharees are home sick people. This might be true to the extent that they do not want to cut off from their indegenious dialects, their own food habits, their own way of simple and unsophisticated living and very much attached to their family members but they are very much enterprising in the sense that we can find Biharee breathen engaged in hard work whether it is Jammu and Kashmir,

Punjab, Delhi or in the North Eastern states either playing a hand rickshaw, or carrying the heavy weight of bags for transportation, or rough agricultural work or in construction work etc. They go out of their state in trains without reservation and lead almost a normal life but they bring money to Bihar like the NRIs.

It shows their undaunted struggle for existence. Even while living in flood-prone areas, they have been accustomed to live in a very difficult conditions. The density of population, the recurring ravages draught and flood have not deterred them and they have been able to maintain record production in agriculture.

Amidst so many physical difficulties and deprivations, they maintain their full interest in grass root politics of the panchyats. Though Bihar went to the polls of the panchyats after over two decades, but it has shown fresh vigour and interest in community work. The Panchayat system in Bihar has further smashed the old leadership hegemony of upper caste people in Bihar to a great extent and the emergence of Janta-R.J.D. power has weakened the traditional Congress leadership of the high caste people who are mostly elites. Thus Bihar has once more established the Shudra-politics of the proletariate and B.J.P. with high caste orientation and predominance have failed to seize power. This reminds of Chandra Gupta tradition in Indian polity. This Shudra-Politics based on the power of the backward classes people have not only theoarted the blacklash of high caste and economically better off sections under B.J.P. leadership in Bihar but has also checked the marching chariot of Jai Sri Ram in Bihar making a safer place for secular and social justice politics in Bihar.

Biharee mind-set longs for something big and great, not restricted to Bihar. It aspires for an upheaval of all India frame for example, seeds of India Kisan movement was ingrained in Champaran. Bihar was the laboratory of socialist struggle, J.P.'s movement found its crucial and potential thurst from Bihar and even Vinoba's Bhoodan flourished in Bihar. It might left to Bihar to fill the political vacuum by ushering a **real** third force combining all the progressive forces in the country through coordinating the forces of grass root organizations and those who are really dedicated to the cause of total revolution.

At present, Bihar is in a state of quandary and crisis. The present set up of R.J.D. under Laloo Prasad is corrupt from top to the bottom as it has institutionalized corruption in all walks of life. It has also injected caste politics under the cloak of social justice. It has wiped out all intra-party democracy and instituted most vulgar personalized dynastic politics. The worst feature is that it has also institutionalized criminalisation of politics under state patronage. But its alternative is B.J.P. which is equally corrupt, anti-social justice, anti-Muslim and anti-Christian. This will strengthen facist and communal forces at the national level. Besides, it is bound to strengthen the forces in favour of liberalization, privatization and globalization in the country. Hence, both the alternatives are undesirable and dangerous. Naxalism cannot become a mass-movement in Bihar. It has failed in Telegana, in Bengal, so it has no prospect in Bihar as there are hardly big land owners left to make a demarcation between the " haves and have nots". Besides the method of violence has become out of date and against the taste of the people. Hence, Bihar must provide a new front to fulfil the unfinished task of J.P. The scattered forced of vigilant concerned citizens, constructive workers, dedicated N.G.O.'s and youth organizations and the intellengentia be coordinated on a non-party, non-sectarian and non-authoritarian basis to prepare a common minimum programme with a common platform. Once the united voice of the people is raised on a non-party national level, it will develop into a powerful moral and people's force for which the entire country has been aspiring for. People are not only fed up with political parties, they have begun to hate politicians. Hence a non-party people's forum is the need of the hour. But for this we have to put up atleast a decade of collective authority, voluntary social service and public work without vested interest.

15

The Message of Silent Revolution in Bihar

The world has witnessed non-violent revolutions during its freedom struggle against British imperialism a first grade world-power spreading over such a vast region that sun did not set in its territory. Not to mention about smaller "non-violent resistance movements" called "local satyagraha" in **Champaran, Kheda, Ahmedabad, Bardoli** etc., the All India **Non-Cooperation Movement** in 1921-22 with triple boycott of foreign goods, foreign system of justice and courts and foreign system of education. After a decade, the non-violent revolution had in greater teeth and claws leading to **Civil Disobedience movement** breaking the unjust law of a foreign power in 1931-32. In the third phase of non-violent revolution there was a man upsurge asking the Britishers to **Quit India** in 1942, which ultimately forced the foreign rulers to grant independence to India. We may call it a **"bloodless victory."**

But after independence and accepting a democratic structure of polity based on system of elections, the people of India true to its genius, adopted the method of **"silent revolution"** to elect change their representatives without blood-shed. No doubt we have not been able to adopt either the method of **Recall or Referendum** in our constitution, but the demand for 'recall' has often been voiced by senior statesmen and prophet of change like Jaya Prakash Narain and Dr. Ram Manohar Lohia. In a characteristic forceful manner Dr. Lohia had openly said that "a living community cannot wait as a silent spectator for full five years" or until the regular election takes place, if the present rulers turn defiant and deaf to the voice of justice and the cause of the people. However, there is provision in our constitution to table **"no confidence"** motion or any form of censure, cut motions, adjournment motion etc., to check any form of autocracy developing in our system. Even at lower levels of grass root democracy or local bodies, we have been given this provision to change the Mukhias/Sarpanch or Chairman etc., this is also not in force at the levels of State Assemblies or Loksabha, although a Bill for the "Recall" has been tabled by me in the VIth Loksabha in the Indian Parliament on the "Right of Recall."

What the written Indian constitution has not been able to provide for the "Recall" of representative, the people of India has achieved through non-violent "silent revolutions" in India. The more striking example can be shown during 1977 General Election, when the people overthrew the ruling Congress into the dustbin of history and even the charismatic leader. Smt. Indira Gandhi and heir apparent Sri Sanjaya Gandhi faced Waterloo. The entire northern India was in utter revolt through a silent revolution. Similarly, only years ago when National Democratic Front under the able leadership of Sri Atal Bihari Vajpayee and his team had announced premature General Election, almost all exit polls surveys and the elites were confident about the return of N.D.A. with somewhat greater majority. But alas! the people of India again staged a silent revolution and proved that millions of rupees on electronic and print media failed to convince the so-called "illiterate" people of India. All loud slogans about the 'shinning India' and high growth of G.D.P. and foreign reserve currency could not win support of the people in Andhra, the dynamic herolder of computer revolution was unceremoniously thrown out of power because both N.D.A. and Telegudesam followed a pro-capitalist policy of retrenchment and disinvestment abolition of urban ceiling, moving towards corporate and farm agriculture and pro-MNC's economic order.

The third Silent Revolution was herolded in Bihar, which

was under almost inefficient dynastic, corrupt casteist rule under direct or proxy rule of Sri Laloo Prasad since last 15 years. True, Lalooji had become the symbol of **"social justice"** against the high courts dominated feudal rule in Bihar since the days of permanent settlement under Lord Cornwallis. The upper caste had monopolized not only the bureaucratic but political structure as well educational frame work. Feudalism under the zamindari system and machinations with half-hearted Land Reform measures in Bihar, forced the Backward classes people under a system of semi-slavery. Janta rule during 1977-79 with a strongman like Chaudhry Charan Singh at the Centre and Karpoori Thakur in Bihar and Ram Naresh Yadav in U.P. vigorously awakened the Backward Classes to protect their rights and self-respect. Lalooji exploited the sentiments of the oppressed and suppressed called Backward casts most skill fully aligning with the Muslim voters by putting anti-R.S.S.—B.J.P.'s teeth and nails. They had no option but to vote for Laloo as the formidable champion against the B.J.P. rule in the name of N.D.A. The demolition of the Mosque in Ayodhya and the most unfortunate genocide in B.J.P. ruled state of Gujarat and the vaccilation and finally stubborn refusal of the N.D.A. government even by changing the Chief Minister of Gujarat. Hence Laloo's card of M (Muslim) and y (Casteism) was most pragmatic and expedient.

But Laloo's achievements gradually faded into verbal jugglery and false promises, firstly because of malgovernance leading to virtual collapse of civil administration. It went ahead to criminalization of politics and politicalisation of criminals because so compute that there was a virtual **"jungle raj"** in Bihar. In the garb of fighting, he encouraged nacked casteism and dynastic rule. It was a vulgar and distasteful to find his wife being enthroned in his place when he was caught in the **"fodder scandal"**. He lost all sense of decency to hand over the reigns of Bihar government to his wife who was just an innocent and semi-literate house wife to rule Bihar through proxy. Had he chosen any good backward class or even a senior able honest Yadav of his own confidence he would not have been of a blatant dynastic rule. Besides, charge against him about the fodder-scam and many other crimes, Lalooji institutionalized corruption in the very fabric of administration, whose it be education, medical field, police or Public Service Commission or other Selection Bodies. Last but not the least, he reduced election as a toying force "managing" the Election officers, capturing booths, tampering with the voter list and even the counting of votes. To add to all his failures, his record of non-development of Bihar is the last straw of his downfall. Bihar is at least 25 years back in education, irrigation, roads, medical facilities etc. According to the survey of India today, Bihar stands at the last or one but last in the ladder of development. Crores of even Central Government funds get lapsed, misused and misappropriated. Hence 1½ lakhs of unemployed persons migrate to for western provinces like Punjab, Haryana, Uttaranchal, Gujarat, Rajasthan and even to far eastern states like Manipur, Assam, West Bengal etc. Thousands of posts of college or school teachers, policemen, clerks etc., are vacant, hence the young people are constrained to join M.C.C. or P.W.G. or other mafia groups. Less spoken, the better.

The verdict of the people of Bihar was a 'silent revolution', as Lalooji with the clout in the U.P.A. managed to form a 'united front' with the Congress, the C.P.I.(M) and N.C.P. With the result that not only Laloo's R.J.D. but all its allies were forced to taste the shameless defeat C.P.I.(M) the strongest Marxist party got only **one** seat, N.C.P.**zero**, the Indian National Congress 9. Whereas the C.P.I., C.P.I.(ML) had better performances. In a democracy, people is the sovereign. Only they have to be awakened and a workable alternative should be presented. People did not vote for the B.J.P. or even J.D.(U) but against the dynastic, criminalized non-developmental rule of the R.J.D. under Laloo. One example is enough. Saharsa-Madhepura and Supaul, the Vatican of Laloo's Bastile collapsed like a house of cards—all the 16 candidates of Laloo-Papu configuration were no where non won. Had Congress fought the battle without aligning with Lalooji such a shameful tragedy would not have been to its fate.

To conclude, Indian democracy, inspite of many structural and functional drawbacks is rooted in the power of strong common sense of the common people. The so-called educated and elitist people have to learn this message that the so-called ill-educated and illiterate people of India have their sixth sense intact and comparatively they are more honest, less castists and far less communalists. They are not even pro-capitalist as 50% people live below the poverty line development to be real should not be in the 'sky' or 'flyovers' it must come to the doorsteps of the rural poor and urban slum-dwellers. The Congress Prime Minister, a fire brand pro-globalisation economist is constraint to side with agriculturist loby at Hongkong Conference, restore the subsidies on food, enact even half-hearted Rural Employment Scheme etc. It is why people has not been yet dischanted so much rared forced to move towards B.J.P. axis. This is no political ideology but compulsions of hard reality. Non-issues like Ayodhya, Article 370, Common Civil Code commit provide even a morsel of food in our hungry stomach. Hence even a rejected virulent B.J.P. leader like Uma Bharati has combined **Roti** with **Ram**. Infact, the service of the **lowliest** and the **lost**, the **Daridra Narain** is the **worship of Ram**. Ram did not fight for throne but for **Ram Rajya**. People of India do not relish conflict of caste, creed or religion because we inherit a synthetic culture. To become an Indian, we have to work out a synthesis between the Aryans and Non-Aryans, Dravidians, Nishads and Kirats, the Vedic and the Sraman as well as the Lokayats are the three ancient strands of Indian culture. So also the Greeks, the Sethians the Sakas, the Yavans, Pathnon and Mugals and the Christians all are under the Indian umbrella. Any particular race or religion has no-monopoly. India is a unity in diversity Swami Vivekanand uttered a prophetic voice of synthetic culture—"The destiny of India lies in the synthesis of Islamic body and the Vedantic mind." Did not Rahim spoke about Ram Charitmanas "is the **Vedas** for Hindus and exactly **Quran** for the Muslims"? Did not Raskhan sang with same devotion like Surdas or Meera Bai about Lord Krishna? Darasikoh translated the Upanisads in Persian and all Muslim and Mugal Emperors from Babar (**Babarnama**) to Aurangzeb **Ruskat Alamgiri** amd (**Adbe Alamgiri**) forbade slaughter of cows by royal proclamation. Even during Hyder Ali + Tipoo, the punishment for cow-slaughter was cutting the hands of the man who slaughtered them. Did not Jhansiki Rani, Tatya Tope etc., be fought against the Britisher hand in hand with the Muslims under Bahadur Shah Jafar. Even today, Abulji had started dialogue with Pakistan and installed a Muslim scholar and scientist as the President of India. Today all Sikh is our Prime Minister and an Italian by birth Sonia Gandhi is President of the ruling U.P.A. We have to remember that Annie Besant was twice President of Indian National Congress and sister Nivedita was so dear to Swami Vivekanand and Miss Sladeor Meera Behan spent her whole life for the cause of our freedom. This is the secret of Indian culture which disfavors smallness and narrowness and also the cult of violence.

16

Reminiscences of Freedom Movement

Even as a small boy reading in class V of my village school (Indrukh Dt. Munger, Bihar). I had tantalizing awareness of freedom struggle because of the environment and sense of partriotism taught by our primary school teachers who were all regular wearier of Khadi. I was class monitor in class V and my revered teacher late Sri Ayodhaya Lal inspired us to wear khadi cap. I was asked to keep a record of every student of my class who came to class wearing khadi cap and award 1/2 marks daily. There was weekly debating society meeting where I had lessons in patriotism. Every week, we used to clean the dirt including the night soils on the village road and we purposely visited Harijan locality in our village and ask for a glass of water to break the bane of untouchability. When 9th August, 1942 came, I was a student of class VIII at Jamalpur, which is a small town near my village. I only remember that it was some Saturday, in and around 9th August. Along with a band of militant friends, we came to R.B.H.E. School Jamalpur, where Saturday morning mass-drill was in full swing. Some of us went to the roof of the school building and unfuled tri-colour flag and chanted our favourite slogans—Qauminara (national slogan) : *Vandematram; Hindustand Azad Hai* and *Inquilab-Zindabad*. We sang the national song—Vijayi Vishwa Tiranga Pyara. Then we made a procession and went round the whole town though British war troops were stationed heavily there as it was a war camp. But though we were small children, we had not even an iota of fear. Wearing Gandhi caps and holding the national flag, we were marching shouting *Britishers: Quit*

India. Then we went with some of the our seniors to invade another school, took away its Registers and burnt them in our village though a gentleman tried to protest for fear of Govt. aprisals. Then I remember a memorable meeting of the revolutionaries in the place of worship, a little away from village. They had assembled to chalkout a militant programme to blast the Electric Power House of Jamalpur Railway Workshop to paralyse the entire workshop and to derail an engine in the Railway funnel so as to block movement of railway traffic. We children were asked to guard the gate of the meeting place so as to keep an eye on the C.I.D. or police.

Then my old father got scared and took me to my sister's place at Jamshedpur. The railway tracks were broken so it took two days to reach. There were other memories. But when the movement subsided and all my class-friends joined the school in December to appear at the Annual Examination, I also went to the Headmaster. He asked me to tender apology in writing like other students which I refused. Then I moved to another place Mokama 50-60 miles away from my house and there I got admitted in a newly started High School (Sri Krishna Marwari School, Mokama, Patna). But I had to change my name as well of my father's name in order to avoid legal difficulties. I was formerly Ramchandar Singh which was changed into Ramjee Singh. Though the Freedom Movement was suppressed but our spirit was always very high. We used to sit in small numbers and plan strategies to block assistance to War Fund—"Do not give a pie, do not send a brother..." Some of my class-friends were subjected to worst tortures who had gone to unfurl tri-colour on 26th January 1943, Some of them were packed up in a military truck, their clothes were torn, their bodies were coloured red with some sort of pump and then thrown one by one from the running truck into the dreadful jungles. One group was bundled and their hands and feed tied down and then thrown into the high river. Thanks to the patriotic-minded boatsmen that they were rescued anyhow. When there was formation of Provisional Govt., Worst Communal riots broke out in our area but as true volunteers of Congress Seva Dal we tried to protect the minorities. We lived with them. We did not even celebrate Holi at our homes but slept in Muslim houses so that they might be safe. Everyday, we had parades and play. On 14th/15th August—the memorable night of Independence is clear in our vision. I did not sleep for a moment till 12 p.m. We sounded a bugle from the top of my house to make the whole village awake at the dawn of freedom. I remember to have prepared a flag 15 meters long and 4 ½ metres wide tied into big and long bamboos. After hoisting the flag in our village, we walked whole day in the nearest cities of Jamalpur and Munger. Freedom! O Freedom! let it be eternal and imperishable.

17

Gandhian World Order and World Peace

1. Introduction

Peace is far more than an absence of war. Peace is a state of positive and constructive both of world-view and world-order, where individuals, groups and nations eschew to dominate or exploit each other and like in cooperation and mutual aid. Hence, there cannot be any delinking of peace and democracy, peace and development, and peace and decentralisation. Not only this, peace cannot be delinked with technology, ecology and psychology. In short peace needs a holistic outlook and a radical life-style and culture. To say that world peace is only linked with disarmament and not with 'equality' or with the concept of 'national sovereignty' or 'personal religion' and 'unfettered possession' is a mischievous thought. Even in terms of pedagogy, peace has a great stake. In our total crisis of civilization, education has its full share. We have to learn to choose between Atom and Ahimsa, Military Science and Peace Research, Military Training (N.C.C.) and Shanti Sena. Even in the field of jurisprudence, we have to choose between retribution and reformation, death penalty and something better. Violence does not only bring a bad image to our nation, it also weakens its very fabric. Hence, the concept of World Peace can be achieved through a culture of non-violence.

2. Individual Peace vs. Social Peace

There have been many apostles of peace from the time

immemorial and throughout the world. Had they not taught us the value of peace, love and compassion, our world would have been more vicious than of the savage animals. Their efforts have been two-fold—firstly to acquire internal peace and then to propagate peace. The result is that we have moved from savagery to civilization, from cannibalism to vegetarianism, from cruelty to compassion. The teachings of religious saints, no doubt, are rooted in peace. But it is a paradox that we have forsaken or even forgotten our animal nature. Our human ingenuity and intelligence have made us more ferocious than tigers and vultures, more dealier than scorpions and cobras. Today, men themselves have become, perhaps, the greatest enemy of men. From Buddha to Jesus, Zoraster to Jevoah, Confusius to Nanak have been sincerely preaching the message of peace and non-violence, but there has been no end to religious conflicts so much so that more than 60% wars in human history have been fought in the name of religion. It means that either there is no close relation between the prophecy by the prophets and practice by their followers or perhaps man is by nature a beast.

To me, there is no fault with the noble lives and character of these religious seers or any flaw in their teachings nor we can accept that man (woman) is by nature evil, nasty, brutish and even incorrigible. To think that man, by nature, is bad is not only an insult to the entire mankind who live in peace on all week days and it is only on Sundays that he goes violent and wild and indulges in conflicts and quarrel, it is also pessimism par excellence. If we accept that by nature, human beings are evil, there is no scope for any reform. All educative efforts become useless. Hence, the malaise seems to be deeper. On the level of spiritual engineering or ethical elevation, moral teachings in ethical virtues like peace and compassion are alright but on the level of social engineering, we have not been able to develop social non-violence. Hence there is a wide chasm between our individual ideals and social structure. Man lives in society. He is born and brought up in family where he is face to face with worst kinds of domestic violence. Further, there is his neighbourhood, where again he faces violence, conflict, hatred etc. It becomes a matter of routine. He goes to school and is taught the theory of 'Survival of the Fittest', 'Class-Struggle', 'doctrine of inevitability of war' and 'excellence through competition'. In political life, the situation is still worse where 'goodness', 'honesty' and 'peace' are treated either as outdated utopias or 'politics of the unpolitical'. Instead of will, force is said to be the basis of the state and machiavellian methods are treated as the guiding principle of practical polity. It means that entire societal structure is repugnant to peace. If the real world order is differentiated, structured and stratified, any correspondence to the real world can be only metaphorical in character. Gandhi, therefore, did not adopt a Utopian but a constructivist and experimentalist view. Hence, as a practical idealist, he took seriously structural and developmental violence into consideration.

3. Constructivist Non-violence

Gandhi's concept of world peace follows from his concept of world-order, which is comprehensive, constructive and forward looking. He is radical enough to break the age-old idolas in politics, economics, religion and even in the fields of education and health.

For time and space constraint, I propose to pick up only three such idols of the present world order and their Gandhian alternatives which can provide some hints to the ideological-cum-structural basis of Gandhi's concept of world peace.

(a) Paradox of National Sovereignty and World Peace

The concept of nation and nationhood is perhaps the strongest nation of sentimental attachment in the world as it often crosses the border of race and religion, language and culture. This is because the strong bond of political government backed by the coercive power of police, military and courts on the one hand and the charter of ownership, trade and other forms of livelihood on the other hand help to consolidate and channelise the wrong sentiments into unipolar recognition of nation and

State. There might have been imperatives for the creation of the institution known as nation or State or nation-States, in the past but today, it has not only become outdated but also pernicious and dangerous for the world peace. The sentiment of patriotism as well as the lust of power cemented through the Austinian concept of inalienable sovereignty and the false umbrella of internal peace and external security, it has made the institution more, mighty than the Leviathan and more authoritarian than that of the most despot kings or the dictators. There are multiple factors like the territorial space, citizenship, governance for safety and security and the sense of identity attached to the nation of State. However, there were also very small States called the city-States among the ancient Greeks and the Licchavis and the large empires of the Romans, Magadh and the Mughals. These States, due to various reasons either for exploitation, or dominance or imperial extension, have been fighting with one another and leading to catastrophe.

Hence, in order to find out an alternative, the concept of "One World" has emerged. Windel Welkie's book entitled "One World", H.G. Wells' and Pt. Rahul Sanskrityayana's idea about it have been very popular Utopias. But as one world war followed by other and the dread of an atomic war has pushed the mankind not only to set up world organisations like the League of Nations and the United Nations Organisations but various other international institutions. Perhaps, the world has become too small to allow the nation-States to live in isolation. Even in the realm of economics and information technology, national boundaries are loosing their hardline postures. The recent trend of unification of two Vietnams and two Germanys and creation of an European Parliament, European Market with one Visa and one currency of 21 East European Sovereign States are significant achievements towards world federation. Gandhi, therefore while addressing the Inter-Asian Relations Conference just before India's independence while replying to a question he had explicitly answered : "I would not like to live in this world, if it is not to be One World." He has always denounced narrow nationalism and religious sectarianism. He further said : "Nations cohere because there is mutual regard among individuals composing them. Some day we must extend the national law to the universe, even as we have extended the family law to form a nation" (Young India, 2.3.1922). He emphatically said that "India's freedom as conceived by me can never be a menace to the world (Young India, 3.4.1924). In an extraordinary lofty moral voice Gandhi further said : "My country may become free, that if need be, the whole country may die, so that the human races may live". He openly reiterated : "Isolated independence is not my goal of the world states. It is voluntary interdependence (Young India 15.7.1924). His "Nationalism. fierce though it is, is not exclusive" (Young India, 12.11.1931).

(*b*) Paradox of Religion and Pax Mundi

Along with the concept of nation, unfortunately, the prevalent religious dogmas have also been serious hurdles in the path of world peace. There has been at least as many wars in the name of religion as in the nation of politics and nation. One hundred years of war between two sects of Christianity, were fought. Hindus and Muslims, as well as Muslims and Jesus have been fighting each other since half a century. Today, we listen to have a clash of civilization in the name of religion. Religious fanaticism either in Afghanistan or Iraq or in Gujarat are some of the examples of inhuman cruelty. They might lead even to regional or world wars.

Hence either we mend these religions or end them. Secularism, as the cult of negation of any religious faith cannot be a solution. Religion is the inner nature of man, it is said to be the yearning of our soul. Hence to end it will be like throwing the baby with the bath-water. But it requires a serious surgical operation. Swami Vivekanand, being a religious apostle had therefore realized that the days of "ersional religion"are over. Instead we must have 'universal religion'. This is what the ancient Vedic Scripture says : "Reality is one, the wise people call it by different names". Tagore also advocated the "Religion of Man" instead of "religion of a sect society". Gandhi has taken exactly this line. To him "all religions, at bottom are one, though they differed in detail and outward form even like the leaves on a tree". Even as "the tree has a single trunk, but many branches and leaves, there is one religion, but any number of faiths." In order to avoid misunderstanding and religious conflicts, Gandhi following the Indian tradition had advocated a special vow called "Equal Respect for All Religions". This means that he went further than mere religious 'tolerance'. To him, all faiths constitute a revelation of Truth, but all are imperfect. Reverence for other faiths need not blind to the defects to their faults. "If a man reaches the heart of his own religion, he has reached the heart of the others too" (Polak, H.S.; *Mr. Gandhi : The Man,* London, 1931, p. 41). Gandhi's personal attitude is that *(a)* all religions are true; *(b)* all religions have some error in them; *(c)* all religions are almost as dear to him as his own Hinduism (Report of International Fellowships, Sevagram, 1928, p. 17-19). To him, religion was entirely a personal affair. Each one could approach his Creator as he liked.

(c) Economic Disorder and World Peace

"Human Society is not a water tight compartment called social, political and religious. All act and react upon one another." (Gandhi, M.K.; *Young India,* 2.3.1922). But Marxian theory of Economic Interpretation of History is valid to a great extent. We have seen in the story of the Mahabharata that even the great savants and moral personalities like Bhisma, Drona, Kripacharya etc. had to remain as silent spectators even when the lady queen of the Pandavas were being made naked in the full view of the assembly. Even if we do not go so far, we must say that economic factors determine our actions and reactions very much. Hence Gandhi, on the one hand stressed upon the 'Gospel of Work' and the doctrine of 'Bread Labour', he was always for service to the Last Man—The Daridranarayan or the starving millions of India through Khadi and village industries as national constructive programme. Economic equality, according to Gandhi is the master key to non-violent independence.

Working for economic equality means abolishing the eternal conflict between capital and labour. It means the levelling down of the few rich in whose hands is concentrated the bulk of the nation's wealth on the one hand and levelling up of the semi-starved naked millions on the other. This is also the panorama of the world today. The U.S.A. with a world population of only 6% consumes about 40 to 45% of consumer goods of the entire mankind, while nearly half of the world population live in poverty. Hence the present policy of 'globalization' is only so called. It is in fact world capitalism with nails and teeth of merciless exploitation, profiteering and domination through W.T.O. Gandhi's ideal was 'equal distribution', but so far it may not be realized. He worked for 'equitable distribution' through Trusteeship on the one hand and through non-violent mass action (Satyagraha) on the other. Even his Trusteeship theory was not to be left alone on the assumption of mere change of heart of simply by verbal persuation but must be backed by non-violent non-cooperation. No person can amass wealth without the cooperation willing or forced of the people concerned. Even the tyranny of W.T.O. would be over, if all the member nations refuse to cooperate with it. Gandhi had shown non-violent method of fighting capitalism through practicing Swadeshi and self-sufficiency. He also emphasised limitation of wants. Nature's plan support it. Nature has enough to meet our needs but not our greed. Multiplication of wants bring blind consumerism and cruel exploitation of nature nature leading to ecological disasters. It is being said that the third world war might start on the problem of 'water'. Even today, blatant U.S. invasion of Iraq is to appropriate its rich oil. World Capitalism need monopoly of world-market which can lead to war. Today wars are not waged to annex territories but to capture consumer markets. Hence in the name of L.P.G., a new form of sophisticated but more dangerous capitalism has emerged. Had Gandhi been alive, he would have fought it tooth and nail, first on the national level and then on the global plane.

Conclusion

World Peace is a sine qua non for human progress, nay for the human survival. But it cannot be only through religious sermons or through benevolent charity. Had it been so, these techniques have been going on all over the world since last two or three Mellenia. Communism did adopt a method of mass action including violent class struggle. But it has neither achieved equalisation of wealth nor world peace. On the other hand, human rights and individual freedom were its casualties. The impregnable bulwark of Soviet Communism have collapsed. Even Chinese Communist State has joined the wand wagon of W.T.O. or World Capitalism. Hence, Gandhian ideology and Gandhian method remains the only alternative. Today, Gandhism is not a fed but an imperative. Like the capitalist States, the so-called Communist States of U.S.S.R. and P.R.D. China have been caught in the coils of narrow nationalism, invading Poland and Hungry or Vietnam like the neo-imperialists. Hence world peace has become willo-the-wisp. So far religion is concerned, this is rejected by the Communists but it does not satisfy the yearning of the people. On the other hand, the capitalism has made religion and religious institution, its hand maid. Hence Gandhian alternative of 'ethical religion' and treating "all religions with equal respects" remains the only rational solution to stop religious fratricide endangering world peace. Gandhi should not be taken as the full-stop of Gandhian thought. We must add and improve upon Gandhi as he himself magnimously said : "There is no such thing like Gandhism".

18

In Lieu of a Foreword for 'Shanti-Sena'

Indeed it is with considerable hesitation that I venture to write a few lines about Professor Thomas Weber's monograph on Shanti-Sena (Peace Army). I am driven between two loyalties loyalty to the republic of letters and my humble love for Shanti-Sena. I had suggested more competent authorities also because I have been undergoing treatment for blood haemorrhage of my eyes. This work is a labour of love and hence as a Shanti-Sena activist and a humble student of Gandhian Thought, I take it as a privilege to associate myself with this mission of the *Mahatma* which is a mission of Peace. Perhaps, this is the first systematic and scholarly monograph on this subject with this specific title. Of course, there is a book by Acharya Vinoba Bhave (spiritual disciple of Gandhi) on Shanti-Sena but it is a collection of his speeches. No doubt a few booklets also are there.

Two of my Ph.D. students have worked and earned their doctorate degrees on Shanti-Sena—Dr. William Bhaskaran (Gandhigram Rural Institute (G.R.I.), Gandhigram) and Dr. Manoj (Bhagalpur University) while the third research scholar is yet to complete his work. With our humble efforts, an independent Post Graduate Department of Gandhian Thought and *Shanti-Sena* has also been started at G.R.I. long ago but it has yet to catch up speed.

Hence this book is a base book for future research and references on the subject in English. Although, the present work is an extension of author's earlier various research papers on various dimensions of *Shanti-Sena*, the author must be credited for the publication of this book.

THE CENTRAL IDEA OF SHANTI-SENA

Satyagraha is the vortex, out of which the ideas of *Shanti-Sena* has emerged. *Satyagraha* is *Truth-Force* plus *Love-Force* combined into one. Without truth-force, rhetoric of peace is a camouflage or merely a peace of the grave-yard. Tolstoy called it also Soul-Force, which is different from *brute-force*. Physical Force or violence is the negation of the great spiritual force. Its universal applicability is the demonstration of its permanence and invincibility—that is Socrates, Jesus and Mansoor. Gandhi's credit lies only in making this powerful instrument to the easy reach of men, women and children, or a successful weapon of mass action. Only those who realize that there is something in man which is superior to the brute-nature in him, and that the latter always yields to it, can effectively be a *Satyagrahi*. As light is to darkness, force of violence, injustice and tyranny just in like "the owl of Minerva" which takes its flight when the twilight shades of soul-force begins to fall. So the birth of *Satyagraha* in 1906 in South Africa is also the birth of *Shanti-Sena*. Gandhi had referred to the "*Armies of Peace*" in a meeting of British India Association held in Johannesburg on 27th April, 1913 to consider action against unjust and discrimination of Immigration Bill. When Gandhi returned to India and plunged himself into the freedom struggle, he took first step "towards its reorganization of *Peace Brigade* (Shanti-Sena) following outburst of communal riots in Bombay on 17th of November, 1921. He at once went on a fast until the disturbances subsided. Following the enlistment of *Shanti-Sainiks*, Khan Abdul Gaffar Khan seized the first opportunity to set up *Khudai Khidmatgar* (Servants of God) organization on the pattern of *Shanti-Sena* in 1929 among the tribal pathans of North-Western Frontier Province.

To my mind, *Shanti-Sena*, being a progeny of *Satyagraha* adopts both its ideology and methodology in its working against structural and ideological violence. But if it is so, why there should a separate outfit such as *Shanti-Sena*? The first reason was to have a well-trained volunteer force like the military police, with very high state of discipline as first grade *peace-army*, which is very smart, punctual, fearless, obedient and prepared to take the highest risk.

This is why, Gandhi suffixed the word *Sena* (army) with *Shanti* (Peace), that ordinarily sound contradictory as the word "army" is associated with weapons, war and violence. Like Gandhi, his spiritual disciple Acharya Vinoba Bhave who has justified, the use of "army" (*Sena*) along with "Peace" quotes a verse from the Vedas where the word *Sena* means "power" (*asenyah Panyo Vachansi*). Non-violence is the virtue of the strong not of the week. It is like walking on the blade of a sword which requires extensive courage and strong determination. It is path of the brave. Hence Gandhi distinguishes *Satyagraha* from "Passive Resistance" because it is intensely an active state of action, more active than passive resistance or violence. "Passive resistance is a misnomer". (*Young India,* 25.8.1920). A Satyagrahi is subject to a 'higher law' so "disobedience to the law of the State becomes a peremptory duty when it comes to conflict with the Law of God" (M.K. Gandhi, *Ethical Religion,* Madras, Ganeshan & Co., 1930, p. 45). This is why Gandhi had to wage *Non-cooperation* and *Civil Disobedience Movements* against the unjust and immoral foreign rule. However, there is no room for violence as Satyagraha is not only Truth-Force but also Love-Force. Satyagraha postulates the conquest of the adversary through justness of the cause, love and suffering. Hence non-violence is not a method of coercion, it is one of conversion. (*Harijan,* 8.7.1930). Love, not hatred is the motive and guiding principle of Satyagraha. Hence the basic assumptions for a successful *Satyagrahi* are four-fold :

1. There must be common honesty among *Satyagrahis*.
2. They must observe heart-discipline without any reservation.
3. He should be prepared to pay the highest price, even slow death.

4. They must not be violent in word, thought and deed.

There are other guidelines for *Satyagrahis* like cultivation of democratic spirit, a respecting differences of opinion among co-workers etc. Hence there is no compulsion or coercion in *Satyagraha*. The task of leadership is great. He must command respect on account of his unblemished and selfless life and character. He must live a life of truth, because we cannot serve God and Mammon both. He shall have to take up both sackleth and ashes. He should have thoroughness, punctuality and order, fearlessness, humility and maximum amount of self-restraint and simple living and high thinking. In short, he should be servant of God having renunciation and joy.

Violence, though pervasive and intense is getting out of date and practically more and more counter-productive in practice, because modern science and technology have bestowed upon the State with immense power to suppress sporadic violence. So those who had subscribed to the theory of "inevitability of war" have accepted the "doctrine of peaceful co-existence". Infact, the world is getting weary of hate. There is no taste for killing of innocent persons in war and terror-blasts. Maoist violence is more a reaction against the structural violence like unemployment, poverty, exploitation and inequality rather than ideology of violence. Terrorist violence of the *Al-Quaida, Hizbullah*, and the *Talibans* are one-fourth due to religious bigotry and the three-fourths against desire for global hegemony by some world powers, exploitation and usurpation of national sovereignty.

NON-VIOLENCE : THE MOTHER OF SHANTI-SENA

The world is fed up with violence and bloodshed. We see the fatigues overcoming even the West. The 20th century was a century of conflict. There were about 1000 bloody wars and two World Wars. To cap them all, we had use of atom bombs over Hiroshima and Nagasaki. At present, we have been dreadfully watching terrorism taking ugliest form and shape all over the world. Hence, we have to choose between "non-violence" and "non-existence". Non-violence has not been merely an ethical virtue but a hard necessity of life. Secondly, non-violence is no more an individual virtue but must be made a "social and cultural value" and a world force. It is an error to suppose that white non-violence is good for the individual, it is not good for the masses. It is a moral equivalence of war and a safety-valve for a safe and peaceful world. It is the law of human nature. It is a power which can be wielded by all children, old and women. This is true that perfect non-violence is impossible so long we have a physical body but there is no road block to try progressive non-violence. Non-violence is not negative but positive virtue. Hence we cannot equate non-killing with non-violence. In positive form, Ahimsa (Non-violence) means *Love* and *Patience*. "Love is the strongest force the world possess and it is the humblest imaginable". (M.K. Gandhi, *Young India,* 10.2.1925). "Love has special quality of attracting abundances of love in return". (M.K. Gandhi, & L.M. Desai, *With Gandhiji in Ceylon,* Madras, 1938, p. 150). It is a prejudice and superstition to think that non-violence means weakness. It is the virtue of the strong. It presupposes ability to strike. There is a conscious, deliberate restraint put upon one's desire for restraint for vengeance. (M.K. Gandhi, *Young India,* 12.8.1926). Hence non-violence is the extreme limit of forgiveness and is therefore a quality of the brave. Non-violence and cowardice go ill together. True non-violence is impossible without the possession of unadulterated forgiveness (Gandhi, M.K., *Harijan,* 15.7.1939). Non-violence is the noble way and according to Gandhi, it is also the swifter way as it is the surest. Gandhi has also dwelt upon the role of non-violence during criminal assaults. (Gandhi, M.K., *Harijan,* 1.3.1942, 9.2.1947) and non-violence against aggression (*Young India,* 31.12.1931) and even during the war (*Young India,* 17.11.1921, 13.9.1928, *Young India,* 19.9.1940, *Gandhi's Correspondence with Government,* 2.30 etc.)

At the end, I can say that Shanti-Sena has a larger role in the world from domestic violence to world-war, from structural violence to ideological and revolutionary violence. The learned author has discussed about Shanti-Sena in 6 chapters divided and sub-divided into sub-chapters, 3 Appendices and a smart bibliography and an Introduction. My impression is that this work will be useful reference book for further studies and research in Shanti-Sena. It has discussed both its theoretical as well as practical dimensions. But the author has perhaps left to the researches to approach the subject from a critical point of view. Secondly, there should have been more emphasis upon how Shanti-Sena meets with Structural Violence. There are many other organizations in India like Seva Dal, Rastriya Yuva Sangathan, Ahimsa Vahini, etc. who have been engaged in training youth on the pattern of Shanti Sena but coordination is lacking. I hope, the learned and dedicated author will look into these point for further writing.

Simply congratulations is not enough. I extend my heartfelt thanks and gratitude to the author to take up this important but neglected task. If compulsory military training can be a part of national politics, why not introduction of Shanti-Sena in Schools and Colleges be made a part of extension programme to make our society safe and peaceful. The author deserves blessings of millions of people for carrying the torch of Peace.

Blessed are the peace makers.
Peace ! Peace ! Peace.

19

In Defence of Value Education

1. Education is itself a Value

Alexander Pope has said :

"Its education that forms the common mind. Just as twig is bent, the trees inclined." Humanity is indeed facing a value crisis, which is crisis per-excellence. This is energy-crisis, water crisis, resource crisis, etc. But they are all the direct outcome of a value crisis. However, we feel reluctant and hesitant to adopt and appreciate the traditional values of simplicity, reduction of wants concern to follow feeling sacrifice, non-exploitation of nature from reckless individualism etc. in the name of modern and program. A blind persusal of science divorced from humanity and a spirituality has become as the modern Frankenstien and a source of all wills. Atom and Ahimsa must meet to save the ugly existence of humanity. I do not have any must awaken the spiritual strength of man in culcatugy in him greater awareness—physical, moral and spiritual. Education can be regarded meaningful only when it fosters synthesis in the contradiction of social life. Comparison in economic life and sacrifice in political life. Infact, the quest of meaningfulness in education is the quest of human existence. Sacrifice, truth and ethical truths are complementary and not contradictory. Education must open up the hearts and minds of the young and the old alike so that one would communicate and live in harmony and peace in a society fulfiling one's duties towards the whole society and humanity. The destiny of India is now being shaped in her class rooms, no doubt. But we have to see whether educational growth is a consonance with the growth in moral values. Knowledge with lack of moral values is dangerous both to the individual as well as to the society. Even Dr. Mallons Adigeshiah laments that despite an impressive increase in the number of students and institutions, this is a teet need for a qualitative improvement in all spheres. The very much opposition arousing in long-standing remedy of delinking jobs from degrees not being actual upon. There has been a wider chasm between the normative educational framework and the actual attainments. National development is not identical with public works development or in short materials development. The concept of economic growth with social justice, material development with human resource development have emerged as the important parameteres of educational planning. Development is not just about factories, dams and roads, it is basically about the people. The goal is the people's material, cultural and spiritual fulfillment. The human factor is the of the supreme value. The National policy on Education adopted in 1968. Which among other things had declared that the cultivation of moral and social values would help the radical reconstruction of education under the section "University Education", of the Seventh Plan (1985-90), there was a special emphasis upon science and environment and on "value orientation". A "national value system" is the greatest pedagogical need of the hour. The major objective is the blossoming of the human personality through a well-thought out programme of education in human values.

2. How is Value Orientation of Education?

The question is not only value Education but how in terms of implementation of programmes and projects. Mahatma Gandhi in his famous Autobiography My Experiments with Truth in Chapter xxxiii (As School Master), says "I have felt that the true text book for the pupil is his teacher. I remember very little that my teacher Taught me........ books, but I have even now a clear recollection of the things they taught independently of the book." In an educational........., with emphasis on development of humanistic values, a child can boon in many possible ways by voice, by book, by pictures, by machine, by investigation or by sermons but above, by example set by the teacher.

"If the child lives with criticism he learns to condemn. If the child lives with of a learns to be just."

Today, we see the pathetic picture of the youth of our country adopting all sorts of subterfuges to get through the examinations and obtain a certificate, just as a sick man aims at getting a health certificate without getting rid of his sickness of all the factors which determines the quality of education and its contributions to national development, the undoubtedly the most important. It is his personal qualities and character his educational qualifications and his professional competence that the success of all educational endeavours must ultimately depend. The status of the teachers reflects the..........cultural ethes *e.g.* a society, it is said that no people can rise above the level of teachers. Goldsmith's romantic picture of his teacher—poor and not very scholarly but nonetheless noble would bear mention—"Like some tall cliff that lifts its aweful form Swells from the vale and midway leaves the storm. Thought around his breast the rolling clouds are Stread Eternal sun-shine settles on his head." In India a teacher is very respected and adored as the triple. God Brahmas, Vishnu, Mahesh and sometimes it accords a higher place than God. Socrates was a teacher par-excellency, who taught his disciple by virtue of his character. Teachers refer to those who import education fitted for a tree man, tree to order his life according to his well-concerned thoughts and Philosophy of life. Educational only are free hence education is for liberation of the spirit, liberation from all bondages which comes by birth and are imposed by custom and by society. Milton viewed a complete and generous education which fits a man to perform justly, skillfully, and magnimously all offices both private and public of peace and war. Milton emphasised the moral and Descartes the intellectual aspect of freedom. Moral values have bearing on the contact of social life and human relationship.

Education has a crucial contribution to make towards promoting national integration, understanding and a sense of together man and harmony. Hence there is a great need for an integrated and value oriented education with national perspective. The faculty improvement programme will develop a national value system. Education shapes the destiny of our people. It is not the chak and talk, book and the laboratories or the equipments but the teacher with a vision, who has realized his 'self' and loves his students and his subjects, the three S's. Education is the manifestation of the perfection already in man. It is the teacher or Guru, who helps the pupil to discover his own personal philosophy or the invisible sum within him.

Late Professor J.P. Naik, with an anguished heart in his book "The Education Commission And After" (1982) wrote "The main litch has been that the implementation." The proposal were also generally accepted in as well as non-official circles. But experiment is very limited.

The N.C.E.R.T. in its publications "Documentations on Social and Moral and Spiritual Values in Education (January 1979) attempted to compile a list of value on.........Of the study of the constitution of India and reports, submitted by various Committees and Commissions of Education. They are 82 in number with extra sub-values. When we talk about moral and ethic values etc. we come to the irristable conclusion that these different types of values together constitute the totality of human values which reflect the major five facts of human personality. The key, however to the development of human Personality is the.................. of universal human Values such as Peace, Truth, Love, Non-Violence and Rightous Conduct. After considering the hierarchy of values, presented in the NCE document, the SIMLA Seminar (1981) clarified the concept of value-oriented education and recommended that it should be regarded as an education for becoming "and self-exceeding". Value-education should not only provide information on values to students, but what is very important that it should enable them to grow into beings and transcend narrowness, selfishness and portial ideas and attitudes and promote human values in totality.

We should also not overlook the other important recommendation of Shimla Seminar that there should be an integrated approach in the value oriented education programme. Instead of tackling piece-meal such as arosenesss of ecology 'environmental protection', population stablisation, aesthetic education, national integration and international understanding etc. they should be handled in a comprehensive manner under the broad spectrum of "social responsibility" and "inner development of human personality" etc. The NEP 1986 suggested that the national system of education should be based on national curricular framework, besides flexible components containing common core which would include history of India's freedom movement, constitution obligations and other contents essential to..............national identity. In a pluralistic society like me it is accepted to emphasise upon universal human values acceptable to a pluralistic society in........... The education Commission (1964-68) put act of three values, *viz,* moral, social and spiritual values. The UNESCO's famous FAURE COMMISS in its report "Learning to Be" The world of Edu Today and Tomorrow (1972) referred to two question the first is as to what is this real substance be language in which they are formulated and second which defined the ultimate aims of education system. The five basic core human values are universal and transcend all distinctions of country religions castes, and creed. This is the process of merging the "I" in the "We" and finally "He", one has to pass through compassion, enunciation, rectitude, tortitude and patience. These five are the counterparts of Truth, Rightious conduct, Peace, Love and non-violence corresponding to knowledge, skill, balance, vision and oneness. Sri Sathya Sai Baba of Prasant Nlyame emphasized the five universal human values Swami Vivekananda also emphasised the value of love in a very comprehensible sense. The Report of the U.G.C. Committee on the involvement of the Universities and College in the Promotion of National Integration under the

Chairmanship of Justice M.H. Beg (1985) upheld the Gita spirit of synthesis of science and spiritual progress. Knowing more is important but similarly in living more. And in order to know more and live more loving more in important. The true progress of man on earth is the progress of an inner vision (p. 10) Love is hidden in the treasure of soul-spirit. The Working Group to Review Teacher Training Programme (1983) also emphasised the "inner development of human personality" on the right liner hence of value orientation of education with particular reference to the basic core values. It also regarded as "true-selfhood" as integrated centre in which varied personalities are harmonized ideal that the Indian educational thought has held out as one of the supreme spiritual values-wisdom, power. Love and skill in work. Universal.............values are based on world Religions and Faith Natural Cultures, lives and teachings of prophets Sages, Scientists, great Teachers and men of eminence in several fields.

The urgent need for value education should not be merely a matter of brave declarations. It needs patience, careful and comprehensive planning. An intensive study of the Reports of..........Committees and Commissions have always been an alternative to action. Mere brave declaration is not enough. What is required in the political will and determination and firm committee then "we shall overcome". It is a question of now or never. This is crucial for our survival. Broadly, we can suggest the following steps to achieve the goal of value education :

1. Values are not static but have to be realize as values in action from time to time by individual value system different from individual to individual. Family to family, society to society and nation to nation. A value becomes a value only when the individual experiences it as a value.
2. We should reaffirm our faith in the value orientation of education.
3. The curriculum should be revamped to integrate the values.

4. The synthesis of science and spirituality, or blendny of material prosperity with human values be emphasised.
5. Adequate reading materials be prepared and students to encouraged to read.
6. Extension programmes of Peace, National Integration etc. be encouraged as part of co-curricular activities.
7. Students should be taken to historical and cultural sites.
8. Collective celebrations of festivals of different regions be organized.
9. Examination system must be reformed propers.
10. Students should be encondensed to participate in dignity of labour, work-experience and mediation and yoga programmes, group prayers, daily assembly etc.

3. Conclusion

There can be no life without education and education in its real sense cannot be diverced from life. Education should give meaning and direction to life. While knowledge gives information, true education transforms the knowledge into wisdom life should be measured in terms of wholeness. Hence value education must begin with awareness of not only the immediate environs but also of cosmic laws and forces. There has been distortion in the sense of values and prompted self-destructive competition and has materialistic leading to the destruction of spiritual values what we need is creative interdependence and a synthesis of science and spirituality.

The school has almost ceased to be an extension of home and hence the child is treated as an almost as an object to be fashioned in the faceless image of text-book lessons and what we call modernity in neither rooted in tradition nor in new-found wisdom. Our young men do not develop from their educational idealism to fight injustice untruth and inequalities. Values is not like a mask to be worn. It manifests itself in the socio-political and cultural behaviour of individuals. A society wallowing in luxury, dissipation, corruption, exploitation, dispariters, hatred and violence can not......... hope to attain economic development. Similarly neither social scientists nor a genius engaged in the study of development have undertaken scientific measurement in respect of values both among the youth and the children. Fifty years age, the family and society maintained the traditional values. Family ties were cohesive. Today, there has been great strain on all relativeships of society. Respect for legally constituted authority has greatly weakened, and we even lack a burning sense of patriotism. We have created a generation of youth who are neither Indian nor Western. Thus values are not a synthesis between what is good in tradition and modernity but and anti-thesis of traditional values. We have built an economic society with an 'economic man'. We are neither true Indians nor purely western. Our task is to forge a synthesis between the East and the West, between modernity and traditional values.

We have three alternatives :

(a) Not teach everything at all

(b) Teach values in a proper, accountable, manner

(c) Or leave it to religious heads.

The first and the last alternatives are no alternatives. Hence the only alternative is to teach value in a proper and accountable manner. Unlesss our education can create "concern for other people, our society will become of jungle of ferocious creatures of human beings." Reveren for other is not a matter of gospel but necessary ingredient for good social life. Unless we learn to speak in terms of humanity and place service above self. Whatever, we should work, we should do with a positive angle. We must learn to live in harmony with Nature by following the principle of Rta. The first condition of growth in children is............With the least possible imposition on the child. The child must be taught not only to grow in freedom but also grow in inner strength. To achieve this, we need faith in the child and the destiny of man we must think of ideal for life both at the school and the house. The home has to play an **im**portant role in the education of the child.

'Value' no doubt seems to be an western imported term, which means "ought to be". Therefore values are not treated as factual and real. Hence, there has been an attempt to offer a naturalistic interpretation of values, so that values are interpreted sometimes as "object of desire" or object of pleasure", or "object of aptitude" but all of them being related to psychological traits cannot clearly bring out the true, import of values. Values are infact not psychological but normative something. In Indian Philosophy, there is no equivalent term for values but if we combine pleasure (Preys) and happiness (sreya), we can react some, approximation. The real equivalent would be Purusartha, which is a richer concept having four-fold climengons—Dutein (Dharma), Wealth (Artha), Lust (Karma) and Liberation (Mokse). Our aims of life depend upon our values of life. The highest aim or the supreme value of our life is the quest for liberation or emonicipalies "Almano Mokshartham, Jagat Litaya echa"-we need complete self-purification and good of the world."

We are what our thoughts have made us. Even thought is a little hammer below on the tump of iron which our bodies are, manufacturing out of it what we want to be. If a man thinks good and does good works, the sum total of these impressions will be good and will force him to do good inspite of himself. Great occasions arouse even the lowest of human beings to some kind of greatness, but he alone is really great where character is great always. As a small candle wipes out the entire darkness, so cultivation of good will drive away evil. If we can bring the light and evil goes in a moment. If we build our character, we can win the whole world. There should be an education for the instrument of law. A code of conduct for every class of person should be developed and value-education programme for the whole of society should be designed that everybody learns to respect the social order. The pursuit of material affluence and power has been the dominant thing no doubt but to pursue higher values and fulfilment of them is more important if man can escape nuclear holocaust. Today, the outer space air the inner space within the skull are not in balance. It is this embalance which mankind must seek to redress. Man now faces himself. He faces the choice of rolling down as abyss to partial extinction or raising himself to new heights of fulfilment as yet unimagined. The duably of the two worlds external and internal, 'atom' and 'self' should be accepted equally significant for human life. Today the reality of the inner world is a flat negation of all that is immediate in existence, to minimize its significance is to depreciate the very purpose of living, and to explain it away as a product of natural selection, is a plain fallacy. Earlier, whenever question of value was brought in either in Economics or Education, it was rejected as belonging to some other field of analysis. But this conceated a death trap for the subject itself and hence began a search for alternative paradigm. Today, education without "value" or "character" is itself a death-trap.

20

Inspiring Martyrdom of Mahatma Gandhi

Gandhi's life was no doubt inspiring but his death was much more majestic and memorable as it was not an ordinary death but a martyrdom. Socrates died as a philosopher, Jesus Christ died as a God but Gandhi died as a warrior saint on the battle front fighting fanaticism and hatred. He had earlier said : "Death is at anytime blessed but is twice blessed for a warrior who dies for the cause, that is truth".[1] For him death was no fiend, he is the truest friends for it delivers from agony. Replying to the abusive letters of the fanatic Hindu communalists, he had valiantly replied in his modest manner, "Only my death will determine whether I am 'Muhammed Gandhi', 'Jinah's slave', 'destroyer of Hindu religion', "or its true servant and protector".[2] He was rather pained to be addressed with the title *Mahatma* (Great soul). Once he poignantly said : If I am shot point blank by any assassin and if I have name of God on my lips and I do not bear any ill will against my assassin, you can call me *Mahatma* or else a fraud, like Jesus, who had his last prayer : "God forgive them, they know not what they have done". So Gandhi, when shot while going to the evening prayer did not show any sign of anguish or ill-will against his assassin. He simply uttered peacefully the name of God—"He Ram!" To him, 'history is replete with instances of men who by dying with courage and compassion on their lips converted the hearts of their violent opponents.[3] It was both his humility and greatness that he never in his dream, thought that he was a *Mahatma* (great soul) and others were *alpatma* (little souls).[4]

There are some sound basis of his inspiring martyrdom :

***(a)* Invincible Faith in God :** Firstly, according to Gandhi, we are living in the midst of death. Man proposes God disposes. What is the value of working for own schemes when they might be reduced to naught in the twinkling of an eye, or whom we may equally swiftly and unaware by taken away from them? But we may feel strong as a rock, if we could truthfully say, "We work for God and His Schemes". Then nothing perishes. "Death and destruction have then, but only then no reality about them. For death and destruction is then but a change".[5] Gandhi's fearlessness from death emerged from his absolute faith in God. He says : "You may pluck out my eyes, but cannot kill me. You may chop off my nose, but that will not kill me. But blast my belief in God, and I am dead."[6] The pursuit of Truth *i.e.* God is the talisman by which death itself becomes the portal to life eternal.[7] God as Truth had been for Gandhi a treasure beyond price, may he be so to every one of us.[8] "Devotion to this Truth is the sole justification for our existence"—says Gandhi.[9] Unshakable faith in God, and insistence on the primacy of spirit is the basis of his fearlessness. It is this unshakable faith in God and truth that he waged a war against the biggest imperial power of his time. For him the only weapon of Satyagraha is God. Without Him, the Satyagrahi is devoid of strength before an opponent armed with monstrous weapons. But he accepts God as his only protector who will remain unbent before the mightiest earthly power.[10] So immovable is his faith in God that he feels that he may live without air and water but not without God[11] and that even he were cut to pieces, God would give him the strength not to deny Him.[12] He who denies the existence of God denies the use of that inexhaustible Power and thus remains impotent. The indomitable courage and confidence of a Satyagrahi comes from the belief that God sits in the hearts of all and there should be no fear in the presence of God. The knowledge of the omnipotence of God is reassuring. On the other hand, dismissal or negation of God from common affairs gives rise to a feeling of helplessness and induces people to put their faith in violence. Hence Gandhi wrote—"We have become atheist for all practical purposes. And therefore, we believe that in the long run we must rely upon physical force for our protection.[13] May western pacifists would agree with Gandhi on this point. Max Plowman of the Peace Pledge Union says that for a pacifist, it is essential to believe in God "as the symbol of supreme value" and incarnate in every individual.[14] Gandhi's heart always pined to see God face to face. He had often glimpses of the Absolute Truth, God.[15] "Faith is an unbroken torture to me", Gandhi said "that I am still so far from Him who, as I know, governs every breath of my life."[16] But his intense yearning for God is a proof of his unshakable faith. "I must go with God as my only guide."[17] True there are dark nights of the soul but ultimately he surrenders unconditionally to God as he got spiritual realisation.[18]

(b)* Immortality of Soul :** He who takes refuge in God ought to have glimpse of the ***Atman (Soul) that transcends the body.[19] The Soul is never born nor die at any time, nor having once come to be does he again cease to be.[20] He is born eternal, permanent and primeval. He is not slain when the body is slain.[21] The soul is spoken of as "having come to be". It is everlasting, as a Divine Form and derives existence from God. Those who think that the soul slays or is slain, both of them fail to perceive the truth.[22] To illustrate this point, the Gita says : "Just as a person casts off worn out garments and the others that are new, even so does the embodied soul cast off worn-out bodies and take on others that are new.[23] There is an objective connection between various forms of life—psychic, physical and vital. Embodiment seem to be essential for the soul. But weapons do not cleave this self. Fire does not burn him, waters do not make him wet, nor does the wind make him dry.[24] Like corn a mortal ripens and like corn is be born again.[25] Even if it is held that the self is perpetually born and perpetually dies, even then, one should not grieve. Thus inevitability of death should induce us to poise and proportion.

Gautama, the Buddha had consoled a mother who had lost his only child by making her realise that this is the law of all things to pass away. Beings are unmanifest in their beginnings, manifest in the middle and unmanifest in this end. So what is there in this for lamentation?[26] Just as this body gets childhood, youth and old age, so also there is change of bodies. All the things connected with the senses are affected by hot and cold, by happiness and misery. They are transient, they come and go. Hence we must bear with them and maintain our equanimity. We should try to know what is eternal. No body can destroy what is imperishable. One who considers it as destroyed, does not know the reality. It is not born, nor does it die. It cannot be destroyed even though it is in a destructible body.[27] Hence, if one knows that the soul is indestructible, he cannot have an iota of fear. The soul is eternal, all pervading, stable, immovable and permanent. Even we consider it always being born or always getting dead, we should not lament over it because one who is born will certainly die and one who dies will certainly be born again. What cannot, therefore, be avoided must not be worried about or lamented. In short, the soul which lives in all the bodies is eternal and imperishable. Hence there is no cause of fear. This is faith in the immortality of self. Mahatma Gandhi's spiritual experience seems to have begun very early and rose to the culmination toward the end of his career. It developed into three stages. First there was like Anahata sound of mystical experience. In the second stage, we have got some utterances of his which indicate that he received messages from the Inner Voice. In the last stage we have at least two definite utterances of his in which he not merely says that he received messages but also tells us the very words in which they were clothed.[28] Gandhi says "My firm belief is that He reveals Himself daily to every human being but we shut our ears to the still small voice. We shut our eyes to the pillar of fire in front of us. I realise his omnipresence.[29]

***(c)* Faith in Non-violence :** Gandhi's mission is to provide a scar to the world weary of hate and violence. So far violence has been fought with violence. But Gandhi wanted to show to his countrymen and to the world that violent non-cooperation only multiplies evil that as evil can only be sustained by violence. Thus it becomes a vicious circle. Withdrawal of support of evil requires complete abstention from violence. Thus non-violence implies voluntary submission to the penalty for non-cooperation with evil. Non-violence has become toady a world-force. We have to choose between Atom and Ahimsa or Non-existence and Non-violence. Even in matters of social change, violence has become out of date. Today, it is very difficult to fight the State-power. A violent upheaval generally throws a dictator. It so happened in the French Revolution, England, Russia etc. Hence individual freedom is at stake. The more of violence, less democracy and much less of change of idea. If revolution means change of ideas, ideals, values etc., how can it be changed through violence? Hence, non-violence is not only an equivalent of war, it is also a better substitute to violent methods of change. Violence is anti-civilization, anti-culture and anti-man.

But just as one must learn the art of killing in the training for violence, so one must learn the art of dying in the training of non-violence. Violence does not mean emancipation from fear, but discovering the means of combating the cause of fear. The votary of non-violence has to cultivate the capacity for sacrifice of the highest type in order to be free from fear. He has only one fear, that is of God.[30]

Abstract truth has no value unless it incarnates in human beings who represent it by proving their readiness to die for it.[31] The secret of non-violence lies in our realization that it is through suffering that we are to attain our goal. The more we suffer and the more of us suffer, the nearer we are to our cherished goal.[32] According to Gandhi no country has ever risen without being purified through the force of suffering.[33] For a non-violent person there is no emergency, but quite dignified preparation for death.[34] Fearlessness is the first requisite of spirituality—Cowardice can never be motal or spiritual. True strength is inward. Gandhi had deliberately made a supreme attempt to cast out from his heart all fear whatsoever including the fear of death. Non-violence affords the fullest protection to one's self-respect and sense of honour.

It is true that perfect non-violence is impossible as we exist physically but a progressive non-violence is the only practical proposition today. We can only win over the opponents by love, never by hate. Love and patience are the two positive aspects of Ahimsa. Non-violence can be militant in character. Buddha fearlessly carried the war and brought down on knees the arrogant priesthood. Christ drove but the money-changers from the temple of Jerusalem. There is no room for cowardice or even weakness. Non-violence and cowardice go till together. "Where there is choice between cowardice and violence I would advise violence.[35]

Conclusion : For constraint of time, I have tried only to place some principles which made life inspiring and his martyrdom unique. But Gandhi had lived a long life of a living martyr. When he was fighting against racial discrimination in South Africa, he escaped almost fatal assault many times but he bore ill-will against none. He would not go to the court of law against anybody for his personal injury. While fighting for abolition of untouchability of at least of one-fourth population of the Hindus in India, he was often harassed by the priests and brutally assaulted by an orthodox Brahmin. But, he, on the other hand, requested him to share his platform to express his views. He faced at least half a dozen times murderous attempts by the communal Hindu fascists but he refused to have governmental security. He daily went to his prayer meeting. It is unfortunate that even now, there are some Gandhi-haters in India. Gandhi was a saint. He had no enemity with anyone. But his fight against social orthodoxy, communal hatred and because of his many radical views created many enemies. Barring the trial of Socrates and Crucification of Jesus Christ, there is perhaps no example in the history of mankind comparable to that of Gandhi which stimulated so much interest. It seems that Gandhi has risen again from the place of his cremation. Gandhi could have escaped his numerous harassments and finally his final assault had he had shown no compromise to his principles. He had come to the world with a mission of truth and non-violence as instrument of social revolution. He said : "My non-violence does not admit of running a way from danger and leaving dear ones unprotected." He said : What I want to achieve is self-realisation, to see God face to face." He demonstrated that his non-violence is the summit of bravery.

REFERENCES

1. Gandhi, M.K., quoted by D.G. Tendulkar, *Mahatma* (7 vols.) New Delhi Publications Dn.' rev. ed. 1961, vol. II, p. 237.
2. *Ibid.*, Vol. VII, p. 370.
3. Gandhi, M.K., *Complete Works of Mahatma Gandhi* (100 Vols.), New Delhi : Publication Deptt.
4. Gandhi, M.K., quoted in Tendulkar's Mahatma, Vol. V, p. 261.
5. Gandhi, M.K., *Young India,* 23.9.1926.
6. Gandhi, M.K., *Truth is God,* ed. R.K. Prabhu, Ahmedabad, 1955, p. 35.
7. Gandhi, MK., *From Yerveda Mandir,* Ahmedabad; Navajivan Press, 2nd ed. 1935, p. 5.
8. *Ibid.*, p. 6.
9. *Ibid.*, p. 2.
10. Gandhi, M.K., *Harijan,* 19.10.1940.
11. Gandhi, M.K., *Harijan,* 14.5.1938.
12. *Ibid.*, 29.7.1947.
13. Gandhi, M.K., *Young India,* I. p. 720.
14. Gandhi, M.K., *Harijan,* 25.6.1938.
15. Gandhi, M.K., *Young India,* Vol. I, p. 4.
16. Gandhi, M.K., *My Experiment with Truth,* p. 8.
17. *Ibid.*, 3.9.1931.
18. Gandhi, M.K., *Harijan,* 5.9.1936.
19. *Ibid., Young India,* 22.12.1921.
20. *Ibid.*, 16.6.1920.
21. *The Bhagvad Gita,* II.20; See also *Kathopnisad,* II. 183 *Chandogya Upanisad,* VIII.1.5.

22. *Gita,* II.19.
23. *Ibid.,* II.22.
24. *Ibid.,* II.23, 24.
25. *Kathopnisad,* I.6.
26. *Gita,* II.28.
27. *Gita,* II.13 cp. Vishnu Smrti, xx.49.
28. Ranade, R.D., *Spiritual Awakening in Gandhi and Other Indian Saints,* Varanasi Sarva Seva Sangh Prakashan, 2003, p. 83.
29. Gandhi, M.K., *Young India,* 25.5.1921.
30. *Ibid.,* 23.3.22.
31. *Ibid.,* 22.12.21.
32. *Ibid.,* 19.1.21.
33. *Ibid.,* 16.6.20.
34. Gandhi, M.K., *Harijan,* 9.7.
35. Gandhi, M.K., *Young India,* 11.8.1920.

21

Gandhi will Inspire Me even in My Next Birth

I have not seen Gandhi although I was very much in the Quit India Movement under his leadership. Apart from his action programmes against the foreign domination. I do not know how I became deeply involved in his Constructive Programme from the early days of my awareness even before 1942. I still remember that while a student at Primary School level, there was ample inspiration for me from Gandhi for patriotism and social work. I want to be a little nostalgic to say that three of our friends in the primary school had entered into a voluntary contract "not to speak untruth", and if anyone is caught violating it, he would have to pay a fine of one paisa each to rest of two friends. This shows that Gandhi's ideas of Eleven Vows had permeated to the teenagers who had no adequate conception, of morality and ethics. Similarly we observed almost every Sunday village sanitation Programme and visited Harijan locality at the outskirts of our village to establish fraternity and discard apartheid. Hardly, we had any complex of caste and religion as if Gandhi's ethical nationalism had washed away the age old dirt of sectarianism even from the hearts of very very young kiddies like us. In short, though we did not understand what 'Gandhism' meant but actually our life and conduct, our emotion and sentiments were unconsciously influenced by Gandhi.

Later on in 1942, when I was a student of Class-VIII only, the "Quit India" call of Gandhi engulfed our being. Apart from giving up studies and doing odd jobs for the movement, what

Gandhian element was infused in us was tremendous amount of 'fearlessness'. We organised strike in our school while the mass-drill was going on. It was converted into national flag hoisting ceremony. Then we marched into the city full of British and American war soldiers as that city had a big military camp. We never had even an inkling of fear that they can shoot us. I think this sense of fearlessness came from Gandhi.

In 1946, when I was still a student of Class-X, I vowed to wear Khadi to identify myself with Gandhian nationalism which continues upto this day. At this very time, I did not understand about the unconscious prophetic force of the Mahatma that inspired me to become a strict vegetarian, a complete tetoller give up taking even tea or coffee, and chewing pan etc., which continues as yet. Had not Gandhi entered into my life, I would have been different as I was the eldest male child of my parents and I had ample scope for distraction in terms of adopting bad habits. Living a simple life is not imposed on me, it is a veritable gift of Gandhi to me. It is natural, spontaneous and even unconscious.

Similarly as a college student, Gandhian programmes of communal harmony, eradication of untouchability, adult literacy, denying vulgar show of wealth, prohibition, anti-dowry, anti-funeral feast etc. entered into the blood of my veins and cells of my brain under the sole influence of Gandhi, which has been lasting upto this date. So whether it is purification of my personal life and conduct or indulging in social action, more specially to "Constructive Programmes", Gandhi is the fountain spring. After Gandhi's martyrdom, I was automatically led to Vinoba and his mission—Bhoodan, Gramdan, Acharya Kula and Santi Sena. Vinoba overpowered me and my being as he inherited Gandhian ideals and was an embodiment of Gandhian Constructive revolution, political ambition did not flourish in my heart as a result of Vinoba's non-party and not power politics outlook. I did not even cast my vote in any election till 1977. In 1974, J.P.'s influence as a Gandhian was uppermost in my mind as Vinoba's Bhoodan-Gramdan till then had lost its vitality and vigour. Vinoba had no doubt extended the Gandhian non-violent revolution through Bhoodan-

Gramdan movement but because of his many considerations, he could not carry on the Gandhian tradition of non-violent resistance against growing corruption, poverty, unemployment, injustices etc. J.P. with his unflinching faith in truth and non-violence also caught the martial thread of Gandhian non-violent social action. Hence, I participated in J.P.'s movement with my total being, organised perhaps the most formidable movement in Bihar in my locality. In J.P.'s own words—"Bhagalpur (my place) ranked first in the firstline of movement". During the course of the movement, I was always on the guard to give a moral and Constructive tone and a Gandhian base. Though I was detained under Maintenance of Internal Security Act once in 1974 and then during the Emergency, I had never thought to enter politics and seek for a ticket in the Parliament. But thanks to the great insistence of many young friends, Acharya Ram Murti and J.P. himself that I had to accept it. I filed nomination in 1977 on the last date with an application to enter my name in the Electoral Role. Parliamentary Election of 1977 was a continuation of J.P.'s movement. During 2½ years of my stay in the Parliament, I tried my best to project the Gandhian ideals on all issues. I placed before the Parliament about 33 Private Bills including Right to Recall, Right to Work, Trusteeship, Parliamentary Integrity Commission, Cow Protection, Limiting Cricket for Two Hours, Right to Education and so on. My resolution on Banning the Cow Slaughter was adopted by the Lok Sabha by great majority inspite of whip of the Govt. and my Bill on Trusteeship was discussed and sent to illicit public opinion. In the debates, though I had no previous experience even of working in a Panchayat or Political Party, I did try to carve out an image of a Gandhian scholar with no partisan feeling. I had good relations with all members. Even in my Constituency, I travelled through cycles, on foot and through boats listening to their problems. I never recommended any case for gun licence or undue favours. I live in one room of my M.P. flat leaving two rooms for my friends and guests. Thus, when I left Parliament, I had no problem and joined my University duty as a teacher going to my duties on bicycle as usual.

I always felt that we have not been able to carry the message of Gandhi to the young generation so I tried my best to set up a separate Department of Gandhian Thought in my University and worked there with one pointed devotion from 1980 to 1992 when I joined Jain Vishwa Bharti University at Ladnun (Rajasthan). At Bhagalpur, my department has produced more than 350 students with Master Degrees in Gandhian Thought and more than 50 Ph.Ds. Even at Jain Vishwa Bharti, I tried to foster Gandhian ideals through research & extension programnes. Ahimsa Vahini, a Youth Organisation of Peace was floated there. Annual Conference of Gandhian Studies was convened there and we also organized an International Conference on Peace. Later in 1993, I participated in 125 mile trek from Birminghum to London to commemorate 125 birth anniversary of Mahatma Gandhi, participated in Parliament of World Religions at Chicago, World Philosophy Conference at Mascow, Commonwealth Vice-Chancellors' Conference at Brighton (U.K.). But wherever I went I submitted papers or spoke on Gandhism. This has endeared me to all and my identity is recognised as such.

Even during my stay for about three years at Gandhian Institute of Studies, Rajghat, Varanasi, I have tried to promote Gandhian ideals both through academies and action. Here within this short stay we have organised more than 12 National Seminars on Gandhism, one International Seminar, 20 lectures, 8 workshops on Value Education, 11 Camps of Youth Against Violence besides more than a dozen standard publications on Gandhi.

Even if I go back home in two months time, I promise to lend my honorary service to the Department of Gandhian Thought and work for Ahimsa Vahini. Writing has been my passion and it will continue.

Gandhism has not only widened and enriched my intellectual horizon, it has been a source of ever-purifying influence, otherwise I would have been an unsocial being. What to speak of this life, if I am born again, I shall love to work on Gandhian lines and remove my imperfections.

22

Vision of World Poverty : The Gandhian Perspective

The "Poverty Summit" has raised global consciousness and concern that poverty is the greatest threat to international security. Up to these days the attention of the world has been occupied with wars, hot and cold, but only now at the fag end of the century the leaders of the world have expressed their commitment to eradicate poverty and unemployment rather than how to kill or escape killing.

In Indian thought and culture God has traditionally been identified with the poor (Daridranarayana). Therefore, God is said to descend down (Avatar) to the earthly plane to raise it to a higher state by putting Himself into the ocean of miseries. The final state of liberation or Enlightenment (Bodhisattva) is the manifestation of universal love (Maha-Karuna). Swami Vivekananda also raised his voice for the poor to the extent that he advised the Christian missionaries in India "that crying need of the East is not want of religion but want of bread".[1] Mahatma Gandhi inherits this noble heritage of love and compassion mainly from Indian thought, though he owes a lot of inspiration from the life of Lord Jesus and his ideal of crucification. Hence his God as Truth (Satyanarayana) is no different from God as Poor (Daridranarayana). Gandhi said : "I am endeavouring to see God through service in humanity for I know that God is neither in heaven nor down below, but in everyone."[2] In order to emphasise this point, he further says: "If I could persuade myself that I should find Him (God) in

Himalayan cave, I could proceed there immediately, But I know that I cannot find Him apart from humanity."[3] In his own composed prayer, Gandhi addresses God as "Lord of humility", "who dwelleth in the forlorn abodes of the humble, the lowliest and the lost". Gandhi's compatriot Nobel Laureate Tagore sings the same tune : "The famished, the homeless raise their hands towards heaven and utter the name of God. Their call will never be in vain in the land where God's response comes through the heart of man in heroic service and love." In the spiritual tradition of India, Gandhi asserts that he does not believe that "an individual may gain spiritually and those that surround him suffer." In fact, according to him, spiritual law does not work on a field of its own. If there is no application of non-violence and love in everyday life, Gandhi says, "I have no use for them as a means of individual salvation."[4]

Gandhian Ideal of Universal Welfare

While Buddhist ideal of universal love rests on the doctrine of compassion or the Christian ideal rests on the idea of crucification, Gandhian ideal of universal welfare emphasizes the principles of spiritual unity of man. All life in its essence is one. He believed in absolute oneness of God and therefore of humanity.[5] If there is one universal soul, how can one be happy individually? Hence he advocates that "good of the individual is contained in the good of all". However, the "last man" was his first concern so "Unto This Last". His sense of compassion for the starving millions has a overflowing tendency. He says : Hanuman (an ardent mythological devotee of God tore open the heart and showed that there was nothing but Ramanam (name of God). I have none the power of Hanuman to tear open my heart, but if any of you feel inclined to do it, I assure you, you will find nothing there but love for Ram (God) whom I see face to face in the starving millions of India.[6] When he writes for the poor hungry, he becomes almost poetical and sensitive. "The hungry millions ask for one poem—invigorating food".[7] To a people famishing and idle, "the only acceptable form in which God can dare appear a work and promise of food as wages".[8] We can further gauge the extreme concern of

Gandhi for the poor when he offers a Talisman or a testing principle to decide when we are in doubt : "Recall the face of the poorest and the most helpless man whom you may have seen and ask yourself if the step you contemplate is going to be of any use to him? other words, will it lead to Swaraj or self-rule for the hungry and also spiritually starved millions of your country? Then you will find your doubts and yourself melting away".

The Concept of Poverty and Its Meaning

Being poor means being limited, resented, cramped, hemmed in physically, biologically, economically, intellectually and emotionally. It does physical, biological and cultural damage to man. Hence it is destructive.

Being poor means getting inadequate health care leading to shorter expectancy of life, inadequate education leading to mental, intellectual and professional disadvantages. Hence poverty means waste of human potential. It is the result of unjust social structures. However, in the context of major world—religions, poverty is a spiritually desirable state and hence we have the idea of "voluntary poverty".

Gutierrez 9 distinguishes three kinds of poverty : *(a)* Material—the lack of economic goods necessary for a human life worthy of existence. *(b)* Spiritual—an interior attitude of unattachment to the goods of the world. *(c)* Biblical—a scandalous condition inimical to human dignity and therefore contrary to the will of God.

The poor may have different attitudes to poverty :

(a) Confrontational—The poor do think that poverty arises not from any shortcoming of theirs, but from external structural factors which can be changed.

(b) Accommodational—Being reconciled with poverty, there is accommodation (Galbraith).

(c) Self-effort—An attitude to work hard to overcome poverty.

In the Material Poverty, we have diseases and sickness due to malnutrition, starvation, inadequate health care and high death-rates. It also includes inadequate housing or shelter, minimal educational resources or lack of access to education; minimal social resources, dependence on children for support, preference for large number of children and the losses but not the least, the population bomb.

Spiritual poverty has two dimensions—one generated by fatalistic conception of being rich and poor by birth. To me this is unspiritual outlook. Secondly, material possession and property are regarded as hindrance to the growth of spiritual power. There is a tendency to discard the acquisition of material wealth and temporal power for the achievement of higher spiritual excellence. There are two realms : material and the spiritual, pleasure and happiness. The temptation of material wealth and voluntary suffering for the sake of love or for higher noble cause is a spiritual activity. Besides "suffering, cheerfully endured ceases to be suffering and is transmuted into an ineffable joy".[10] Similarly, the virtue of non-possession is the manifestation of spirituality in us. "We must then not wish for anything on this earth which the meanest or the lowliest of human beings cannot have."[11] Possession implies provision for the future. "A seeker after Truth or a truly spiritual soul cannot hold anything against tomorrow because God never stores for tomorrow. Therefore we repose faith in His providence, we should rest assured that He will give us everyday our daily bread".[12] Therefore, according to Gandhi "Love and exclusive possession can never go together".[13]

The Challenge of World Poverty

About one billion people world-wide, mostly in developing countries live in helpless poverty on the edge of starvation, or "absolute poverty".[14] "Absolute poverty is so limited by malnutrition, illiteracy, disease, high infant mortality and low life decency."[15] It is quite degrading and it undermines the possibility of a reasonable and fulfilling existence. "Of these, 10,000 people per day die from lack of nutrition."[16] In developing countries, 40% of the people do not have access to pure water, and this is one of the main factors for widespread disease. More than 300 million people, mainly in the Third World, are unemployed or seriously under-employed. Another feature of poverty is lack of education : there are still 34 countries in the world where over 80% of the people are illiterate.[17] The average income in developing countries in 1975 was 441 dollars as compared to 4831 dollars in western countries; average life expectancy 42 years and 72 years. The richest 30% consume 75% of the world's non-renewable resources. In U.S.A. 17% of one's disposable income is spent on food, while in India it is 67%.

Whatever the precise figure, there was little doubt that "the poverty percentages are high enough to be a matter of grave concern."[18] At one stage, Professor V.R.K.V. Rao, an eminent Gandhian economist (also an ex-Minister of Education, Govt. of India) suggested that in view of norms being currently used in anti-poverty programmes, it was necessary for social scientists to work on the concept of meaning of poverty and its causes. The causes of poverty were not only distributional but also national, social, political and educational and that of the media and communication system : we have also to find out how far poverty was due to causes within the poor. Poverty was not only an economic phenomenon but also social, political, psychological and religious. Hence inter-disciplinary approach was best calculated to understand the nature of the problem.

Culture of Poverty

This culture of poverty makes the poor perceive reality as a closed world, as a prison in which they are trapped or alienating religious or para-religious beliefs. We should refrain ourselves from being overwhelmingly determined by the past and allowing the past to negate or crave out the possibility of creative action in the present. We must refuse to accept the "equilibrium of poverty" (Galbraith) and break loose the blocks of "the culture of poverty" (Lewis). We have to cast away the fatalistic notion about poverty or inequality as something divine or determined by our fate or destiny. The poor need to accrue adequate economic and cultural motivation to ward off "culture of poverty".

Gandhi prescribes "Gospel of Work" and not "Charity" as means of getting of the state of poverty. Gandhi's non-violence could not tolerate the idea of giving a free meal to a healthy person who has not worked for it in some honest way, for it" degrades the nation and it has encouraged laziness, idleness, hypocrisy and even crime".[19]

He was against maintaining the poor on charity. He said : "I must refuse to insult the naked by giving them clothes they do not need, instead of giving them work which they surely need. God created man to work for his food and said that those who ate without work were thieves."[20]

Gandhi has substantiated his idea of "Gospel of Work" with the doctrine of "Bread Labour", which came to him upon reading the writings of Tolstoy, Ruskin and Bondaref from the west and from the Gita. The law is simple : to live man must work. The Bible also supports this idea : "In the sweat of thy brow shalt thou eat thy bread". Gandhi says that even "a millionaire cannot carry on for long, and will so get tired of his life, if he rolls in his bed all day long and is even helped to his food. He therefore induces hunger by exercise, and helps himself to the food he eats." Gandhi further argues, "if everyone whether rich or poor, has thus to take exercise, and helps himself to be food he eats. Why should it not assume the form of productive, *i.e.,* "Bread Labour"?[21] No one asks the cultivator to take breathing exercise or to work his muscles. Aversion to productive physical labour creates division between "hand labourer" and "brain labourer". Thus invidious distinctions of rank would grow.

Poverty and Peace

Today, the global military budget is over 600 billion dollars a year. The armament culture has worse impact on developing countries. Military expenditure of NATO declined from 56.2%

to 42.8% whereas the expenditure of the Third World increased from 6.2% to 13.7%. All these have resulted in poverty which precedes political instability creating a climate of hunger for militarization of social processes, politicization of outlook and a authoritarian political structure. "Hunger in the modern man is more intolerable than past hunger not because it is typically more intense but because it is now unnecessary. If there is universal disarmament, there will be automatic abolition of world poverty. Armament development dichotomy has to be seen not from a bureaucratic Milex/GNP angle, but as a strategy to accelerate nation-building process. As the Thorsson Report says : "The world can either continue to pursue the arms race with characteristic vigour or it can move consciously and with deliberate speed towards a more sustainable international economic and political order, it cannot do both." Hence, there is a need for converting an increasingly militarised global culture into culture of peace and non-violence even we want to wipe out poverty in the world. Gandhi found out the technology of non-violence. Arms race has not helped to solve a single international problem hence disarmament is an imperative need for a peaceful and happy society. The nuclear age has posed a serious dilemma : "Either the great nations of the world must honestly agree to renounce the use of the newest type of weapon, or the world must honestly be brought to an end."[22] Besides, more of expenditure on arms, less of food and clothing for the common man. The struggle for disarmament is a civilizational struggle, it is indeed a struggle for our own existence and peace. To quote President Eisenhower : "Every gun that is made, every warship launched, every rocket fired, signifies in a final sense a theft from those who hunger and are not fed, from those who are cold and are not clothed."[23] However, we must remember, violence is not simply manifested in acts of violence, it is also manifested in our policies and objectives, institutions and structure. In this respect, poverty is institutional violence : exploitation, inequality and arms-trade are all forms of structural violence. Hence Gandhi in order to fight poverty also had to fight militarization and armament and the entire cult of violence.

The famous Brandt Report on world poverty significantly observed, "If reduced to a simple denominator, this Report deals with peace."[24]

Poverty and Social Justice

At present throughout the world the affluent people are under the grip of a sort of consumption-hysteria, although half of the humanity go to bed without even one square meal a day. It is now admitted that growth in GNP does not solve the problem of poverty. The trickle down theory according to which the benefits of development will percolate down to the bottom strata is falsified, at least in developing countries, where industrial development is so much accompanied by rise in prices and inflation, the real income of the large majority diminishes with the rise in prices. Detelf Kantowsky therefore says that, "it has taken only two Development Decades for the western paradigm of development to prove its invalidity in the newly independent countries of the Third World."[25] The benefits of growth are usurped by twenty per cent of population leaving the rest of people in a state of "biological decay".[26]

On the global perspective, the development in U.S.A. has been possible to this extent by using 70% of the global resources for its 6% of world population. Hence it is impossible for 70% of the Third World people to develop with 10% of the resources at their disposal. It seems Darwinian principle of the survival of the fittest has come to be true also among human beings. Deprivation of resources has become acute among the poorer nations and they face hunger and poverty and consequent spurt in violence.[27]

There is a vital point for consideration both for the rich and poor nations, who have been equally caught in the coils of consumerism due to a wrong notion of civilisation and modernity. First, we have equated economic progress with total development. Hence, to achieve a measure of economic progress, cruel exploitation of natural resources is regarded as the only way out. Unlimited consumption is possible through unbridled exploitation of non-renewable resources of nature resulting in environmental hazards. Hence, Gandhi, while disapproving poverty and exploitation also attacks the materialistic craze for ever-growing material standard of life. If we go on increasing our wants and needs, more and more exploitation of natural resources becomes necessary leading to the "rape of earth". Hence Gandhian ideal of simple living or voluntary limitation of wants is not a religious sermon or a fad but an imperative. Pitrim Sorokin, like Gandhi, had named the modern western civilization as "Sensate" and came to the conclusion that there is no future for human survival if we do not abandon our utterly ego-centric and homo-centric stance. To save himself, man must become more altruistic, ecologically conscious and adopt as Rifken, the author of Entropy, simpler life-style in the name of Second Law of Thermodynamics. Perhaps observing all this, Gandhi dissuaded us from luxuries and extravagance. To quote him : "Nature has given enough to meet our needs but not our greed." According to him, true civilization is the mode of conduct which points out to man the path of duty. Performance of duty and observance of morality are convertible terms.

Conclusion

Gandhian understanding of the problem of poverty is multi-dimensional. It cannot be understood only from the point of "growth economy" but it is also linked up with the model of development, gospel of work, disarmament and last but not the least with the life-style of simplicity. Unfortunately, the Third World countries are also moving in the direction of the developed nations in raising their material standards of life. Religious teachers in the past and also saint-philosopher like Socrates have advised us to limit our wants if we want to be happy. Now, it seems that it has became a scientific necessity. The Poverty Summit has rightly echoed the voice of sanity by demanding limitation on extravagance in the life-style of the developed nations. It is the requirement of international social justice not only to alleviate poverty in poorer countries but also put a halt to unbridled consumption. As the Right to Life should have no geographical limits so as to the standard of life should not have trans-national variations and obliquitous inequality. Even "human rights begin with breakfast." Nature doesn't recognise such divisions. She deals with all life as a whole. Nature is limited by Time and Space. Hence, while dealing with the problem of poverty we should not loose sight of the "Economy of Permanence" and the cause of "human good".

REFERENCES

1. World Summit For Social Development, Copenhagen, March, 1995.
2. Gandhi, M.K., *Harijan*, 29.8.1936, Journal edited by M.K. Gandhi.
3. *Ibid.*
4. Gandhi, M.K., *Amrit Bazar Patrika* (English Daily), Calcutta, 30.6.1944.
5. Gandhi, M.K., *Young India*, A Journal edited by M.K. Gandhi 29.9.1944.
6. Gandhi, M.K., *Ibid.*, 24.3.1917.
7. *Ibid.*, 13.10.1921.
8. *Ibid.*, 13.10.21.
9. Mallac Guy De, *Remedies To Man Poverty*, Madurai, Gandhi Museum, 19, p. 34.
10. Gandhi, M.K., *Young India*, 13.10.1921.
11. Gandhi, M.K., *With Gandhi in Ceylon*, ed. M. Desai, Madras, 1928, p. 1310.
12. Gandhi, M.K., *From Yarveda Mandir*, Ahmedabad, Navajivan Press, p. 34.
13. Gandhi, M.K., *Modern Review*, Monthly Magazine, Calcutta, p. 12.
14. Bull, H., "Human Rights and World Politics" in *Moral Claims and World Affairs*, ed. R. Pettman, Croom Helm 1979, quoted by Nigel Dower, *World Poverty: Challenge and Response*, New York : William Sessions Ltd., 1983, p. 1.
15. Macnamara, R., Address to the Board of Governors of the World, 30.9.1980.
16. *New Internationalist*, No. 68, Oct. 1978, p. 8 (periodical) Wallingford, Oxon.

17. Ferguson, *Disarmament The Unanswerable Case,* Heinemann, 1982, p. 78.

18. Social Science Research and the Problem of Poverty, *1st National Conference on Social Sciences,* New Delhi, 12-15 January.

19. Gandhi, M.K., *Young India,* 6.10.1921.

20. *Ibid.*

21. Gandhi, M.K., *The Selected Works of Mahatma Gandhi,* ed. S.N. Agr, Ahmedabad, Navajivan Publishing House, Vol. IV, p. 238.

22. Alexander, Horace, "Nuclear Explosions and The World Peace", in *Gandhi : His Relevance for Modern Times,* New Delhi, Gandhi Peace Foundation, p. 279.

23. Eisenhower, D., quoted in The Coracle, No. 2, Iona Community, 1980.

24. The Brandt Report, *North-South : A Programme for Survival,* Pan Books, 1980, p. 14.

25. Kantowsky, D., Sarvodaya : The Other Development, Bombay : Vikas Publishing House, 1980, p. 167.

26. Sethi, J.D., "Poverty, Alienation and the Gandhian Way Out", in *Gandhi Marg,* Vol. I, No. 6, Sept. 1979, p. 31.

27. Madeley, J., *Human Rights Begin With Breakfast,* Pergamon Press, 1982.

23

Satyagraha : As a Moral Equivalent of Terrorism and Violence

Violence in the 21st century has become so dreadful that it can wipe out not only our civilization and culture but also our existence. No doubt, there is an element of violence inherent in human nature and therefore we have fought with each other with nails and teeth. But later on we invented new weapons of war as stools. During Paleolithic and Neolithic ages we fought with crude stones and pointed stones. Next in the evolutionary framework we invented sticks, arrows and clubs for fighting. In the metallic age we invented spears, swords and many weapons for fighting made of steel and brass. During the gun powder age we had guns, machine guns and bombs for war operations. However, in the 20th and 21st centuries we have atomic weapons. According to rough but reliable estimate there are at present about 40 thousand nuclear weapons which are deadlier than those used at Hiroshima and Nagasaki. If there is an atomic war it can wipe out entire human civilization at least seven times with the atomic arsenals reserved at different places. Though the U.S.A. and some western powers and China have the monopoly of atomic weapons but according to reports forty seven countries have some excess to atomic power. At present though there is only occasional full fledged wars as in Korea, Vietnam, Kampuchia, Iraq, Afghanistan and the middle east countries etc., we have the greatest threat from growing amount of terrorism all over the world whether it is U.S.A. 7/11 or U.K. blasts or India or Pakistan etc. There is every likelihood that through purchase or theft or some other form of help the terrorists may acquire atomic bombs and weapons sooner than later. It is clear they have no international legal binding or moral sense of human safety and they can use these weapons indiscriminately when they are in their hands. It is beyond the control of super powers to control the situation and bring scur to humanity.

Hence either we search out a moral equivalent of war or we prepared for being wiped out of our existence. But what would be the moral equivalent, will it be unabashed and totally illegal invasion on smaller countries by super powers either on Iraq by U.S.A. or on Vietnam by People's Republic of China or anywhere else. So if war is out of question can narrow nationalism or the concept of personal religion come to our rescue. In the name of narrow nationalism we have fought out six thousand five hundred big and small wars in human history and similarly we have about 7 thousand bloody wars fought in the name of religion. Even in the same religion of Christianity the Catholics and Protestants fought for hundred years of war. So also the different sects of Hindus, Muslims etc. have worse records of hatred and violence in the name of religion.

Hence unless we try to discover a substitute for "nationalism" and "personal religion", we cannot save our human existence. Now taking the concept of narrow nationalism we have the concept of world government as a feeling moral substitute. Starting from Socrates and the Vedas and upto Wendel Wilie, 'One World', H.G. Wales, Pt. Rahul his novel 'On 22nd Century. We have been given some hints as Etopia. But one world government is neither an ethopia nor a dreaming paradise. But a hard choice and the only alternative for modern times. We have only one choice either we choose atom or one world. Secondly, we have to reconsider our attitude towards personal and sectarian religions. I do not reject the various contributions of religions professing moral and spiritual virtues. But at present they have become out of date. There has been a virtual clash of civilization "Hutcheson" in the name of personal religions. The middle east, the Kashmir region and the European and African countries have also experienced the bloody hatricidal wars in the name of religion. Hence either we develop a universal religion based on pure morality and spirituality or brush aside religious dogmas enciting violence as the opium of the people.

Next to the outdated concept of nationalism and personal religions we have a new challenge in the face and exploitative concept of so called liberalization, privatization and globalization which is perhaps the greatest threat to world peace and harmony.

In the name of so called Globalization, the I.M.F., the World Bank and the W.T.O. have been creating two worlds—a world of haves and a world of have-nots. There has been subtle attempt to impose new imperialism in the grab of economic reforms. In the recent wealth report of the U.N.O. it is clearly said that the wealth has no doubt increased but it lies only in the hands of a small minority. For example in India only 15% people have become wealthy and rich but the condition of 85% is wretched and poor. Hence with the growth of wealth there has been growth of inequality. This is the state of all over the world in the Third World countries. Hence we have to evolve a new global economic structure based on non-exploitation and equality.

As a footnote on the concept of Satyagraha may I venture to suggest that we need a non-violent war against unjust socio-economic and political structure of our society. Since violence is out of date, self-suicidal and anti-civilization non-violence is the only alternative. Not to bring the theoretical justification for Satyagraha or psychological arguments put forward by Richard Gray in his book 'The Power of Non-violence' and by Lek Velissa etc. I will like the people to consider the miracle of Satyagraha in modern times. Without dwelling upon the martyrdom of Socrates in Greece, of beheading martyrdom of Mansoor, crucification of Jesus Christ and recent martyrdom of Mahatma Gandhi, Lincoln and Martin Luther King. The Indian sub-continent has broken the chains of slavery through non-violence under the then first rate world power of the world.

Even with recent past Martin Luther King won the battle of racial equality in the U.S.A. without weapon of violence. Violence is not only unpractical but it is counter-productive. Violence has brought worst peril in human history and has substituted tyranny and despots with the established weak power.

In France Napolean came after violent revolution during Louis fourteenth. Crownwell rose as a dictator after killing Charles 1st and Stalin seized the power and became a dictator after killing the Czars. Along our neighbourhood Pakistan, Bangladesh, Thailand and Burma have lost their democratic structure because in the name of violent reforms the dictators have always the upper hand. Hence Satyagraha as the path of truth and non-violence has the ingredients of fighting structural violence as well as creating a world of love and peace.

It is apparent that as war has lost its dynamics in this atomic age. Similarly social change through violence has been becoming gradually out of date and unproductive. Hence it is imperative to search an equivalence of change without violence. Satyagraha offers such an alternative which rejects both violence as well as structural injustices of all kinds. If bloodshed is violence social and economic injustice are also violence perhaps more deadlier than over-violence. Hence we need a world without war and society without violence of all kinds. But one can argue that the religious saints and sears have been singing the music of love and non-violence from time immemorial. But violence has not been abolished. There is no doubt about the pure intentions of the saints and sages about their prophecy of love and non-violence. But perhaps they thought that if there is love and non-violence in the hearts of man there will also be reflections of love in social and economic affairs. But history has showed that the vested interests in religion have outweighed the simple and pure intensions of the saints and many forms of exploitations and discrimination including human cruelty have clouded impurity of religion.

Hence we have to free religion from dogmatism and

unnecessary ritualism. In fact only then religion can be acceptable. This brings to us the glimpse of inner spirituality which should be combined with scientific outlook. Satyagraha as a weapon of social change is a science of triple transformation—change of heart, change of ideas and the change of circumstances. This is a task for social sciences to invent a dynomatics of both change of hearts and ideas. Change of heart is no fiction of imagination but it is a reality. It is a psychological truth that there has been real conversion of man from forsaking its evil habits and adopting better mode of behaviour. We have to frame a scientific calculus for change of heart on an individual and on mass level. But changes of heart has to be supplemented in this age of knowledge and science. We find large scale propaganda for both political and ideological changes. Even religion have taken this path of propaganda and the help of several trans media. Even the religious and political extremists have been using this instrument of ideological propaganda and brain-washing to train their cadres to adopt violence. Violence even to this extent of human bombing. Hence if we can develop ideological changes through logics and reason, we can achieve a lot of success. The change of circumstances is in favour of Satyagraha method of war and change. This is more appropriate, effective and humane.

24

Structural and Institutional Dimensions of Global Peace

The traditional approach as early as Socrates who had said—"I am neither an athenian nor a Greek, but a citizen of world." In the same spirit, the Vedas had proclaimed through a Prayer "I am the progeny of the Mother Earth". Similarly almost all religions, the doctrine of the Father or God and the Brotherhood of man has been acclaimed as the supreme commandment. The prayer in the holy Quran clearly says that God is the preserver and the guardian of the entire creation; Almin—Al Fhatiah! But it is a tragedy that the Religion which literally means "to bind together" has been a source of millions of massacres, oppression and exploitation, bigotory and orthodoxy. According to reliable testimony nearly six thousand five hundred small and big wars have been fought in the name of religions in the human history. Islam had its Jehad and the Christianity called it crusades and fight of hundred years of war between two sects of same Christianity. True religions have fought for the mankind to move from savagery to civilization, from cannibalism to vegetarianism, from arsan and anarchy and from hatred and violence to love and peace, but it is also a stark reality that it has also engineered narrowness, rivalry and even different kinds of oppressive discrimination based on superstitions of birth, gender and many artificial cobwebs. This traditional and research approach have been given nearing five thousand years of experimentations in achieving peace making but it has not been able to achieve success. Religion and politics have become two sides of the same phenomena for dividing humanity power with the resulting that both kingship and the peperi and the paple supreme have fought a grievous battle of which the Vatican is the cast vestage of the theocratic power with the secular might of the political power.

Hence peace has become a distant dream. Apart from the traditional religious approach for global peace, we have also efforts of humanitarians and pacifists to establish peace in the world. But because of some fundamental structural and institutional approach the efforts of these well intensioned persons have not brought relief to the mankind.

Structural Peace

War begins in the minds of man, therefore the defences of peace can be built in the minds of man. But this dictum of UNESCO has been regarded more as a religious sermon rather than a programme of action. In fact, violence is ingrained in our societal structure. To start with economic life, one-third of the globe have been enjoying comforts and luxuries while the rest of humanity mostly in Asia and Africa have been ruling under grim poverty, unemployment and inequality. It seems the world is divided between the rich and the poor, developed and developing. Even now either the world body like the U.N.O. have not been able to bridge the great gulf between the have's and the have not's. Earlier capitalist system had mercilessly exploited the raw materials and minerals through imperialistic system based on military force. At present new imperialism has taken its place in the name of liberalism, privatization and globalization. We have an exploitative economic structure which breeds violence and thwarts efforts for global peace. If war for bloodshed is violence, exploitation, inequality and profiteering are also uglier forms of violence. We cannot have global peace if we have such an unfavourable economic structures. Recent examples of invasion of Iraq and Afghanistan and Ugoslavia and threat over Iran, Pakistan and North Korea etc. are invincible proofs of economic causes of war.

Political Structure

Economic system and economic interests influence our political system, whereas political system also influence our economic structure. Hence they go hand in hand. Politics has ceased to be a science of brotherhood. It has become a more machiavellian than dealt in the famous fretory. 'The Prince' Our political system is based on deceit and dishonesty, falsity, fraud, exploitation and bossism. Hence it is bound to usher violence in the world. Perhaps with grab of nationalism modern political state has usurped the power of the people and has become more autocratic and dictatorial even the sacred cow of narrow nationalism has been the most potent cause of violence in the world. The 20th century has been a century of nationalism. Following the foot-steps of Julius Caesar and Alexander the Great, Hitler in the modern time wanted to be a world conqueror through savage war. Even now the great powers specially U.S.A. has been behaving as a world policeman. In the case of Iraq and other places it seems that our political system based on sovenistic nationalism has become outdated. For world peace we urgently need a world governance and a world polity based on equality and non-exploitation. Tolstoy and Gandhi had rightly advocated purification of politics because true politics is brotherhood which is a branch of ethics. Gandhi therefore advocated spiritualization of politics. But today there is not only politics for power and self-interest but it is also a cult of criminalization. From much centralization breeds violence whether it is in politics or economics. Hence a world government will be a decentralized federal Govt. of different states enjoying utmost freedom and equality. World peace is impossible with the existence of either military pacts like NATO or Atlantic nor it is possible with super powers like G-8 or G-4.

Cultural Structure

Like economics and politics our educational and cultural systems are also rooted in violence. We need a world where the mind is free and the head is high. At present our educational system is based on the spirit of competition which legacy of the Darvinian systems of struggle for existence and survival of the fittest. Any educational system based on the cult of competition cannot create a society of peace and harmony and man can not and should not have competition with another man because it only create an atmosphere of hatred, jealousy and envy. Therefore the entire educational system should be based on co-operation and non-violence aid rather than co-operation of one man with other.

To treat one's religion as the most conducive for the development of human progress and the rest others in the clutches of the devils is perverted absolutalism and degenerated intellectual violence. Hence the only way out to treat all religions with equal respects and evolve a kind of universal religion which will be the real religion of man.

Social Violence in Social Structure

Though the mankind is one and undivided and the human race is one and only one but our folly have led us to divide ourselves on the basis of race and religion, birth and colour, nationality and gender etc. If humanity is one any attempt for such distinction is anti-man and anti-civilization.

Institutional Dimension of Peace

India has achieved perhaps the greatest height in the field of spiritual engineering but it is not so in the realm of social engineering and organizational engineering. At the level of the world we have to create such institutions of organizations which can further cause of global peace. During the last century we had hundreds of smaller and big conflicts. One, deadlier than the other. Besides, there have been two world wars and we are on the brink of the third world war which will mean total annihilation of human species. Hence the League of Nations and the UNO have not been able to fulfill the aspirations of the mankind for abolishing the fear of war. Even now almost every state of the world have smaller and bigger armies and modern weapons of destination. Nearly it is a sad commentary for educational world to carry on education of war and military science instead of teaching military science to the young generation. We should enforce syllabi in peace education, conflict resolution and peace research. Alexander Pope said—It is education that forms the common mind.

Just as the twig is bent, the tree is inclined. In short, peace education is the foundation for a peaceful world. Education is also a very important component of our culture because it not only moulds our mind and trains our intellect. It goes to create a new frame of personality for a new world. Like education we have accepted the dynamics of competition as the only efficient method for progress in our cultural life and therefore we have adopted competition in the field of sports, music, dance and drama etc. In short, our whole cultural system is based on competition which breeds psychological and intellectual violence.

In the field of religion the concept of personal religion have become outdated. Every religious sect regards its own religion, the oldest and best.

20 billion dollars are being spent over the military and its hardware. There are about a dozen countries having nuclear weapons in their possessions but the UNO has become a tool of consolidating the vested interests of a few super powers. Hence it is imperative to create institutions of peace and harmony in the world. We have to set up a UNO of peace and instead of sending a cadre of peace army (Shanti Sena). Similarly we have to establish universities or institutes of these all over the world in good number.

In short, global peace needs a new civilization and a new culture. Unless we are able to attack structural violence peace will remain a day dream. Similarly instead of establishing temples, mosques, churches etc. of different religions we should set up temple of peace and harmony everywhere. The most optimistic note about global peace is based on the logic that violence has lost its dynamics. War has become out of date because world war with atomic weapons will leave none alive. Both sides will be completely annihilated in an atomic war. Hence there is no choice and the peace is only alternative. Similarly for eliminating violence in society violence has become productive because it leads either to fundamentalism and extremism or it leads to dictatorship. Hence we have to develop moral equivalence of violence even for social and political change. We must not tolerate social and economic inequality but we should also not take the help of violence which is self defeating. Gandhi, mutual can be revised through non-violence that is Satyagraha. Satyagraha therefore is a positive instrument to fight structural violence and institutional violence.

25

Global Resistence Against the Globalisation : The Gandhian Way

Recently Indian Prime Minister Dr. Man Mohan Singh, during his crucial visit to U.S.A. has, perhaps, boastfully declared that the process of Democratic reforms is irreversible. Outside India, Russia had already accepted the Principle of Globalisation following the Prestroika and the Glassnost revolution. The strongest fulwork of Communism *i.e.* China has surrendered to the W.T.O. In India, Azadi Bachao Andolan in particular and National Alliance of people's Movements in general and some other organisations have severely and tenaciously been spear heading their movement against the M.N.Cs. in India. Accepting the Patent Bill of the W.T.O. Indian agriculture and water are next important target of the M.N.Cs. Compulsory sale and purchase of iodine salt from Independence Day (15th August 2005) has been enforced thus giving a serious stroke to Gandhi in the heaven. Outside India, discontent has been spreading. Afro-Asian Countries are almost for sale—whether it is Banking, Industry, Agriculture, Natural resources including water. There has been people's resistence in Venenzula, Brazil, Chile, South Africa, South American countries etc. Last year we had a mega world social Forum Conference at Mumbai, which dealt with the wages and means of developing global resistence for justice, and preservation of nature resources. Indeed it is a collective task because the energies very is well organised. Protest, of other terms of resistence are there. However, Gandhi had some novel and effective methods of resistence, which require serious consideration. They are backed by the activists as well as by the social scients. Let us enumerate and discuss a few of them :

1. Back to Swadeshi : Since globalisation is a kind of new-cold war, it has to be fought through the same dynamics. The teeth and claws of M.N.Cs. are rooted in consumerist culture modernity and the so-called scientific progress in high-tech increase in G.N.P., or nation's wealth. Hence an alternative calculus and an alternative basic ideology has to be evolved, 'Swadeshi' may be such an ideology with an appropriate Technology. Fight against globalisation may start with salt. If we can create a climate of commitment not to use or boycott M.N.Cs. goods, they will die a natural death without an overt struggle. It also does not involve any serious or even ordinary violation of the law of the land. Therefore, Gandhi in his first phase of his non-violent movement had started with NON-COOPERATION. He taught us to say and stick to 'NO'-NO to foreign clothes, 'NO' to British *Courts* 'NO' to British systems of schools and colleges. This is called *Tripple Boycott.* When he achieved success in mobilizing the people's cooperation in *Non-cooperation,* he moved to a more force battle of *Civil Disobedience.* Today we are jumping upon the second leg of protest without commitment to self Non-cooperation through *Swadeshi.*

2. Civil Disobedience Movement : If we can achieve atleast 60% success in *Swadeshi* movement, it is very easy to organise 100% successful Civil Disobedience Movement against globalisation or M.N.Cs. Today for example, C.D. Movement will be very catching and relevant against obligatory use and sale of iodine *Salt* against which Gandhi had staged a Satyagraha. We can chose any such issue of common interest and organise mass civil disobedience.

3. Swarajist Model of Politics : Politics is like the coil of snake, which we cannot escape. Therefore, we must wrestle with it said Gandhi. It means that he did not minimise the importance of politics which determines important aspects of our life. But today politics has lost its worth and character.

Hence unless we strive for "politics with principle" or "goodness politics". We cannot win a battle of Swadeshi or Civil Disobedience' Gandhian method of protest is impossible without personal commitment to the cause and faith in the triumph of truth and justice. We can successfully organise people's resistence against corporate empire only if we make this issue, not as a profession but a mission of our life.

If we study the experience of the last 10 years of W.T.O.'s working, we will find dangers of unemployment and growing inequality in the world. It is why countries like Argentina. Venenzula etc. are coming out of the trap of I.M.F. The U.S. is the super-boss of these so-called International bodies so when it does not suit its own interest does not care to bypass them. The asymmetrical power relationship and disproportionate force has a dominating interest on the others. The ruling power exercised control and order both locally and globally. For example the role of veto between 1946 to 1989 is U.S. dominated and after 1989 the veto has been rare and scare, which reflects the active and dominant role of the U.S. in peace and defence treaties throughout the world. The U.S. has also power unbalance over the globalisation of economics. It enteres into one treaty, while out from trade pacts as has been in the case International Criminal Courts. Even in case of Non-prolification Treaty, the U.S. assumed responsibility and legitimacy in designing and practicing guidelines for the sole possession of atomic Agency. There are examples of the cause of disregard for other neighbours by the U.S. like U.S. refusal to pay the full dues to the U.N. and other Agencies, misusing them behind performance of the I.M.F. and the world Bank. It has refused to go with the majority of countries to enter into the treaty for creating international Criminal Court. It unilaterally withdraw from the UNESCO in 1994, to ratify the International agreement on green house effect, banning land mines, and doing many things, even like Iraqui invasion without any consent of the world body. It imposed war not only in Iraq but also Afganistan etc. which may be branded as necked international terrorism. Even now the U.S. is threatening Iran and other oil countries just for oil control. This erodes the very relevance of U.N. we can vividly find the impact of flegeminized culture on global societies.

During 10 years of W.T.O. *Hunger, unemployment AND INEQUALITY HAVE INCREASED IN THE WORLD*, besides increase in economic instability, destruction of agriculture, control of M.N.Cs. and imposed globalism. Hence Civil disobedience and adoption of the cult of Swadeshi is an urgent necessity. After destroying the national and cottage industries, the M.N.Cs next targets is agriculture. They try to tempt us dole out money provided the privatise agriculture in the name of raising production. They are selling seeds that will give germination of only 75%. This is slow poison to agriculture. Thus introduction of Monsanto seeds is the death knell of Indian agriculture. These seeds are seeds of farmers suicide on a large scale. Then the government policy of deregulation input, the entry of seed M.N.Cs. and the creation of seed monopolies increased the cost of seed and the risk of crops failure. For example, in Bihar in 2002 the cost due to failure of Monosanto hybrid seed, rose to 400 crores of rupees. This seed sovereignty is therefore an important cause of farmer's suicide. Our rice has already gone in the hand of Swiss multinational syngenta, the world under neo-imperialis. Hunger is seen in plenty and when seeds of M.N.Cs. are they can stoop down to any low for profit and economic slavery. No wonder the western Medicine Mart have created AIDS bogey to earning money as well as to wipe out black population like Turkee which had spread between 1932 to 1972. Where as their scientists made the Blacks believe that they are being treated for syphilis but this was not the fact. They were administered lacebos for better study of or the development of their evil designs. This is reported in the *Washington Post.* In the name of Parliament, they are blocking resistence and revolution. In the name of welfare they are conspiring to get water monopoly. Water bottle M.N.Cs. are posing great threat to public utility. Privatisation of water is on their card. If we loose water we loose land and Ultimately our liberty and freedom.

Globalisation : The True Perspective :

The ideal of human unity has been perenial aspiration of man. It is also the logical and inevitable for both *Material* and *spiritual* PROGRESS OF HUMAN Civilization. Hence from Socrates to Gandhi, we find a hunger and thirst after global unity. However, mere slogan of globalisation won't do. It needs a new desire, a new asceticism. Globalisation is a means as well as an end. We must always remember that man is the supreme consideration. So whether it is liberalisation or privatisation or globalisation, they are for man, not man for them. If globalisation is an exercise in neo-imperialism or world capitalism, based on exploitation and profiteering of the common man dangerous. Globalisation should not be understood as a new edition of Industrialisation or consumerisation. So Gandhi advocates 'globalisation' for human unity rather than human exploitation. This concept of globalisation stands for maximum equalisation of natural resources and their preservation. E.F. Schumacher following the Gandhian spirit discards the craze of 'limitless growth' and 'limitless consumption'. Unfortunately, the western economists from Adam Smith to Marx and Keynes and upto the stage of the so-called 'globalisation' rest on wrong notion of maximum production and maximum consumption as a 'Science of wealth' not of 'man'. For this, maximum exploitation of nature and natural resources become necessary and natural with the result that we are bound to face ecological disasters and dangerous environmental pollution leading to holes in the ozone layer and even acid rains, and depletion of natural resources. Hence we need optimum consumption through simple life style, appropriate technology and economics of permanence. Gandhi rightly said "Nature has enough to meet our needs but not our greed". Hence we need are alternative development model and a new development goal *i.e.,* man rather than commodity.

The so called globalisation today does not rest on the concept of equalisation or sharing. For example, Australia with plenty of space would never like to share the overgrowth of population of neighbouring countries. So the middle east will never share the their treasure of oil with poorer countries. According to Gandhian concept of Globalisation, the natural resources is a common treasure. So in the arena of scientific knowledge there is no need of any patent or monopoly right.

Thereby, with the concept of limitation of growth and consumption there must be maximum self-sufficiency and self-realiance in a poor country like India. A costly Mercedes Car of 70 to 80 lakhs is imported for any individual Officer or Minister, is virtually a social crime and an act of anti-globalisation. Gandhi says My notion of Poorna Swaraj is not isolated independence (Young India 26.1.1921). Through Swaraj we serve the whole world (Young India 13.10.1921) Indian nationalisation is not exclusive, not aggressive not destructive. It is breath giving religious cult and spiritual, therefore humanitarian. He further emphases that "India must learn to live before she can aspire to die for humanity" (Young India, 13.10.1921). He again says "I would like to sea India free and strong so that she may offer a willing and pure sacrifice for the betterment of the world" (Young India 16.4.1941). Gandhi says that "my idea of nationalisation is that my country may die so that the human race may live" (Mahadeo Desai, Gandhi in Village, p. 170). Gandhi wanted national Independence before international co-operation because cooperation can be only among the equals and not between the slaves and the masters. By national freedom, Gandhi does not mean absolute independence which is inconsistent with aggressive nationalisation. Hence he frankly hits at some sort of world federation, when he says that "the better mind of the world despite today not absolutely independent States warring one against another but a federation of friendly inter-dependent states" (Young India 16.12.1924). According to him "the only condition on which world can live is being united under one central governing body coroposed of representations of the component parts" (Harijan 8.6.1947). Today, nationalisation has been assuming the form of a dreadful dragon. Nuclear nationalism is the worst of all. The world has to choose between non-violence and non-existence, *atom* and *Ahinsa*. Hence globalisation can not be real if it is forced by military violence and exploitation.

26

Strategies and Stratagems in Gandhian Thought

It is most welcome to share my ideas in an intellectual enterprise to examine the status of Gandhian Strategies in this century-year of writing Hind Swaraj which is an undisputable manifesto of Gandhian ideology. At the outset, I may submit that Gandhian thought is an open an ever-evolving system based on practical experience. But it is important to note that Gandhian Strategies can not be considered at the cost of Gandhian fundamental postulates of truth and non-violence. Even his truth and non-violence are not absolute and static concepts. Hence, Gandhi does not prefer to be a bonded-slave of so called 'consistency'. To him, such an undynamic concept of truth is not his ideal. Therefore, he grew from truth to truth and also his concept of non-violence had been growing and progressing. But this does not mean that he had ever sacrificed is principle for opportunistic gains. As a matter of fact, he was always ready for compromises but never at the cost of cause. Hence he adopted only those strategies which were in conformity with his fundamental principles. The 'Eleven Vows' were his basic moral postulates and '18 Point Constructive Programmes' were his practical guide lines determining his strategies. Even in matters of Satyagraha the basic principles of truths and non-violence determined all his actions and his strategies. This means that there is an integral and intimate relationship between ends and means.

Ends and Means

So instead of cleverness or cunningness, he stuck steadfast to honesty, sincerity and humility. Unlike Machiavellian politics, he believed and practiced 'Spiritualisation of politics' or 'Goodness Politics'. Without moral and spiritual basis, politics has become a refuge of the scoundrels. Hence, they adopted political strategies based on falsity and fraud, deceit and dishonestly violence and bloodshed.

The questions of purity of means cannot be properly conceived without understanding the nature of man.

Nature of Man

If we think that man is nasty, brutish and selfish, we cannot think of any reform of human society. If man is regarded essentially as evil in nature it is an insult to entire humanity. Besides this is a gospel of utter pessimism. History of mankind is a record of its march from violence to non-violence from cannibalism to animal protection. No doubt, we started our conflicts with fellow-beings with our nails and teeth, then we quarrelled with each other with stones in Paleolithic and Neolithic Ages, with bamboo sticks, arrows etc. Later on, with sword, spear etc., in metal age, with guns, machine guns and bombs of different verities during gun powder stage and now with atomic arsenals in this atomic age. Now we cannot move further. We have come to a dead end. It seems that war has lost its dynamics.

Dynamics of Non-Violence

The USA with 30 thousands nuclear warheads could not use them during Vietnam war in spite of the fact that fifty five thousand precious American Soldiers were killed. USA could not use atomic weapons even in Afghanistan, Iraq and Yugoslav wars. Even the Marxist minds adhering to the principle of inevitability of war have revised their doctrine and have accepted the doctrine of coexistence for world politics. Even in matters of social change violence is becoming outdated.

In France when Louise XIV was killed, the reins of governmental and administration did not came to the people. But it was taken over by a dictator called Napoleon. In England, the spineless monarch Charles 1st was slaughtered, but the power did not go to the people and was taken over by another dictator Cromwell. In Soviet Russia Czar was murdered with all his family members, but then power went to the most powerful dictator of modern human history, Josheph Stalin. In our neighborhood the father of Bangladesh with many of his family members was brutally killed in a violent coup. But the power went to the military dictators. It means that "the more of violence, the less of revolution." At the international plane we have to choose between Atom & Ahinsa, nonexistence and existence. In matters of social change we have to discover a moral equivalent of violence. Here we have to choose between blood-bath-cum-dictatorship and Satyagraha. If revolution means change of our idea & ideals, values & philosophy of life. Violence will be counter productive, because we can not change any body's value of life with physical force.

Ecological Challenges and Gandhian Strategies of Life

The 21st century is facing great threat to entire human existence not so much because of terrorism and impending wars but more because of dangerous environmental pollution, acid rains, growing holes in the Ozone layers, rape of the earth, heating of earth, rising of water level in seas and change of seasons etc. The diagnosis is simple. "Nature has enough to meet our needs, but not our greed." If we cannot put limitation to our growing wants we shall be constrained to exploit nature and natural resources in the most cruel manner with the result. There is bound to be disastrous effects in environment. Unless we change our style of life and accept voluntary limitation of our wants we cannot avoid the ecological deluge. Hence Gandhian strategies of simple living and high thinking is not a religious fad or a sermon on the mount from ivory tower, but a necessity for our life.

Gandhian Strategies of Culture

According to Toffler power, wealth and knowledge are the three important features of modern civilization, but modern civilization is facing a paradox. If we move blindly in pursuit of power, wealth and knowledge without any moral and spiritual safeguards, we are likely to face a Dooms day. Hence Arnold Toynbee after examining about 30 cultures of human history has come to the conclusion that moral and spiritual elements have the greatest survival value for any civilization. Gandhi also from his common sense perception of human history has come to the conclusion, that those civilizations which had serious lack of moral and spiritual ingradients have faded away. He cites the example of ancient civilization of Sodom and Gomarah which have been wiped out of their existence because they lacked moral values and moral life. The ultimate goal of life is happiness. But whereas wealth, power and knowledge have been increasing, human happiness has been miserably decreasing. Therefore a Noble Laureate Alexis Carrel has observed that we must find out 'Science of Man' which can give him happiness and peace of mind.

Synthesis of Science and Spirituality

When people saw Gandhi playing his spinning wheel, living in a small room of a thatched cottage and wearing a loin cloth and working with kerosene lamp, generally called him ascetic, mediaeval, anti-science and anti-progress. But Gandhi is not only the spinning wheel or living half clad life, but also a man leading a relentless war against racial discrimination in South Africa, untouchability in India, Satyagraha for the poor farmers in Champran; Kheda, Bardoli in India and fighting British imperialism without any hatred or sense of enmity with the British people. His message was to fight with the evil not with the evil-doers.

In short, Gandhi combined science with spirituality, politics with morality and fight without hatred. Science without spirituality is blind and a curse for humanity. But spirituality and religion without rationality and scientific temper lead to religious fundamentalism, lifeless ritualism and in human social and cultural practices.

Conclusion

Gandhi was not a system builder like Kant or Hegal, Shankar or Ramanuj, but he was never a one-sided arm chair thinker. To him, life is not a water-tight compartment, which can be divided into political, social, economic departments. It is an integral whole. But the most important question is : What should be the fundamental basis of human life and society? Here Gandhi discovered the twin principle of truth and non-violence. Which have been tested as pure gold during the long course of human history. Hence any consideration about the exclusion and inclusion in Gandhian Strategies must take into account the basic tenets of Gandhian thought. This does not mean that we should not try to discover new Strategies and brush aside those which have been become lifeless and obsolete. But we must be careful that the yard-stick of human progress and true civilization is not contained in plentiful extravagant living at the cost of grin poverty and inequality throughout the world. To my mind Satyagraha is the best contribution of Gandhijee for the 21st century and beyond. But Satyagraha is not something new, it is as old as Prahalada and Dhruva in India and Socrates and Jesus outside. Even in present day, we have examples of Martin Luther King, Fuji Guruji, Sol-zens-tein and many others. But they were mostly limited to the individual levels. Gandhi tried to convert the individual to the mass level of non-violent action. Satyagraha has become a science. Hence it has universal application. It can be applied in all aspects of human life—social, political, economic etc. In the matter of Peace-Science, there has been great progress in the field of conflicts-resolution in the west. There are about seventeen hundreds Peace-Science and Peace-Research Institutes in different parts of the world but mostly in the west. This is a new strategy of Satyagraha. In India, a part from various experiments made by Mahatama Gandhi, Gaffar Khan and others in the life-time of Gandhi. We have new ideas in post-Gandhian era. Doctor R.M. Lohia introduce "Gherao." But this has not found universal acceptance as there is an element of coercion in it which is a form of material violence. Gandhi's spiritual disciple Vinoba Bhaway has however tried to argue a case for subtle, subtler and subtlest form of Satyagraha to meet the horrid nature of violence. It has not been experimented on a mass level as yet. However another tallest Gandhian Jaya Prakash Narayan has demonstrated a successful mass non-violent action against temporary dictatorship and curtailment of human-rights during 74-77. There have been isolated experiments both in India and abroad in Satyagraha. Therefore, during the Satyagraha Centenary International Seminar held last year in Delhi the great octogenarian Polish leader Leh Walesa and the African leader J.M. Kunda had expressed themselves in favour of the relevance of Satyagraha in modern times. Last but not the least, Nelson Mandela had also supported the idea of Satyagraha as the only way-out for it peaceful social change in this nuclear age, in his memorable message. The Power of Satyagraha is the power of non-violence and we have to make a choice between non-violence and non-existence.

27

The Relevance of Gandhian Economics for Modern Times

1. Total View of Human Life

To Gandhi, life is not like a water-tight compartment.[1] Hence it cannot be divided into social, political, economic etc. Thus he had an integral vision of man's life and society. Each aspect of life act and react upon each other. Hence any piecemeal study of Gandhian Economics is not only bound to create a partisan or partial view but also a distorted vision. Now it is high time to free oneself from the notion of one-dimensional man or the Economic Man and move towards the new horizon.

2. Gandhi as an Economist

It is no denying the fact that Gandhi was not an economist like Adam Smith, Marshall, Robins, Pigou, Keynes or even Marx. Nor he ever claimed it. Hence, J.B. Kripalani rightly said that "if there was a planner without elaborate blue-print, Gandhi was one of them".[2] Unlike other economists, Gandhi, he did not study economics academically. It was not in his nature too. He himself says, "I am not built for academic writings, Action is my domain".[3] He was not a theorist but primarily an activist. According to him, "solutions do not arise out of dogmatic, and doctrinaire approach but out of experience and struggle. Hence to borrow Tyonbee's expression, Gandhi's economic ideas was "a response to challenge that poverty-ridden India flung to him".

3. Method

His method was to understand the scientific principles in the form of conditions that give rise to them. This means that in order to understand the economic problems we should see the conditions of the time.[4] It is why Gandhi studied in depth the impact of industrial revolution as well as modern civilization, which he has depicted in his Hind Swaraj. His method is therefore based on his experience and not on the basis of bookish knowledge. He saw the miserable conditions of the industrial labourers from India and other Asian countries brought to South Africa. Between 1550-1650, Black labour was used in mines in Bolivia in the most cruel and inhuman manner, so much so that the labourers were used in the 760 ft. deep in the mines for a week. Their average working life was therefore 3 to 4 months only. During 1500-1650, the Spanish colonialists, virtually looted 200 tons of gold worth 125 crores from the colonies. During 1800-1830, international trade increased from 30 crore sterling pound to 40 crores. Between 1840-70, it multiplied to 200 crore sterling pounds. Farmers too were exploited. Hence, we can easily understand new ways of plunder by World Bank, International Monetary Fund and the W.T.O. Western nations accumulated wealth through the worst forms of exploitation and because they combined trade with politics. All these provided Gandhi materials to express appropriate response to economics.

4. Concepts

However, Gandhi could discover the appropriate concepts of economics. But then, he did not treat them as absolute concepts but relative and without finality. He himself kept on elaborating, codifying, enriching the old context, as he was ever-growing. He grew from "truth to truth".[5] His thoughts and ideas were never static but we cannot ever miss a direction in his fundamentals. He courageously ignored consistency in his earlier and later thoughts and allowed his readers to pick up his stand from his later writings if they differ from his earlier ones.[6] Like a scientist, he was in eternal quest of truth.

5. System without System-building

Like the classical and academic thinkers hence he was not an absolutist or finalist which is the true spirit of a scientist. His "Collected Works" is a vast mass of materials spread over 7-8 decades, which have been skulled from different journals and papers and his speeches. There are hardly a few books, which he had the patience and time to write out like his *Autobiography* or *My Experiments with Truth, Satyagraha in South Africa* and *Hind Swaraj* (1909). But if we try to find out a system, we can have it from Dialectics to Dietectics, from Economics to Philosophy, Politics to Sociology, Nature Cure to meditation, metaphysics to morals etc. In this way, he had a comprehensive vision and therefore an integral approach.

6. Forerunners of Gandhi's Ideas

Gandhi did not come out of vacuum. He inherited both his family-culture as well as the political-social culture of his time. In his family, he was influenced by his mother's life as a devout Vaishnaiva of the *Pranami-cult* which have taught to practice a life of purity, austerity and service. He was also influenced by the Jain doctrine of *non-possession* and limitation of wants. Similarly Buddha's life taught him to practice good to other following his doctrine of compassion. In the west, the life of Socrates and teachings of Lord Jesus had profound influences upon him. They inspired him to adopt a life of love and simplicity which were strengthened by Tolstoy concept of Bread Labour, Ruskin's emphasis upon dignity of labour and so on. John Ruskin's *Unto This Last* was a great critique of modern civilization and technology. Ruskin had challenged the very conception of modern economics and called it as a "dismal science of darkness" and more so as a "science of illth rather than wealth". *Ruskin's Unto This Last* became Gandhi's "Bible of Economics", where he got lessons in equality of wages for a band-labourer and a brain labourer." But he learnt the deep meaning of Ruskin's third principle that "the life of a manual labourer like the farmer is ideal" from Tolstoy. These two principles—equal wages of a brain-labourer and a hand-labourer and the preference of the like of physical labourer have radicalised Gandhi's economic thought by shunning elitism. The traditional economics, by recognising "organisation" and "enterprise" provided justification for both capitalism and social elitism. Even Marxism could not abolish the divide between the 'classes' and the 'masses' or through the concept of "bourgeois" and the "proletariate", with the result there was at least 9 times inequality in the income in U.S.S.R. Gandhi by following Ruskin, has moved ahead towards equalisation in the economic and social fabric. Industrialisation and rapid introduction of high-technology has contributed in widening this divide. Hence, Gandhi introduced the principle of "Bread-labour" as one of his eleven vows. Social equality without economic equality or more so without the equality of wages cannot be achieved. Of course the various scriptures do mention about the equality of human beings, but it remained only spiritual idealism but Gandhi brought it at the level of social and organisational engineering. A small experiment of equal wages was introduced among all classes of Khadi workers in Bihar at the behest of Acharya Vinoba but the vested interests could not allow this system beyond two decades.

7. Some Basic Principles of Gandhi Economics

***(a)* Meta-Economics of Mahatma Gandhi or Moral and Spiritual Approach to Economics :** Gandhi, like a rebel, challenged the very foundation of modern economics based upon "wealth" or "money". According to him, economics and ethics are vitally related. Economic order presupposes a social order which further involves a moral order also "True economics never militates against the highest ethical standard". An economics that inculcates Mammon worship and believes in the Darwinian doctrine of the survival of the fittest, is a dismal science which enables the strong to a mass at the expense of the weak. True, economics, therefore, stands for social and economic justice and universal welfare. Hence, Gandhi never drew a sharp line of demarcation between economics and ethics. That economics is untrue which ignores or disregards moral values. Hence in his epoch making speech in 1916 at Muir College, Allahabad where he said that the scripture of the world are safer and sounder treatises on laws of economics than many modern text books. He (Jesus) is himself the greatest economist of his time".[7] So Marshall's theory of demand and supply or Lord Keyne's theory of Liquidity Preference Theory of Rate of Interest are neutral about the value judgement. It means that we should become rich even by exploitation and robbing others. If we follow the so-called Law of Demand and Supply bereft of moral compunction, some supplier might have created artificial scarcity to decrease the supply so that the price may increase. But this is bad economics equal to robbery.

***(b)* Economics of Man** : Hence Gandhi propounded economics of man rather than an "enquiry into nature and causes of wealth of nations". Adam Smith put wealth in the forefront and man in the background. Hence writers like Carlyle, Ruskin or Gandhi condemned this mammon worship. Marshall improved this definition as "a study of man's action" and so did Robbins defined Economics as "study of human behaviour" but as a relationship between "scarce end and means" to get maximum material satisfaction. However the centre of Gandhian economic thought is "man", not "material prosperity". It is true, man cannot live without bread but this is also true that he cannot live with bread alone. Hence Gandhi takes a totalistic view of happiness because like Wordsworth, he was true to the kindred points of heaven and earth. He did understand the importance of material necessities and comforts of life but he did not stop there and took adequate note of psychological and spiritual aspects of human life.

***(c)* Economics of Permanence** : However, he was not in favour of an unbridled consumerism. There can be use and misuse of his free will. By wrong use of will, man displaces this natural function by allaying his thirst with ever increasing wants. "Nature has enough to meet his needs but not his greed", says Gandhi. This has caused both ecological and social problems like parasitic Economy and an unscientific exploitation of nature. Hence Gandhi advocated an Economy of Permanence and Sustainable Development. There are two models of development—1. Transient-Destructive and 2. Permanent-Creative. The first is based on 'Rights' with the absence of altruistic values. There are three stages of them *(a)* Parasitic Economy *(b)* Economy of Perdition and *(c)* Economy of Enterprise. The second model is that of Economy of Gregation and Economy of Service. In short, this is Economy of Values. In fact, this is the Economy of Permanence. Unless we put a control upon our desires and wants, we shall have to exploit nature as cruelly as possible leading to the rapid erosion of natural wealth as well as environmental problems. We have seen the dreadful reports of the Club of Rome. There has been rape of the earth, water and other natural resources. Due to extreme pollution, there have been dangerous holes in the ozone and even acid rains. The threat of nuclear holocaust is also there. Hence, we have to limit our craze for over consumerism. Due to brutal exploitation of nature, we have already exhausted coal, petrol etc. There is water-crisis in the offing. Hence, use must return to less and less consumption not as a spiritual demand but as our compulsion. Our emphasis upon limitation of wants or a sort of voluntary poverty if not wantlessness is the demand of the time.

***(d)* Economics of Peace** : Peace is not only an absence of war. There are good structural causes of violence like poverty, unemployment, wrong use of political power and social injustices etc. Not only this, even inequality breeds violence. Hence Gandhi through his gospel of work, decentralisation and small and cottage industries tried to achieve social peace. Violence is ingrained in a centralised economy.

Large-scale industries need large capital, big technology and bigger markets which are bound to create fierce and unhealthy competition and consequently war. It was Great Britain, France, Spain etc. who practiced cut throat competition for capturing market. This involved big and small wars. Hence industrialization brought an economy of war. Today arms and ammunition worth over 10 thousand billion dollars are manufactured every year and sold mostly to Asian and African countries, while the masses remain hungry, half clad and illiterate.

***(e)* Economics of High Technology : Industrialization :** Industrial Revolution, no doubt, came as a blessing. We learnt "to ride the waves of the wind, to harness the rivers, watering deserts, to master the earth and the creatures thereof and with the earth as our foot stool reach out to the stars"[9] but today it has become a curse. Even western thinkers like Tolstoy categorized the grave evils of machinery and industrial civilization. Gandhi was very critical of industrial civilization for exploitation, alienation, and dehumanization of man. He did not want large-scale production but production by the masses. Then decentralisation and non-violence go together. In fact, Gandhi was not against machinery as such. He advocated appropriate technology. For example, a big country like India with a big population but small capital, small-scale industries are more suitable to ease unemployment and under-employment. That use of machinery is lawful, moral and practical "which subserves the interest of all".[10] Hence he is on record to say mat he would favour the use of the "most elaborate machinery if thereby India's pauperism and resulting idleness is avoided."[11] Gandhi would distinguish between machine and machine. For example he is totally against those machines which produce arms and armaments for the destruction of mankind. Similarly, he is also against the use of those machines, which create unemployment. But he is in favour of those machines which provide employment and removes human drudgery etc. He is also critical of industrial civilization as it has created unmanageable and unwildy cities, consumerism, pollution and a culture of exploitation, crime and corruption. So his picture of Swaraj is the picture of a small but beautiful habitation where people have got some employment and live in peace and harmony.

***(f)* Economic of Swadeshi and Swaraj :** Swaraj is not only freedom from foreign rule. It is not simply political freedom. National independence go along with national self-reliance or Swaraj. He was in favour of freedom of Self and also of the nation. What to speak of our sovereignty, even our democracy, our culture and our life-styles are not safe under economic dependence. However, this is not possible without self-reliance and Swadeshi. Swadeshi must not be misconstrued in the narrow sense of national chauvinism. We must admit that only a free, independent and self-sufficient India can serve the world. But his patriotism is not exclusive, it is not only not to hurt another nation but to benefit all in the true sense of the word. Hence Gandhi clearly said "India's freedom as conceived by me can never be a menace to the world".[12] Freedom is our birth right but non-exploitation of other countries is our most sacred duty. Hence the modern slogan of globalisation is not an anathema but unfortunately it is a retrial of liberalisation, privatisation and exploitation by three capitalist agencies of World Bank, International Monetary Fund and World Trade Organization. The first era of so called globalisation started in 1890-1913, the second phase during 1950-1980 and the third phase of globalisation came in 1980 with high-technology. It is neither universalism nor liberalism. It is pure a corporate scheme of the vested interest for the purpose of exploitation of the developing countries and with the veiled purpose of political dominance in the world-politics. Economically, it creates "Jobless growth", poverty, insecurity in the developing countries, hence violence and anarchy have increased while world output growth has dropped by 2%, world trade has diminished in the Asian-African countries. The so called Asian Tigers, which were show pieces of models of 'globalisation' turned to Pusy Cats during the depression and the masters had to rush with massive loan to save their edifice from crumbling and collapse. Even in U.S.A. in 2003 there were 40 million people below poverty line. In India, during this period of so-called economic reforms, the world trade has gone down from 195.59 lakhs in 1997 to 191.38 lakhs in 2001. So it is a myth that globalisation creates economic progress. Even it creates wealth, it is usurped by only 20% of the population. This is because the economic planning in India has ignored the critical question of demographic and social factor in the development.

Apart from these glaring economic defects, there are serious political drawbacks also. Western nations have accumulated wealth while the third-world countries have lost. On the other hand, W.T.O. has invaded upon human rights and even constitutional rights of these countries under pretext of international agreement. There has been weakening of labour unions; world monopoly through Patent laws and farmers' exploitation by compelling them to purchase seeds, manures and pesticides from them. There has been very ugly interference with the sovereignty of nations like Brazil, Bolivia etc. On social plane, the entire world has been turned into a big market where corruption, addiction, blackmarketing, criminalisation and vulgar consumerism abound. There has been no guarantee of job in a factory and with no human dignity.

"Poorna Swaraj means full freedom for the toiling millions. It is no unholy alliance with any interest for their exploitation".[13] It is complete freedom from alien yoke in every sense of the term and this is for the sake of dumb millions.[14] Hence Swaraj is impossible with Swadeshi. But there are true as well as false Swadeshi. Any article is Swadeshi if it subserves the interests of the million, even though the capital and talent may be all foreign but under effective Indian control. It means that Swadeshi should not be made a fetish. To reject foreign, and to go on wasting national time and energy will be a criminal folly.[16] In fact he want rational and balanced Swadeshi.

***(g)* Economics of Bread Labour :** According to traditional Economics, there are four factors of production—land, labour, capital and organization. We can add even enterprise as the fifth one. But, there has been a chasm between the physical labour and the mental labour with superiority and prestige given to brain-labourer. Although the scriptures like the Bible and the Gita do eulogise the dignity of labour but in common use there is difference between the 'wages' of a labourer and 'salary' of a supervisor or manager. But Gandhi did not want to discriminate between the two as the theory of Bread Labour was both a philosophy and economics to Gandhi—"That to live man must work". This idea came to Gandhi first from reading Tolstoy, then from Ruskin's *Unto This Last.* However, this was first stressed by a Russian writer named T.M. Bondaref and also in the 3rd chapter of the Gita—"He who eats without offering sacrifices eat stolen food".[19] According to Gandhi, the violation of this principle is the root cause of economic disequilibrium. He regards it as a natural law binding on all. It is compulsory duty. Its neglect creates social division between the Elites and the Proletariates. Gandhi's insistence is enforced by the Bible—"In the sweat of thy brow thou shalt eat thy bread". A millionaire cannot carry on for long, and will soon get tired of his life, if he rolls in his bed all day along, and is even helped to his food. He, therefore, induces hunger by taking exercise. Even from social standpoint, a worldwide conflict between capital and labour, and the poor envy the rich. If all worked for their bread, distinctions of rank would be obliterated. This might be unattainable ideal, but we need not cease to strive for it. A question arises—May not men earn their livelihood by intellectual labour? The answer is : The needs of the body must be supplied by the body. Render unto Caesar which is Caeser's. Mere intellectual labour is for the soul and is its own satisfaction. In that case if it should never demand payment. In the ideal state, the doctors, lawyers and others work for the benefit of society, not for self. "Obedience to the law of Bread Labour will bring about a silent revolution in the structure of society. Men's triumph will consist in substituting the struggle for existence by the struggle for mutual service. The law of the brute will be replaced by the law of man".[20] One may ask, why should we insist on Rabindranath or Raman earning their bread by manual labour? Is it not sheer wastage? Why should not brain worker be considered on a par with manual workers, for both of them perform useful social work? Gandhi replies "Intellectual work is important and has an undoubted place in the scheme of life. But what I insist on is the necessity of physical labour. No man, I claim to be free from that obligation. It will serve to improve even the quality of his intellectual output".[21] Even in ancient times, the Brahmin Gurus worked with their body as with their mind. Even Lord Ram collected fire wood for his teacher Vishwamitra and Lord

Krishna cared and massaged his horses of war. Even Rabindra Nath had set up Sri Niketan as a centre of craft after Santiniketan. Body and mind are complimentary and supplementary to each other. Similarly, the economics of Bread Labour was the living way of life. It meant that every man had to labour with his body for his food and clothings; in that case there would never be any want of food and cloth.[22] However, if we put some compulsory manual labour daily along with mental, it would be more pleasant. Change of occupation is rest. For a man engaged for 8-10 hours in mental work, it is a pleasure and play to work in the field, garden or on some handicraft. It is therefore neither a fad nor a retrograde step but a revolutionary devise to increase production, keep oneself healthy and maintain social equilibrium.

***(h)* Economics of Trusteeship :** We are at the cross-roads of our history. There is both rigour and relevance in a changing institutional setting. We have witnessed the collapse of bi-polar extreme economic systems—capitalism and communism. Even the "so called economic reforms in the name of LPG have failed to remove poverty of the masses and unemployment. There is jobless growth. Marxism also failed to remove inequality and instead deprived us of our liberty and individual freedom. Even mixed economy could not also succeed. Hence we have to find out a system which would guarantee individual freedom and economic prosperity. Modern economists have no answer as to what would be appropriate institutional set up for combining economic efficiency and individual freedom.

Here Gandhi provides Trusteeship model which is India's gift to the world. Here not only the capital is socialised but labour has also been socialised. He brought ethics to Economics and gave dignity to the rich by making them trustees. They would give up private ownership of their property and create out of it a trust valid in the eyes of the law court and managed democratically. Trusteeship provides a means of transformation. The present capitalist order of society into an egalitarian one. It gives no quarter to capitalise but gives the present owning class a chance of reforming itself. It is based on the faith that human nature is never beyond redemption. But it does not recognise any right of private ownership of property except it may be permitted by society. It does not recognise right of inheritance also. It does not exclude legislated regulation of the ownership and use of wealth. Thus under state regulated ownership, an individual will not be free to hold or use his wealth for selfish reason or in disregard of the interest of society. There are the six points of Trusteeship Theory presented by Prof. M.L. Dantwala and approved by Gandhiji.[23] Business is so inextricably woven in the very texture of society that it is inalienable from it. The relation between business and society may be based either on conflict or cooperation. If the private sector realise they have their part as trustees, there is really Ramrajya. Gandhi wanted to take advantage of the skill of the business people devoid of dirty profiteering and black-marketing etc.

To say that such an idea is not practicable, is natural but one should try to learn from the experiments of Gandhi in South Africa and by some other people elsewhere. There may of suitable legislation and finally Mahatma's weapons of non-cooperation and Satyagraha are there. Vinoba had shown that lakhs of acres of land may be donated to the landless and Gramdan is a kind of trusteeship experiment. When capitalism and class war both are despicable trusteeship is the hope for future. E.F. Schumacher has also expressed that "if India should be able to move along the path of equality through trusteeship, she would be a beacon to the world". The success lies in experimentation as both systems of capitalism and socialism have failed.

8. Conclusion

Gandhian Economics is not based on rigid doctrinaire approach, it is based on common sense experience. It has faith in the goodness of man and his rationality. Its goal is welfare not of one section of society but of all. Hence it is not sectional or sectarian. Hence there is least chance of conflict. Similarly, the means are also different *i.e.,* love and non-violence. Hence it is a viable alternative before the world. Gandhi has demonstrated the efficacy of love and non-violence in the field of economics. Vinobaji has tried to show the path. But if we do not wish to take the prescribed means and medicines and simply try to accuse that it is utopian or unpractical, we must face the music of violence, terrorism and bloody revolution. Let economists and thinkers leave the beaten track and think courageously. It is not Utopian but pragmatic, it is not based on ivory-tower but practical and realistic. Lousi Fischer wrote—"If man is to survive, if civilization is to survive and flower in freedom, truth and democracy the remainder of the 20th century and what lies beyond must belong not to Lenin or Trotsky, nor to Marx or Mao or Ho-chi Minh but to Mahatma Gandhi". I would like to add that L.P.G. or the so called globalism cannot save humanity. We require globalism of Mahatma Gandhi with no war, no conquest, no exploitation. We want freedom from want but also limitation of our wants, not unbriddled liberalisation, to save the humanity and our civilization.

REFERENCES

1. Gandhi, M.K., *Selection from Gandhi,* ed. N.K. Bose, Ahmedabad : Navajiwan Prakashan, 1948, *Young India,* 2.3.22.
2. Kripalani, J.B., *Gandhi : His Life and Thought,* Calcutta, Orient Longmans, 1961, p. 262.
3. *Harijan,* A Journal of Applied Gandhism, 1933-55, New York, 3.1.46, p. 28.
4. Bhattacharya, B., *Evolution of the Political Philosophy of Mahatma Gandhi,* Calcutta, Indian Associated Publishing Co., 1940, p. 32.
5. *Harijan,* 29.4.1934, p. 260.
6. Harijan, 29.4.1933, p. 2.
7. *Collected Works of Mahatma Gandhi,* Vol. XIII, pp. 311-17.
8. Adam Smith, *An Essay on the Nature and Causes of Wealth of Nations,* New York, The Modern Library, 1937.
9. Radhakrishnan, S., *Speeches and Writings,* Third Series, New Delhi : Publications Division, Govt. of India, 1959-62.
10. Gandhi, M.K., *Young India,* 15.4.26.

11. *Ibid.*, 3.11.21.
12. Gandhi, M.K., *Young India,* 3.4.24.
13. Gandhi, M.K., *Young India,* 16.4.31.
14. Gandhi, M.K., *Young India,* 17.9.31.
15. Gandhi, M.K., *Harijan,* 25.2.39.
16. Gandhi, M.K., From *Yarvada Mandir,* p. 85.
17. Gandhi, M.K., *Young India,* 17.2.27.
18. Gandhi, M.K., From *Yarvada Mandir,* pp. 21.
19. Gandhi, M.K., Bhagvad Gita, III. 12 cp. *Manu Smrti* III.76, 118.
20. Gandhi, M.K., *Harijan,* 29.6.35.
21. Gandhi, M.K., *Harijan,* 23.2.47.
22. Gandhi, M.K., *Harijan,* 7.9.47.
23. Upadhyaya, R.B., *Social Responsibility of Business and Trusteeship Theory of M.K. Gandhi,* p. 71.

Index

A

Abhay, 8
Abhedananda, 31-32, 34
Abhimanyu, 109
Absolute Brahman, 45, 47
Absolute monism, 11
Absolute Truth, 156
Absolutism, 71-72
Acarie, Madam, 38
Acharaya Kula, 93, 163
Adbe Alamgiri, 126
Adhyatma Vidya, 22
Adigeshiah Mallons, 145
Aditi, 39
Adrsha of Vaisesika, 46
Advat Asharam, 69
Advaita Vedanta of Sankar, 7, 19
Advaitic philosophy, 13
Aesthetics, 30
Afghanistan, 86, 134, 177, 183, 190, 195
African countries, 63, 178
Agamas, 29
Agra, 45
Ahalaya, 48
Ahimsa, 130, 142, 144, 158-59, 193, 196
Ahimsa Vahini, 143, 165
Ahmedabad, 90, 109, 121
AIDS, 76, 191
Akbar, 60
Alexander, 56, 104
All India Labour Movement, 109
Almin Al Shatiah, 182
Al-Quaida, 141
Alpatma, 155
Alternative development model, 105
Ambika, 39
America, 13
Anahata, 157
Andhra, 122
Angels of Foligno, 38-39
Anger, 10
Annapurna, 43
Anna Saheb Sahasra Buddha, 95
Annual Conference of Gandhian Studies, 165
Anxiety, 3
Apala, 39
Apara, 22, 38
Apta-vachana, 27
Ardha Narishwar, 34
Aristotle, 24, 26, 54
Artha, 152
Aryans, 18, 125
Arya Samaj, 18, 57

Asanana, 3
Asang, 27
Asian Development Bank, 104
Asian Tigers, 207
Assam, 124
Association of Asian people, 82
Asuras, 47
Athenian, 10, 63, 86, 182
Atlanta, 184
Atlee Clement, 64
Atma Jnana, 22
Atman, 51, 156, 193
Atom, 144, 158, 196
Atomic age, 64, 180
Atomic war, 177
Aung Swi, 83
Auprva of Mimansa, 46
Aurangzeb, 126
Aurobindo, 16, 64
Australia, 192
Austiman, 133
Austrian power, 90
Autocracy, 103
AVARD, 109
Avatara, 33-34, 36, 166
Avidya, 21-22, 25, 38
Ayodhya, 45, 48, 123, 125
Ayodhya Lal, 127
Ayub Khan, 113
Azadi Bachao Andolan, 188

B

Babar, 126
Babarnama, 126
Backward classes, 117-18, 123
Backward Classes Commission, 115
Baghele Sankar Singh, 99
Bangladesh, 89, 109, 180
Bardoli, 90, 115, 121, 197
Becoming, 22
Beg, M.H., 149
Being, 123, 157
Belief, 19, 29
Bengal, 120
Bergson, 22, 24-75
Besant Annie, 126
Bhagalpur, 165
Bagat Singh, 109
Bhagawan Das, 72
Bharadwaj, 49
Bharata, 48
Bhaskaran, William, 138
Bhavabhuti, 44-45
Bhave, Vinoba, 17, 39, 64, 86, 91, 93-94, 108-12, 115, 117, 119, 140, 163, 199, 203, 211-12
Bhoodan Gramdan Movement, 17, 94-96, 108-09, 111, 115, 117, 163
Bhubneshwari, 31
Bhuleshananda, 36
Bhumihar, 117
Bible, 8, 18, 57
Bihar, 94, 116-26, 191
Bihar movement, 50, 109, 112-20, 164
Bihar Pradesh Congress Committee, 117
BJP, 98, 100, 119-20, 124-25

Blissful Mother, 39
Bloodless Victory, 121
Bodha Struggle, 118
Bodhi, 23
Bodhi Sattva, 166
Bodily postures, 3
Body, 21
Bolivia, 201
Bondarif, T.M., 181, 209
Bood Gaya Math, 118
Borsad, 90
Bose Charlottee, 41
Bose Subhas Chandra, 88, 109
Boycott of foreign courts, 106, 121
Boycott of foreign goods, 106, 121
Boycott of foreign system of education, 106, 121
Bradley, 22-24
Brahadaranyaka Upanisad, 8, 10
Brahma, 20, 24, 146
Brahman, 10-11, 41, 46, 159
Brahman realisation, 8
Brahma Samaj, 18
Brahma Sutra, 25
Brahmavadins, 39
Brandt Report, 173
Brazil, 188
Bread labour, 135, 171, 202-03
British colonialism, 87
British East India, 6, 76
British Imperialism, 68
British withdrawal, 68
Brotherhood, 8, 72, 182
Brown, Jame, 41
Buddha, 7, 16, 23, 40, 46, 88, 90, 133, 157, 202
Buddhism, 18, 24, 56
Buddhist, 19, 21, 71
Buddhist Five Moral Conducts, 47
Burma, 63, 86
Butler, Josephine, 39
Byron, 50

C

Camps of Youth against violence, 165
Capturing booths, 124
Carlyle, 204
Caste, 1, 115
Categorial Imperative, 13
Catholics, 178
Ceremonies, 19
Ceylon, 86
Champaran, 90, 115, 119, 121, 197
Chandogya Upanisad, 10
Chandragupta, 119
Charan Singh, 123
Charity, 171
Charles I, 89, 180, 196
Chiang Kai-Shek Generalissmo, 69
Chile, 188
China, 68, 74, 81, 139, 177, 188
Chitrakoot, 45
Chitta, 4
Christ, 40

Christian, 4, 7, 18, 59, 70, 74, 125
Christian brotherhood, 71
Christianity, 10, 29, 34, 37, 39, 56, 60, 134, 178, 182
Christian Missionaries, 56-57, 166
Civil disobedience movement, 90, 106, 121, 140, 189, 191
Civilization, 17, 54-55, 64, 79, 197
Class conflict, 96
Class struggle, 132
Code, Marron, 41
Common Civil Code, 81, 125
Commonwealth Vice-Chancellor's Conference at Brighton, 165
Communal forces, 120
Communal harmony, 163
Communal riots, 80, 128
Communism, 16, 101-02, 137-188
Communists, 73-74, 116-17
Compassion, 4, 75, 154, 166-67
Complete independence, 88
Confession of faith, 41
Confusian, 71
Confusicries, 7, 21, 27, 131
Congress, 96-98, 100
Congress CPI (M), 99, 110
Congress Seva Dal, 128, 143
Conscience of Paris, 38
Consciousness, 1, 3, 5
Constitution, 121-22
Consumerism, 76, 78, 91
Constructive programme, 162-63, 194
Cornwallis, 115
Cosmic life, 74
Corruption, 96, 164
Cosmic community knowledge, 55
Cosmic energy, 33
Cosmic life, 74
CTBT, 17
Council of Europe, 75
Cowardiee, 158
Cow protection movement, 93, 164
CPI, 124
CPI(M), 99, 110, 124
Creator, 37
Cromwell, 89
Crownwell, 180
Crucification, 159, 167
Cultural renaissence, 17
Cultural structure, 184-85
Culture, 157
Czar in Russia, 89, 180, 196
Czechoslovakia, 109
Czech people, 68

D

Dakhineshwar, 35
Dalai Lama, 83
Dante, 26
Dantwala, M.L., 211
Darasikoh, 125
Daridra Narain, 125, 135, 168
Darshana, 23
Darvinian system, 184, 203
Darwin, 52

Datta, D.M., 13-17
David, Saril N., 41
Davidson Elizabeth, 41
Dawkins, Richard, 75
Deak, Ferare, 90
Death, 20, 156
Decentralisation of power, 82
De-chantal, Jeanne, 38
De Gaulle, 113
Delhi, 45, 119
Democracy, 16, 90, 103
Democratic ruralism, 82
Demolition of Mosque in Ayodhya, 123
Denmark, 90
Derby, Ida, 41
Desai, L.M., 142
Desai, Mahadeo, 173
Descartes, 26, 146
Desires, 2
Despande, Nirmala, 97-99
Deusses Paual, 8, 30
Devalera, 89
Devaluation, 76
Devi, 39
Dhama Krist, 27
Dhamma, 30, 46
Dharma, 152
Dhruva, 198
Dhyana, 4
Dialectics, 25-26
Dictatorship, 98, 102-03
Dignaq, 27
Din-a-elahi, 60
Disarmament, 60, 130, 172, 174
Disinvestment policy, 98
Ditheism, 6
Divine, 11, 33-34
Divine of pure, 7
Divine power, 31, 38
Divinity, 34-35, 37, 73
Dock Workers Union, 111
Domestic violence, 131
Dravidians, 125
Drona, 135
Dualism, 6
Duality, 6, 10
Durga, 31, 34, 39
Duty, 13

E

East-West divide, 79
Ecological challenges, 196
Economic compulsions of world govt., 66
Economic disorder and world peace, 135-36
Economic imperialism and globalisation, 74-78
Economic man, 52
Ecosystem, 77
Eddington, 17
Education, 186
Educational challenges and world govt., 67
Education itself a value, 144-45
Education-Today and Tomorrow, 148
Egoism, 3, 72
Egypt, 81

Egyptian mummies, 70
Einstein, Albert, 17, 58, 60, 67, 78
Ekmeva dvitiyam, 11
Election battle, 99
Electoral reform, 104
Electoral strategy, 98
Electronic technology, 73
Emergency, 90, 97, 164
Emerson, 103
Emotional distinction between I and me, 7
End and means, 195
Engels, 102
England, 89, 196
Enlightenment, 21, 23, 166
Entropy, 174
Environment protection, 148
Epistemology problem, 27-30
Equal respect for All Religions, 72, 135, 137
Equity, 21
Essential Unity of All Religions, 72
Ethical humanism, 55
Ethical religion, 7, 137
Ethopia, 178
European Bank for Reconstruction, 105
European Market, 133
European Parliament, 133
Evangelial, 18
Existence of God, 19, 60
Exit Poll Survey, 122

F

Facism, 98-99, 110
Faith, 46, 56-57, 60
Fatherhood, 35, 37
Father's grace, 32
Fear, 8
Fearlessness, 8, 158, 163
Federal World State, 64
Female power, 32, 40, 93
Feudalism, 73
Feudal landlords, 115
Finite, 33
Fooder Scandal, 123-24
Food habits, 53
Forum of Don in Thailand, 76
France, 180, 196
Freedom movement, 127-29
Freedom struggle, 14
Freedom through non-violence, 87-90
Free from desires and body consciousness, 36
French polity, 64
French revolution, 89
Freud, 52, 55
Fry, Elizabeth, 39

G

Gadadhara, 9
Galbraith, 168, 170
Gandhian concept of spiritualisation of politics, 108-09
Gandhian economics relavance for modern times, 200-13

Basic principles of, 203-11
Economics of Bread labour, 208-10
Economics of high technology, 206
Economics of man, 204
Economics of peace, 205-06
Economics of performance, 204-05
Economics of Swadeshi and Swaraj, 206-08
Economics of Trusteeship, 210-11
Economics of war, 203-04
Concepts, 201
Forerunners of Gandhi ideas, 202-03
Gandhi as an economist, 200
Method, 201
System without system building, 202
Total view of human life, 200
Gandhian ideal of universal welfare, 167-68
Gandhian initiative in Bihar-restrospect and prospect, 114-20
Gandhian institutions, 99
Gandhian thought-strategies and stratagems, 194-97
Ecological challenges and, 196
End and means, 195
Gandhian strategies of culture, 197
Nature of man, 195
Non-violence, 195-96
Science and spirituality, 197-98
Gandhian world order and world peace, 130-37
Constructurist non-violence, 132
Economic disorder and world peace, 135-36
Individual peace vs social peace, 130-32
National sovereignity and world peace, 132-34
Paradox of religion of Pax Mundi, 134-35
Gandhi Ashram, 57
Gandhigram Rural Institute, Gandhigram, 138
Gandhi, Indira, 97, 113, 122
Gandhi Institute of Studies, Rajghat, 165
Gandhi, M.K., 7, 10, 15-17, 29, 39, 56-57, 63-64, 68-69, 72-73, 76, 79-80, 87-93, 96-97, 100, 102-03, 106, 108, 110, 114-15, 133-42, 145, 154-76, 187-90, 192-93, 197-212
Marturdom of, 154-61
Gandhi, Rajiv, 97, 100
Gandhi, Sanjaya, 121
Gandhism, 91, 137, 165
Gandhi, Sonia, 126
Gandhi will inspire me even in my next birth, 162-65
Ganeshan, A., 68

Ganga Mukti Andolan, 118
Ganges, 33
Gargi, 27, 39
Garrel, Alexis, 197
Garuda, 49
GATT, 77
Gautama, 27, 157
Genetic system, 75
George, 99
German Nazism, 68
Germans, 68
Germany, 63, 133
Gherao, 198
Ghosa, 39
Gita, 11, 13, 19, 22, 29, 33, 46, 149, 156, 209
Glassmost, 188
Global citizen, 78
Global Forum of Poverty Eradication, 76
Globalization, 75-79, 98, 106, 120, 136, 179, 188-93
Global peace, 182-87
  Cultural structure, 184-85
  Institutional dimension of peace, 185-87
  Political structure, 183-84
  Social violence in social structure, 185
  Structural peace, 183
Global resistance against globalisation, 188-93
  Back to swadeshi, 189
  Civil disobedience movement, 189
  Globalisation—True perspective, 192-93
  Swarajist model of politics, 189-91
Goa, 109
Gobana Nyaya-Suba, 28
God, 7, 9, 15, 19-21, 30, 44-45, 52, 56, 58, 154-56, 166-68, 182
  Belief in, 19
  Faith in, 45, 155-56
Goddess of learning, 36
Godha, 39
Godhead, 21, 38
God realisation, 36
Goetha, 103
Go-hatya bandi, 93
Golapma, 37
Goldsmith, 146
Good governance, 102-07
Good Government, 102-07
Govind, 57
Grama bhimukh khadi, 93
Gramdan, 93-94, 96, 111, 164
Gramdan Gramsabha, 95
Gramsabhas, 93
Gram Swarajya, 93
Grass root panchayat democracy, 109, 119
Gray, Richard, 179
Great Britain, 15
Greece, 179
Greek, 10, 63, 86, 125, 133, 182
Greek language, 12
Green, T.H., 25
Greg, Richard, 57

Gujral, I.K., 83
Gujrat, 99, 123-24, 134
Gupta, Malika Clare, 42
Gupta Maithili Saran, 44
Guru Mata, 31
Gutierrez, 166
Guyard Marie, 38

H

Hanuman, 48, 167
Hanuman Chalisa, 19
Han-yavyun, 88
Haribhadra, 27
Harijan, 68-69, 73, 140, 142, 193
Harijan locality, 127, 162
Harmony, 55
Haryana, 124
Hatred, 10
Hazaribagh, 109
Hegel, 25, 27, 54, 198
Hemchandon, 27
Harigedoing, 17
Hill, Elinor, 41
Himachal, 99
Himalayas, 33
Hindu, 4, 19, 21, 71, 74, 134, 178
Hindu brotherhood, 71
Hindu communalists, 150
Hindu fascists, 159
Hindu idea of life and knowledge, 21-28
Hinduism, 18-20, 28-29, 38-39, 56-57, 60
Hinduism is its own best critic, 28
Hindu monetheism, 7
Hindu-Muslim communal relations, 81-82
Hindu-Muslim harmony, 81
Hindu Rastra, 98-99
Hind Swaraj, 91, 194, 201
Hindu thought, 18
Hindu view of religion, 19-20
Hinshelwood, Cyril, 60
Hiroshima, 90, 147, 177
Hitler, Herr, 68, 18, 184
Hizbullah, 141
Ho-Chi-Minh, 212
Holiness of Mother, 31-32
Holy Mother, 31-43
Honkong Conference, 125
Hugo, Victor, 64
Humanism, 23, 73-74
Humanity, 4, 73, 77, 166
Human life, 1
Human mind, 24
Human nature, 53
Human rights, 73-74, 76
Human rights and democratic principles, 105
Hunger, 191
Hungry, 89-90, 109, 137
Hutcheson, 178
Econoclastic reforms, 71

I

Identity, 8-9
Identity between I and Thou, 10
Ignorance, 21-22, 38
Illiterate, 170

Illusion, 6-12, 47
Illusion and Reality, 6-12
Ill-will, 10
Immigration Bill, 139
Immortality, 22
Immortality of soul, 156-57
Imperishable Brahman, 10
Incarnation of God in the form of mother, 37
Incarnations, 33-34
Independence Day, 188
India, 80-86, 89
Indian civilization, 18
Indian culture, 15
Indian epistemology, 14
Indian freedom struggle, 88
Indian Independence, 87-89
Indian National Army, 88
Indian National Congress, 110, 114, 116, 126
Indian philosophical tradition, 13
Indian philosophy, 14, 16-17, 26-27, 47, 50, 152
Indian revolutionaries, 114
Indian thought, 18-30
Indian thought and culture, 17
Indian womanhood, 39
Individual Peace vs Social Conference, 133
Individual soul, 7
Indonesia, 81
Indo-Pak Conflict—A Gandhian Approach, 80-86
  Loose political models, 85-86
  Model for, 83
  People to people relations, 84-85
  Proposal for mediation for, 83-84
  To start meaningful dialogue, 83
Indo-Pak friendship, 99
Indo-Pak Solutions, 101
Indo-Pak war, 81
Indus Valley Civilization, 18
Infinite, 33
Inner life, 21
Intellectual, 21, 25-26
Inter-Asian Relations Conference, 133
International Conference on Peace, 165
International Criminal Courts, 190
International Fellowship Sevagram, 135
Internationalism, 15
International Monetary Fund, 63, 74, 98, 104-05, 190, 201
International Working Man's Association, 64
Intuition, 22-28, 30
Intuitive, 24-25, 27
Invincible faith in God, 155-56
Iran, 81, 183, 190
Iraq, 81, 134, 177-78, 183-84, 195
Isa Upanishad, 22, 29
Islam, 7, 10, 29, 34, 37, 56, 60, 125, 182

Istapurtam, 29
Italy, 63

J

Jacobi, 27
Jaganthaji, 95
Jaina, 18
Jainsa, 19, 21, 34
Jainism, 18, 56
Jain Vishwa Bharti Union, Lednun, 165
Jamalpur, 127, 129
James, William, 14, 17
Jammu and Kashmir, 118
Jamshedpur, 109, 128
Janta govt., 115
Japan, 63, 87
Japanese aggression against China, 68
Jaya Prakash Narain, 17, 85, 95-97, 106, 108-13, 115, 118-21, 164, 199
  Practical idealist, 108-13
JDU, 124
Jeans, 17
Jehad, 80, 182
Jesus, 16, 131, 134, 154, 159, 179, 198
Jevandan, 109
Jevoah, 131
Jha, Hari Mohan, 13
Jhana Yoga, 69
Jhan Vijnanam Sahitam, 25
Johnson, 8
Josef, Franz, 89
Judaism, 37, 56
Julian of Norwich, 38
Julious caeser, 56, 184
Justice, 21

K

Kakavusundi, 49
Kali, 31, 34-35, 42
Kalidasa, 44-45
Kampuchia, 177
Kant, 13, 25-26, 198
Kantowsky Detell, 173
Kargil conflict, 80
Karma, 46, 152
Karnatak, 95
Kashmir, 80, 86, 109, 178
Kathopnisad, 25, 29
Kelekar, Kaka, 115
Kallapan, 95
Kerala, 95
Keynes, 192, 200, 204
Khadi, 93, 115, 127, 203
Khadi cap, 127
Khan Abdul Gaffar Khan, 139, 198
Kheda, 90, 121, 163, 197
Kher Bhawani, 36
Khudai Khidmatgar, 139
Killing Bali, 48
King Martin Luther, 17, 90, 178-80
Kiratas, 18, 125
Kisan movements, 111
Kisan Sabhas, 94, 116
Kisan struggle, 109

Knowledge, 3, 19, 21-28, 145
Know thyself, 52
Korea, 57, 87-89, 177
Korean Independence, 87
Kripacharya, 135
Kripalani, J.B., 200
Krishna, 32-33, 125, 210
Kunda, J.M., 199

L

Laski, Harold, 64
Lakshman, 48
Land gift mission, 91
Land reform measures, 94, 115, 117, 123
Law of demand and supply, 204
Law of Karma, 46
Law of morality, 7
League of Nations, 133, 185
Leibniz, 26
Lenin, 89, 212
Leviathan, 133
Lewis, Jane, 42, 170
Liberalisation, 75, 90, 106, 115, 120, 179, 212
Liberation, 74
Lichhvees, 114, 133
Life, 21-28
Life is Brahman, 10
Life opposed to death, 26
Lincoln, 68, 179
Linconian Jefforsonian, 111
Logic, 22-23, 30
Logical knowledge, 24-25
Logic and logic calculus, 62-69
Lohia, Ram Manohar, 85, 121, 198
Louis, 89
Lokayat, 18
Lokayuts, 125
Lok Pal, 104
Lok Sevak Sangh, 93, 100
Lomamudra, 39
Louise XIV, 180, 196
Love, 4, 75, 166, 180
Love force, 139
Lucie-cristine, 38-39

M

Macca, 82
Machiavellian politics, 195
Magadh, 133
Mahabharata, 135
Maha Karuna, 166
Mahasamadhi, 32, 35
Mahasaya, 41
Mahavira, 16
Mahendra Pratap, 88
Mahesh, 146
Maintenance of Internal Security Act, 164
Maitreyi, 27, 39
Mammon worship, 203
Manav Seva is Madhava Seva, 40
Manchuria, 88
Mandal, S.P., 116
Mandela, Nelson, 82
Manipur, 124
Man is God, 8

Mankind, 53, 71
Manmohan Bhai, 95
Manmohan Singh, 98, 188
Manoj, 138
Mansoor, 139, 179
Mao, 212
Marie de Incarnation, 38
Market philosophy, 16
Marshall, 200, 204
Martens, Hartna, 41
Martial Law Regime in Poland, 90
Martime, Madame, 38
Martin, Madame, 39
Martyrdoom of Mahatma Gandhi, 154-61, 179
  Faith in non-violence, 157-59
  Immortality of soul, 156-57
  Invincible faith in God, 155-56
Marx, 54-55, 63-64, 68, 102, 192, 212
Marxian theory of economic interpretation of history, 135
Marxism, 203, 210
Marxist, 99
Materialism, 18
Material poverty, 169
Mathematical logic, 24
Matter, 15
Maturity, 75
Maya, 34
Mayarga, Pope, 41-42
May power of God, 33
Meditation, 1-5
Meera Bai, 125
Meera Behan, Sladeor, 126
Mellenia, 137
Memasa, 28
Metaphysical monism, 6
Metaphysical truth, 27
Metaphysics, 6, 50
Military expenditure of NATO, 171-72
Military Science and Peace Research, 130
Military Training, 130
Milton, 146
Mimamsa, 19-46
Mind, 2-4, 21, 26
Mind is Brahma, 10
Mine, 10
Minorities, 129
Misery, 3
Missionary, 18
Mohanjodaro, 18
Moksa, 47, 152
Molecular biology, 73
Monistic faith, 8
Monotheism, 61
Moore Charles, A., 14
Moral, 56-57
Moral equivalent of war, 178
Morality, 16
Motherhood, 35
Motherhood of God, 32-35, 37, 42
Mother's grace, 32
Mother worship of India, 39
Muhamad, 40
Muir College, 204
Multilateral Agreement on Investment, 77

Multinational Corporations, 77, 188, 191
Multi-party system, 96
Mundake Upanishad, 10, 29
Munger, 127, 129
Mushari block, 111
Musharaf, 81
Muslim, 4, 18, 71, 125, 134, 178
Muslim brotherhood, 71
Mussolini, 98
Muzaffarpur, 95, 109, 111
Muzibur Raham, 89
Mysticism, 38
Mystics, 22
Mythology, 59, 70

N

Nagaland, 109
Nagarjuna, 22
Nagashakti, 90, 141, 177
Nagpur, 90
Nahabat, 35
Naik, J.P., 147
Nanak, 131
Nancy, Blenko, 41
Napolean, 89, 180, 196
Narada, 22
Narsing Rao, 98
Narrow nationalism, 178
Nation, 1, 62
National Alliance of People's Movement, 188
National Congress, 124
National consciousness, 17
National defence, 105
National Democratic Front, 122
National flag, 127, 163
Nationalism, 64-65, 68, 79, 134, 162-63, 178-80
National Policy on Education, 145
National Seminars on Gandhism, 165
National Sovereignity and World Peace, 132-34
Nation States, 62-63, 65
NATO, 184
Nature of man, 195
Navya-Nayaya, 28
Naxalism, 120
Naxalite, 94
Naxal movement, 117
Naxal threat, 109
Nazis, 90
Nazism Party, 110
NCERT, 147
NCP, 124
NDA, 99, 122
Nehru Jawaharlal, 64, 68, 101
Neo-imperialism, 192
Neo liberal model of development, 66
Neolithic, 177, 195
Nepal, 109
New Economic Policy, 98, 148
New Economic World Order, 75
New order, 39
New Platonists, 24
Nigamas, 29
Nisads, 18, 125

Niskama Karma Yoga, 13
Nitya Swarupananda, 77
Nivedita, 39, 42, 126
Niyam, 3
Noakhali, 95
No-confidence motion, 122
Non-absolutistic attitude, 56
Non-attachment, 95
Non-cooperaion, 90, 94, 106, 121, 140, 158
Non-duality, 11
Non-existence, 158
Non-exploitation, 69
Non-possession, 202
Non-prolification Treaty, 190
Non-violence, 10, 17, 57, 69, 87-90, 92, 97, 106, 130-31, 140-43, 157-59, 171-72, 189, 194-96, 199, 211
Non-violent freedom struggle, 89-90
Non-violent mass action, 90
Non-violent resistance, 17, 90, 117, 135-36, 163-64
NORSIS, 24
North-West Frontier Province, 139
Norwagion peace negotiation, 83
Norway, 90
Nuclear Age, 172
Nuclear exploism, 66
Nuclear physics, 73
Nun-Goddess, 36
Nyaya-vaisesika, 28
Nyland, Anna, 41

O

Object, 19-20
Omnipresent, 52
Omniscent, 71
Oneness of Reality, 8
Oneself, 12
One unit existence, 51
One world, 133, 178
Opposition unity, 108
Organization for Economic Cooperation and Development, 104-05
Orissa, 95
Others, 6, 12

P

Pacifism, 53
Padambinodi, 42
Pak ISI, 99
Pakistan, 80-86, 177, 180, 183
Palcolithic, 177, 195
Panchayat, 169
Panchayat System in Bihar, 119
Panch Mahavrata, 47
Panchshilla, 47, 88
Pantheism, 7
Para, 22
Paratva, 33
Paris revlution, 64
Parliamentary democracy, 92
Parliament Integrity Commission, 164
Parliament of World Religion, 69, 165

Parmanent settlement, 115
Parmenides, 22
Partyless democracy, 108, 111
Party politics, 92
Party system, 92-93, 111
Parvati, 34, 49
Pasa, Mustafa Kamal, 89
Pascal, 26
Passions, 52
Passive resistance, 140
Patent Bill, 188-208
Patriotism, 127-28
Pax Mundi, 134-35
Peace, 10, 67, 73, 130, 138, 198
Peace Army, 93
Peace Mission, 109
Peace Pledge Union, 156
Peace Summit, 166
Perfect being, 52
Perfect God, 7, 52
Perfect knowledge, 25
Personal religion, 7, 10, 58, 69, 74, 178-79
Phenomenal world, 38
Philistine sentimentalism, 63
Philosophy, 15-16, 70
Philostratus, 19
Physical pleasure, 38
Pigou, 200
Plato, 22, 24-26
Platonists, 24
Pleasures, 8
Plebiscite, 104
Plao, 81
Plowman Max, 156
Pluralistic, metaphysics, 6
Pluralistic theology, 6
Pobinus, 22
Polak, 135
Poland, 17, 90, 137
Political communalisation, 80
Political imperative of world Government, 60-66
Political party, 166
Political power, 102
Political structure, 183-84
Politics, 5
Polygamy, 82
Polytheism, 6
Poorna Swaraj, 68, 208
Pope, Alexander, 50, 144, 186
Post and Telegraph Employee Union, 111
Poverty, 75, 96, 164, 168-69
Poverty and peace, 171-73
Poverty summit, 174
Prahalada, 198
Prajna, 24
Pranami cult, 202
Pranayama, 3
Prasastbado, 27
Prathana Samaj, 18
Pratibodh viditam, 11
Pratt, J.B., 14
Pratyahara, 4
Prestroika, 188
Prithvi, 39
Private capitalism, 74
Privatisation, 75, 98, 106, 120, 179
Privatisation of foreign currency, 105

Privatization of tax collection, 105
Prophet, 34, 58
Protestants, 178
Pseudo-globalization, 75, 78
Psychologists, 50
Public Service Commission, 124
Punjab, 119, 124
Pure consciousness, 9, 47
Pure reason, 26
Purification, 53
Purity and divinity, 31
Purnananda, 32
Purusartha, 152
Purushottama, 47

Q

Qauminara, 127
Quran, 18, 125, 182
Quit India, 90, 113, 121, 128

R

Racial discrimination, 17, 30
Racial equality in USA, 180
Radcliff, 84
Radha, 32
Radhakrishnan, 5, 14
Radha Swami Vijnanand, 32
Raghunath Siromani, 27
Railway Men's Federation, 11
Raja of Hathwa, 116
Rajasthan, 99, 124
Rakshasar, 47
Rama, 32-33, 44-49, 125, 209
Ram Charita Manas, 44-49
Spirituality of, 44-49
Raman, 20
Ramanam, 167
Ramanuja, 7, 198
Ramanuja (Buddhist), 27
Ramayan, 19, 44
Ramjee Singh, 128
Ram Krishna, 31-35, 38, 42-43, 60
Ram Rajya, 48, 125, 211
Ranchi, 109
Rao, V.K.R.V., 170
Rastriya Yuva Sangathan, 99
Rationalism, 73
Rationalistic, 27
Ravana, 46-47, 89
Rayne, Joan, 41
Reality, 6-12, 23-24, 60, 72-73
Reason and Intuition in Indian thought, 18-30
Referendum, 104, 121
Relativity, 58
Religion, 1, 4-5, 7, 10, 19-20, 55-57, 60, 70, 72-74, 134-35, 182
Religion of man, 7, 10
Religious fundamentalism, 20, 73, 134, 198
Religious harmony, 59
Religious mixtures, 30
Representative democracy, 110
Republic Day, 88
Reservation of jobs in government services, 116
Reves Energy, 65
Revolution, 15
Rifken, 174

Right conduct, 47
Righteousness, 28, 48, 73
Right faith, 47
Right knowledge, 47
Right to education, 164
Right to life, 174
Right to recall, 122, 164
Right to work, 164
Rigveda, 30, 46
Rites, 19
Rituals, 70
RJD, 120
Robbinhood, 109
Rolland, Romain, 42
Romans, 133
Romasa, 39
Roosevelt, 68
Roti with Ram, 125
Rourkela, 109
Roy, Raja Ram Mohan, 17
RSS, 98, 123
RSS-BJP Combine, 98, 100
Rta, 46
Rural Employment Scheme, 125
Ruskat Alamgiri, 126
Ruskin John, 79, 171, 202, 204, 209
Russel, Bertrand, 67
Russell Comple, 24, 55
Russia, 81, 188, 209

S

SAARC, 86
Sabri, 48
Sacrificial ritual, 29
Sadhana, 43
Sahara Mahepura, 124
Sahjhanand Sarswati, 116
Saivas, 29
Sakas, 125
Saktas, 29
Sakti, 31
Salt Satyagraha, 90, 106
Salvation, 8, 19
Samadhi, 3, 37
Samdarsinar, 41
Samta Bhadra, 27
Samyak Jnana, 25
Sanghai, 88
Sankara, 16, 22-23, 25, 27-28, 34, 198
Sankhya, 19, 28
Sankrityana, Rahul, 133, 178
Santiniketan, 210
Santi Sena, 93
Saraswati, 31-32, 34, 39
Sarat, 41
Saravanumati, 93
Sarda Devi, 31-34, 36, 40-42
Sardanandji, 32
Sarva Mukti, 8
Sarva Samiti, 93
Sarva Sena Sangh, 92, 97-100
Sarvodaya movement, 91-101, 109
Sarvoday Samaj, 92
Sathya Sai Baba, 148
Satyagraha, 17, 96, 106, 136, 139-42, 177-81, 187, 189, 196-99
Satyagraha as a moral

equivalent of lemonism and violence, 177-81
Satyagraha Centenary International Seminar, 199
Satyagrahi, 139-41
Satyanarayana, 166
Saulabhava, 33
Savitri, 32
Sexlund, Edle Alma, 41
Schumacher, E.F., 192, 211
Schoringder, 75
Science, 15, 23, 61
Science and spirituality, 60, 78, 197-98
Science and technology, 89
Science of yoga, 2
Sectarian patriotism, 56
Sectarian religion, 55, 60
Sectarianism, 73, 134
Secularism, 73
Self, 9-11, 40, 47, 51-52
Self control, 41
Self government, 96
Self is Brahman, 10
Self knowledge, 2, 21-22, 24
Self purification, 72
Self realization, 19, 47, 160
Self sufficiency, 15
Sense experience, 24
Sensate, 174
Sethians, 125
Sexual creature, 52
Shakespeare, 50
Shakti, 32, 34-35, 38, 42
Shakta, 18
Shanti Sena, 130, 138-43, 186
Central idea of, 139-41
Non-violence, 141-43
Sharad, 99
Shava, 34
Shiva, 18, 34, 49
Siberia, 88
Sidhsena, 27
Sikhism, 18
Silent Revolution in Bihar, 121-26
Simla Seminar, 147-48
Singh, V.P., 83
Sita, 32, 48
Siva mahimma stotra, 11
Six ways of knowing, 14
Skylorck, 13
Slade, 57
Slaughter of cows, 126
Smith, Adam, 52, 192, 200, 204
Social justice, 123
Socio-political resurgence, 15
Socialist party, 110
Socialists, 73-74, 99, 116
Social violence in social structure, 185
Socrates, 16, 24-26, 52, 63, 68, 139, 146, 154, 159, 178, 182, 192, 198, 202, 211
Sodam, 197
Sodshi, 31, 34, 39, 42
Soekarno, 113
Sophistication of intellect, 24
Sorokin, Pitnm, 174
Sorrow, 8
Soul, 9, 15, 24, 52-53, 156-57

South Africa, 57, 66, 89, 159, 188, 197
South America, 188
Sovereign Democratic Republic, 92
Soviets, 74
Spainish colonialists, 201
Spinoza, 22, 26
Spirit is man, 28-29
Spiritual, 10, 20-21
Spiritual experience, 20
Spiritualism, 19
Spirituality, 1-6, 17, 32, 52, 72-73, 197
Spirituality of Mother's love, 37-40
Spirituality of Ram Charita Manas, 44-49
Spiritual poverty, 109
Spiritual power, 39
Spiritual realisation, 16, 36
Spiritual renunciation, 34
Spiritual unity, 11
Sradha, 14
Sraman, 125
Sramania, 18
Sri Lanka, 83
Sri Yantra, 34
State, 102, 104-05
State power, 158
St. Paul, 21
St. Teresa, 38
Structural peace, 183
Sudra, 48
Suffering, 158
Sufis, 60
Summun Bonum of life, 47
Supali, 124
Superconscious state, 3
Supernatural, 24, 60
Superstitions, 5, 74
Supreme deity, 31
Supreme Divinity, 33
Supreme God, 52
Supreme Prakriti, 34
Supreme Reality, 11
Supreme Self, 47
SVD, 115
Swadeshi, 106, 189-91
Swaraj, 68, 106
Swarajist model of politics, 189-91

T

Tadatmya, 9
Tagore, Ravindranath, 10, 16, 60, 72, 87, 134, 167, 209-10
Taittiriya Upanisad, 10
Taliban, 98, 141
Talisman, 168
Tamilnadu, 95
Tantrik tradition, 34
Tapas, 30
Tat Tvam Asi, 8
Telegudesam, 122
Telangana, 91, 117, 120
Temporal world, 22
Teresa of France, 38
Terrorism, 20, 90, 177
Thailand, 180

That Those Art, 8, 13, 40
That Thou Art, 8-9
Theology, 6-7
Theory of Liquidity Preference, 204
Theory of Rate of Interest, 204
Theosophy, 72
Thermo dynamics, 174
Thine, 10
Thomas, Cwenddyn, 41
Thoreune David, 102
Thorsson report, 172
Thoughts, 2
Thukar, Karpoori, 123
Tibet, 109
Tilak, 17, 114
Tirthankaras, 34
Toffler Elvin, 91, 97
Tolerance, 57, 70
Tolstoy, 139, 171, 184, 202
Total revolution of JP in Bihar, 118
Toynbee, Arnold, 64, 67, 77, 197, 200
Transcendence, 54
Transcendental marriage, 35-37
Transhumanism, 55
Trotsky, 212
True globalization, 75, 78
True knowledge, 57
Trusteeship, 164, 210-11
Truth, 4, 9, 15, 45, 57, 59, 71, 73, 97, 155, 194
Truth consciousness, 45
Truth force, 139
Tulsidas, 44-46
Turkee, 191
Tutu Ara Bishop, 83

U

UK, 177
Ultimate reality, 27
Uma, 39
Uma Bharati, 125
UNDP, 104
Unemployment, 96, 124, 164
UNESCO, 17, 148, 183, 190
United Nations, 64, 66, 133, 183, 185-86, 191
Unity of existence, 24
Unity of religions, 60
Universal brotherhood, 59
Universal cosmic entity, 51
Universality, 20
Universal love, 166
Universal man, 50, 58
Universal person, 54
Universal philosophy, 59
Universal religion, 7, 10, 50-60, 69-71, 179
Universal religion-difficulties and solutions, 58-61
Universal welfare, 167-68
Universe, 6, 11, 51-52
University education, 145
University Grants Commission Committee, 148
Untouchability, 163, 197
Upadhya Gangesh, 27

Upanisad, 10, 11, 13, 16, 21, 27, 35, 39, 52, 75, 125
Urdu, 82
USA, 66, 81, 88, 90, 136, 173, 177-78, 184, 188, 190, 195
US invasion of Fraq, 136
USSR, 137, 203
Utopian, 64, 66, 132-33
Uttaranchal, 124
Utter Roberts, P., 42

V

Vaishnava, 18, 202
Vajpayee, Atal Bihari, 122
Vak, 39
Valmiki, 45-46, 48
Value education, 144-53
  Education without value, 155
  How is value orientation, 145-50
  No life without education, 150
  Vasubavodhu, 27
  Vasudhaiva kutumbkam, 55, 64, 78, 86
  Veda, 27, 63
  Vedanta, 38, 40
  Vedantic Absolutism, 11
  Vedas, 8-10, 16, 18-19, 27, 29, 39-40, 42, 57, 125, 178
  Vedic, 18
  Vedic Aryans, 29
  Vedic religion, 18, 30
  Vegetarianism, 53, 163, 182
  Velissa, Lek, 179
  Venenzula, 188
Vedict of people of Bihar—a silent revolution, 126
Vibhisana, 48
Vidya, 21-22
Vietnam, 133, 177
Vijayrath, 46
Vinay Patrika, 45
Vinoba Ashram at Daunar, 97
Violence, 73, 89-90, 96, 103, 141, 158, 172, 177, 180-81
Virgin Mother, 36, 42
Virgin nun, 36
Vishnu, 146
Vishnu Purana, 40
Vishwamitra, 209
Vivekanand, 10, 16, 31-32, 34, 41, 60, 69, 72, 80, 125-26, 134, 148, 166
Voters education, 100
Vows, 162, 194
Vratyas, 114
Vyasa, 44-45, 48
Vyakom, 90
Vytpattivada, 9

W

Walessa, Leh, 17, 199
Wardha, 100
War compulsions for world govt., 66-67
War Fund, 128
Weber, Thomas, 138
Wells, H.G., 64, 133, 178
West Bengal, 124
Western philosophy, 66

West minister model of parliamentary democracy, 92
Whirls, 70
Whitehead, A.N., 14
Wilkie, Windel, 64, 178
Wisdom, 25-26
Women power, 34
Women prophet, 34
Wordsworth, 13, 108, 204
Working Groups to Review Teacher Training Programme, 149
World Bank, 63, 98, 104-05, 201
World civilization, 62-79
  Economic imperialism and globalisation, 74-78
  From personal religion to universal religion, 69-74
  Logic and logical calculus, 62-69
World citizen, 86
World government, 63-67, 86-87
World peace, 86, 130
World Parliament Association at Oslo, 64
World philosophy, 14
World Philosophy Conference at Moscow, 165
World poverty-Gandhian perspective, 166-76
  Challenge of, 169-70
  Concept and meaning, 168-69
  Culture of poverty, 170-71
  Gandhian ideal of universal welfare, 167-68
  Poverty and peace, 171-73
  Poverty and social justice, 173-74
  Problem-multidimensional, 174
World Social Forum Conference, Mumbai, 188
World Trade Organization, 63, 74-75, 77, 104-05, 136, 188, 190-91, 201, 208
World War III, 67
World War IV, 67
Worshipping of woman, 39

Y

Yadav, Laloo, 99, 118, 120, 123-24
Yadav, Ram Naresh, 123
Yagnavalkya, 49
Yajna, 30
Yama, 3, 47
Yasovieya, 27
Yavans, 125
Yelwal, 95
Yoga, 2-3, 60
Young India, 134-35, 140, 142, 193
Youth force, 113
Youth power, 113
Yugoslav, 183, 195

Z

Zamindari system, 117
Zamindars, 115, 117
Zand Avesta, 57
Zoraster, 131
Zorastrianism, 56